The Matrix and Philosophy

Popular Culture and Philosophy
General Editor: William Irwin

The Matrix
and Philosophy

Welcome to the
Desert of the Real

Edited by

WILLIAM IRWIN

OPEN COURT
Chicago and La Salle, Illinois

For Peter H. Hare,
Morpheus to many

Volume 3 in the series, Popular Culture and Philosophy

To order books from Open Court, call toll free 1-800-815-2280.

Open Court Publishing Company is a division of Carus Publishing Company.

Copyright © 2002 by Carus Publishing Company

First printing 2002

Printed and bound in the United States of America

Library of Congress Cataloging-in-Publication Data

The matrix and philosophy : welcome to the desert of the real / edited by William Irwin.
    p.   cm. — (Popular culture and philosophy ; v.3)
    Includes bibliographical references and index.
    ISBN 0-8126-9502-X (trade : alk. paper) — ISBN 0-8126-9501-1
(pbk. : alk. paper)
    1. Matrix (Motion picture) 2. Motion pictures — Philosophy.
I. Irwin, William, 1970– II. Series
PN1997.M395 M38 2002
791.43'72—dc21
                                                       2002029041

Contents

Acknowledgments

Many thanks to the contributing authors for their hard work, timely production, and wonderful insights. The good folks at Open Court, especially David Ramsay Steele, Marc Aronson, Kerri Mommer, Lisa Morie, and Jennifer Asmuth provided sage advice, diligent assistance, and bountiful support. My student assistants, Trisha Allen and Jennifer O'Neill, proofread the entire manuscript and saved me from many gaffs and blunders. Those that remain are my fault. Last but not least, I thank my friends, colleagues, and students with whom I discussed *The Matrix* and philosophy, who helped make this book possible, and who offered valuable feedback on the work in progress. A list such as this is almost inevitably incomplete, but among those to whom I am indebted are: Rich Agnello, Adam Albert, Mark Conard, Bill Drumin, Robert Guldner, Peg Hogan, Megan Lloyd, Henry Nardone, the Socratic Society of King's College, Aeon Skoble, Nick Tylenda, and Joe Zeccardi.

Introduction:
Meditations on *The Matrix*

Which pill would you choose, the red or the blue? Is ignorance bliss, or is the truth worth knowing, no matter what? After watching *The Matrix* we are impressed by the action and special effects, and also besieged by questions. Is it possible that we ourselves are prisoners of the Matrix? Is this a Christian film? A Buddhist film? There is no spoon?

A student of mine at King's College, Adam Albert, first drew my attention to *The Matrix*. He immediately saw the connections between the film and Descartes's speculations on the possibility of deception by dreams or an evil deceiver. My experience and his were similar to those of philosophy professors and students around the world. The magazine *Philosophy Now* even held an essay contest for college students. The topic: Which pill would you choose? Why?

With this book, professors follow the trail blazed by their students. Each author asks and answers questions about the philosophical significance of the film. As culture critic Slavoj Žižek suggests, *The Matrix* is a philosopher's Rorschach inkblot test. Philosophers see their favored philosophy in it: existentialism, Marxism, feminism, Buddhism, nihilism, postmodernism. Name your philosophical *ism* and you can find it in *The Matrix*. Still, the film is not just some randomly generated inkblot but has a definite plan behind it and intentionally incorporates much that is philosophical. The Wachowski brothers, college dropout comic-book artists intrigued by the Big Questions, readily acknowledge that they have woven many philosophical themes and allusions into the fabric of the film. *The Matrix and Philosophy* does not in every instance attempt or purport to convey the intended meaning of the writers and artists responsible for *The Matrix*. Rather, the book highlights the philosophical significance of the film.

To paraphrase Trinity, it's the questions that drive us. The contributing authors draw on Plato, Aristotle, Aquinas, Descartes,

Kant, Nietzsche, Sartre, Sellars, Nozick, Baudrillard, and Quine (among other philosophers) to address the questions: What can I know? What should I do? What may I hope? What is real? What is happiness? What is the mind? What is freedom, and do we have it? Is artificial intelligence possible? Answering these questions leads us to explore many of the major branches of philosophy including metaphysics, epistemology, ethics, aesthetics, philosophy of mind, philosophy of religion, and political philosophy. Despite the multitude of questions, there is but one imperative: WAKE UP!

People like popular culture; it is the common language of our time. Did you know that Aaliyah died before completing the sequel to *The Matrix*? Did you know that W.V. Quine died less than a year before that? Many people know about the pop star, Aaliyah, while most people have never even heard of the great philosopher, Quine. The contributing authors of this book aim to bring the reader from pop culture to philosophy. Willie Sutton was a criminal mastermind, a genius of sorts. Once asked, "Willie, why do you rob banks?" he replied straightforwardly, "Because that's where the money is." Why write about pop culture like *The Matrix*? Because that's where the people are.

No one would object if we turned to the works of Homer, Dante, and Shakespeare to raise philosophical questions. *The Matrix* does not belong to the list of Western classics, but nevertheless the film raises the same philosophical questions as the great works of literature. If philosophy could be found only in the writing of philosophers and were relevant only to the lives of professors, then it would be the dull and sterile discipline too many people mistakenly believe it to be. But philosophy is everywhere; it is relevant to and can illuminate everyone's life; like the Matrix, "it is all around us."

This book is not just for philosophers but for all of us who have ever had a "splinter in the mind, driving us mad." Let it be a beginning but by no means an end to your study of philosophy.

Scene 1

How Do You Know?

1

Computers, Caves, and Oracles: Neo and Socrates

WILLIAM IRWIN

I tell them that I'm doing fine
Watching shadows on the wall.
— JOHN LENNON

So often times it happens that we live our lives in chains
And we never even know we have the key.
— THE EAGLES

Many people recognize *The Matrix* as a retelling of "the great-est story ever told." The biblical imagery is clear, and the film's release on Easter weekend 1999 supports the intent. Few peo-ple recognize *The Matrix* as a retelling of "the greatest story *never* told," the story of Socrates, an intellectual hero who con-tinued on his quest despite opposition and ultimately paid for his noble defiance with his life.

Why don't most people know one of the greatest stories our culture has to offer? The main reason is that we leave the job of telling the story to college philosophy professors. Not everyone attends college and, sadly, not everyone who attends college takes a philosophy course. While Philosophy 101 is an ideal set-ting in which to study closely and discuss passionately the life of Socrates, there's no need to wait for an opportunity that may never come. Like the story of Jesus, the story of Socrates should be the subject of children's books, family and classroom discussions, and TV specials. There should be a movie about it. The Wachowski brothers directed Keanu Reeves in a veiled telling of the tale, but I would cast Steve Martin as the lead in an "unapologetic" Socrates cinematic celebration. Spielberg would direct. *The Matrix* is many things; a retelling of the Socrates story is just one of them, and indeed viewers are certain to miss this element of the film unless they already know the story. If you're unfamiliar with the tale, let this essay be your introduction.

Questions and Missions

"We're on a mission from God," said the Blues Brothers. They had a full tank of gas, half a pack of cigarettes, and one hundred and six miles to Chicago. It was dark and they were wearing sunglasses. Their mission? Play a concert to save the orphanage in which they were raised by an "old school" nun, affectionately called the penguin. Neo is on a mission to save the human race from unwitting enslavement to artificial intelligence. Socrates too is on a mission, a mission from (the) God (Apollo), delivered via the Oracle at Delphi to his friend Chaerephon. His mission, should he choose to accept it, is to "wake up" the people of his hometown, Athens.

In a whisper through the din of Rob Zombie in the Goth club from hell, Trinity tells Neo, "It's the question that drives us." Their question: What is the Matrix? Like Neo, Socrates had "a splinter in his mind" and a driving question: What is the good life? Questioning brings trouble to both our heroes. Socrates finds himself on trial, charged with impiety and corrupting the youth, and Neo is accused by the Agents of "committing nearly every cyber crime we have a law for."

Socrates was in the habit of asking his fellow citizens questions, often seemingly straightforward and simple questions whose answers turned out to be elusive. Like a skilled interviewer, Socrates would follow up with more difficult, probing questions which would expose the ignorance of the people he asked. For example, Socrates asks his friend Euthyphro: What is holy? What makes an act holy? Euthryphro's response: "Holiness is what all the gods love and its opposite is what all the gods hate, unholiness" (*Euthyphro* 9e). This seems to be a good answer until Socrates poses the difficult follow-up question. "Is what is holy holy because the gods approve it, or do they approve it because it is holy?" (*Euthyphro* 10a) As you can imagine, Euthyphro has a difficult time answering this one and grows annoyed with Socrates. This process of asking questions until the person either contradicts himself or makes a mistake has become known as the Socratic method (as Bill and Ted learned at San Dimas High). Not only does the method of persistent questioning intimidate students (as in *The Paper Chase*) and embarrass politicians (choose your own example), but it made Socrates popular among the socially conscious youth, and despised among the self-interested elite.

Despite what was often perceived as a rather arrogant conversational style, Socrates was utterly humble concerning his knowledge. He claimed ignorance rather than omniscience with his mantra, "I know nothing." Why does a guy who knows nothing question everyone else so intensely? Like Neo, Socrates's excellent adventure is sparked by the words of an oracle and some insight concerning the nature of knowledge and wisdom.

What Did the Oracles Say?

The Oracle told Morpheus he would find the One, the person who would break the grip of the Matrix and free humanity with the truth. Thus Morpheus unplugs Neo, and, after some rehab and Kung Fu Fighting, takes him to the Oracle for confirmation. Neo resists this grand possibility and rejects the idea that his life is fated in any such way, telling Morpheus that he doesn't believe in fate—that he wants to believe he is in control of his life. Socrates was similarly resistant to his fate. At least so he tells us at his trial, recorded by Plato and entitled the *Apology*.

> [Chaerephon] was a friend of mine . . . [H]e went to Delphi one day, and went so far as to put this question to the oracle . . . he asked if there was anyone wiser than me; and the priestess of Apollo replied that there was no one wiser. (*Apology* 21a)

> When I heard the priestess's reply, my reaction was this: "What on earth is the god saying? What is his hidden meaning? I am well aware that I have no wisdom, great or small. So what can he mean by saying I am so wise?" (*Apology* 21b)

Indeed, how could it be that no one was wiser than he who claimed to know nothing? Socrates tells us he set out to disprove the prophetic words of the oracle.

> What I did was this: I approached one of those who seemed to be wise, thinking that there, if anywhere, I could prove the reply wrong, and say quite clearly to the oracle, "This man is wiser than I am, whereas you said I was the wisest." (*Apology* 21 c)

Socrates was disappointed upon questioning this man, a politician, to find that the man thought he knew much but really didn't know anything. Persistent by nature, Socrates did not give up but proceeded to question the esteemed playwrights and then the skilled craftsmen of Athens. He was similarly disappointed. Ironically, in realizing his own ignorance Socrates was indeed the wisest man in Athens.

Consequently, Socrates took it as his divine charge to question his fellow citizens, to expose them to their own ignorance so that they might wake up and join him in seeking knowledge.

> It is as if the city, to use a slightly absurd simile, were a horse—a large horse, high mettled, but which because of its size is somewhat sluggish, and needs to be stung into action by some kind of horsefly. I think god has caused me to settle on the city as this horsefly, the sort that never stops, all day long, coming to rest on every part of you, stinging each one of you into action, and persuading and criticizing each one of you. (*Apology* 30e)

Like a pest, a horsefly (or gadfly), with constant questioning Socrates aimed to awaken the city at large to the truth—that the glue factory, not bliss, awaits those who rest in idle ignorance.

The homes of the two Oracles are quite different. According to mythology, Zeus released one eagle from the east and another from the west to find the center of the world. They flew until they impaled each other in mid air above a spot in Delphi, thus declared the omphalos, or navel, of the world. At Delphi, a place of majestic beauty at the foot of Mt. Parnassus, Apollo spoke through his priestess, the Oracle, known also as the Pythia. Morpheus takes Neo, not to the omphalos of the world, but into the heart of the Matrix, to a place as unlike Mt.

Parnassus as possible, an inner-city tenement, the home of an unlikely Oracle.

Neo, very unsure of himself asks Morpheus, "She knows what? . . . Everything?" Morpheus responds, "She would say she knows enough." Neo, still skeptical, asks, "And she's never wrong?" Morpheus with aloof, paradoxical assurance replies, "Try not to think of it in terms of right and wrong. She is a guide, Neo. She can help you to find the path."

A visitor to the temple of Apollo at Delphi, after making the appropriate sacrifices and payments, would ask his (no women allowed) question of one of the Oracle's assistants who would ask it of the priestess. Seated on a tripod, the priestess would inhale the breath of Apollo, the fumes (probably ethylene) emanating from a chasm in the earth. Like a midnight toker at Woodstock, the priestess of Apollo would prophesy by speaking in tongues. A priest would then interpret the incoherent babbling and usually put it in hexameter verse. Like the sage advice one gets from calling 1-900-PSYCHIC, the prophecies of the Oracle were usually vague and open to more than one possible interpretation. Socrates, as we know, found puzzling the Oracle's declaration that there was no one wiser than he. Knowing the Oracle's reputation for cryptic prophecies though, he set out to disprove it, only to discover its ironic meaning. Less wise was King Croessus, who wanted to know of the Oracle whether it was an auspicious time for him to make war against the Persians. The Oracle's response was, "If you go into battle now a great kingdom will be destroyed." Taking this as terrific news the King led his troops to war and to the slaughter. He had no genuine grounds of complaint to the Oracle who simply pointed out that he was mistaken about *which* kingdom she had meant.

The Oracle of *The Matrix* not only lives in a rough part of the virtual city, she is a grandmotherly black woman—"not what you expected," much as the Pythia were, for a time, selected from women over 50 rather than from virginal maidens whose virtue would be less secure. Unlike her Delphic counterpart, the inner city Oracle meets face to face with those who seek her. And despite the fact that, sitting on a tripod, she blissfully breathes the cookie fumes issuing from her oven and inhales smoke from her cigarette, she does not speak in tongues. But don't let that fool you; her message, though apparently plain, is Pythian in its purpose. Oddly, this Oracle *asks* the questions. "You know why you're here?" "What do you think? Do you think you're the one?" Neo responds, "I don't know." Socrates had always claimed not to know, but Neo really does not know. As the Oracle quips, he's cute but not too bright. She allows him to conclude for himself that he is not the One and tells him that being the One is like being in love. No one can tell you. "You know it through and through, balls to bones." A poor consolation, she tells him, "You got the gift, but it looks like you're waiting for something." "What?" he asks? Her prophetic reply: "Your next life maybe. Who knows? That's the way these things go."

The Oracle is without malice though, and even offers some free advice in the course of their session. Pointing to a sign above her kitchen door she asks Neo if he knows what it says. It's Latin, she tells him, it means "Know Thyself." This wisdom is in fact the key to making sense of the Oracle's prophecy. The same phrase was inscribed in Greek, γνῶθι σαυτόν, (rather than the "barbaric" Latin, "Temet Nosce") in the temple of Apollo at Delphi, and it was surely more important in interpreting any Pythian prophecy than the actual answer given by the Oracle. Socrates realized this and lived by the related maxim "The unexamined life is not worth living." Cocky King Croessus did not know himself, as we saw, and paid dearly for it. Only in time does Neo come to know himself, and thus believe in himself, and thus fulfill the depth of the Oracle's prophecy—which includes Morpheus finding the One and Trinity falling in love with a dead man who is the One.

Self knowledge is the key, and without it we can unlock no other knowledge worth having. This is a theme important not just to Socrates and *The Matrix* but to other outstanding philosophical films. *Fight Club* poses the seemingly adolescent question, "How much can you know about yourself if you've never been in a fight?" We see, however, as the plot and the "fight" develop, this is not a moronic, testosteronic query. We gain self-knowledge through struggle. Consider also *Boys Don't Cry* with Brandon's deception of himself and others and the disastrous consequences this brings. Finally, *Memento* wrestles with the perplexing question: How is it possible for me to lie to myself? Is memory loss part of the answer? Hollywood and Athens agree, the unexamined life is not worth living.

To complete our look at the urban Oracle, consider another piece of wisdom inscribed at Delphi and practiced in the kitchen, "Nothing in excess" (μηδεν αγαν). "Here, take a cookie," the Oracle says to Neo, not "take some cookies" or "take as many cookies as your heart desires." We know they smell good, perhaps tempting Neo to overindulge. The Oracle is also drinking something strange (quite likely an adult beverage) and smoking a cigarette. Presumably, she can indulge in these things without going to excess. This is in stark contrast to humanity in general, described by Agent Smith as a virus that spreads, using up all the resources in an area before it moves on.

Legend has it that there was a time when the fumes that inspired the Oracle at Delphi were available to all, but the people abused the privilege and harmed themselves, jumping into the hole from which the fumes emanated. In time the Pythia alone was allowed to inhale "the breath of Apollo," and a priest-interpreter had to hear her prophecy and put it into verse for consumption by the seeker, who was thus two levels removed from the god. If fully digested, the wisdom of "Know thyself" and "Nothing in excess" might allow the chosen One to tell the truth to the many. Perhaps then all could "inhale the prophetic smoke" and commune with the god for themselves.

A Tale of Two Caves

Morpheus tells Neo he was "Born into a prison for [his] mind." Even slaves, prisoners of war, and concentration camp victims sometimes manage to keep their minds free. "They may have my body but they'll never have my mind." This resistance to slavery and imprisonment has been implemented through the ages by countless heroes such as Epictetus, Fredrick Douglass, Viktor Frankl, James Bond Stockdale, Nelson Mandela, John McCain, Malcolm X, and Rubin "Hurricane" Carter, to name a few. The only thing worse than a prison for your mind would be a prison for your mind you didn't know you were in, a prison from which, therefore, you would have no urge to escape. How would a person in such a prison even recognize if he were set free?

"Suppose one of them were set free and forced suddenly to stand up, turn his head and walk with his eyes lifted to the light;

all these movements would be painful, and he would be too dazzled to make out the objects whose shadows he had been used to seeing. What do you think he would say, if someone told him what he had formerly seen was meaningless illusion, but now, being somewhat nearer to reality and turned towards more real objects, he was getting a truer view? . . . Would he not be perplexed and believe the objects now shown him to be not so real as what he formerly saw?" These lines are from Plato's *Republic* (514c–d) in which Plato tells a story known as the allegory of the cave (also variously called the simile, myth, or parable of the cave) (514a–521b). The account, however, serves just as well to describe Neo's predicament upon being freed from the Matrix.

The prisoners in the cave are chained by the neck, hands, and legs. They have been this way since birth and so have no conception of any other way of life. Shadows appear on the wall in front of them, as their jailers pass animal figures before the light of a fire in the manner of a puppet show. The prisoners watch shadows on a wall, shadows not of real animals but of carved figures. The light that makes these shadows possible is firelight, not the best possible kind of light, sunlight. Yet these prisoners do not know that they are prisoners and do not suspect there is any reality but that which they experience. One day, however, one of the prisoners is set free of his chains, is dragged to the outside world, and by the light of the sun beholds things as they actually are. Rather than selfishly remaining in the outside world, the prisoner returns to tell the others, who reward his kindness with mockery and resistance, believing he has gone insane.

This story parallels the life of Plato's teacher,[1] Socrates, who was thought mad and ultimately put to death for trying to draw attention to a higher plane of reality. Of course it also parallels the story of Neo, who one day is freed from the Matrix to behold "the desert of the real." Like Plato's prisoner, Neo finds himself in chains or, more precisely, black cable wires that stimulate the

---

[1] Plato uses his teacher Socrates as a character in his writings, including the allegory of the cave in *The Republic*. For a discussion of the complicated connection between Plato and Socrates see my "Jerry and Socrates: The Examined Life?" in *Seinfeld and Philosophy: A Book about Everything and Nothing* (Chicago: Open Court, 2000), pp. 3–5.

illusive shadow show of the Matrix. Who frees the prisoner in Plato's allegory is unclear, though in *The Matrix* it is Morpheus (in Greek mythology the name of the God of sleep, who brings changes in shape via dreams). Like Plato's prisoner who must be dragged upward, Neo is at first horrified by the sight of the other unwitting prisoners who slumber, plugged in gooey pink cave-pods. Neo does not want to accept that what he now sees is real, that previously he had been living in a dream world. "Most of these people are not ready to be unplugged," Morpheus assures him. Like Plato's prisoner's gradual, painful period of adjustment to the world outside the cave, Neo's rehab is painful. "Why do my eyes hurt?" Neo asks. "Because you've never used them," Morpheus replies.

"The roots of education are bitter, but the fruit is sweet," wrote Aristotle. And we do well to keep in mind that "education" literally, etymologically, means "to lead out," as the prisoner is led out of the cave and as Neo is led out of the Matrix. The Hippocratic Oath reminds physicians that they are guardians and trustees, not owners, of medical knowledge. They must share the knowledge to help others. No solemn oath binds those who receive education in philosophy, though the duty to share is no less attendant. Plato's escaped prisoner would prefer to bask in the light of the sun, of goodness and knowledge, but he returns to help others. "Would he not feel like Homer's Achilles, that he would far sooner 'be on earth as a hired servant in the house of a landless man' or endure anything rather than go back to his old beliefs and live in the old way?" (*Republic* 515d) Neo, unlike Cypher, would similarly endure anything rather than return to a false reality.

Knowledge and Reality

The allegory of the cave is not only, or even most importantly, a veiled retelling of the Socrates story. Rather Plato uses it to point to, and encourage openness in the reader to, a higher level of reality, the Forms. We—all of us—are like the prisoners, for we often mistakenly suppose that the reality in which we live is the truest and highest reality there is. According to Plato, all we actually experience at the level of reality available through our five senses, are poor imitations of a higher level of reality, the Forms. We may experience beautiful sunsets, just actions, and really good noodles, but all of these things are mere imitations of the perfect Forms, copies of Beauty itself, Justice itself, Goodness itself, and so on.

What "splinter in the mind" could rouse a person to seek the Forms? And how can they be known? Plato and Socrates teach the importance of understanding not through the senses but through the intellect alone. Morpheus tells Neo that no one can be told what the Matrix is. You have to "see it for yourself." As with the Forms, it is not a literal "seeing" but a direct knowing that brings understanding of the Matrix. This essay cannot truly teach you what the Forms are, not even reading Plato can. This is part of the challenge and frustration of Plato's dialogues. One finds oneself asking, What is Justice? What is Love? What is Goodness? What, after all, is a Form? It was asking such questions that landed Socrates in trouble. So read and proceed with caution.

Neo too learns that intellect is more important than the senses. Mind is more important than matter. As for Plato the physical is not as real as the Form, so for Neo "there is no spoon." Neo is the reincarnation of the man who freed the first humans. Plato held that the intellect and body are so alien to one another that their union at birth traumatically engenders loss of memory, a kind of amnesia. This is not the total loss of memory Cypher traitorously deals for, but rather the kind one might suffer after drinking too much of Dozer's Lethic moonshine. The details can come back with the right prompting and clues. For Plato, *déjà vu* is not evidence of a glitch in the Matrix but a recollection (*anamnesis*) of the Forms. In the time between incarnations, when the soul is free of the body, we behold the Forms. On the earthly plane all learning is actually a process of recollection in which we recall the Forms, cued in by the resemblance mundane objects bare to them. A child does not need to be taught that a flower is pretty, for example, but knows it through recollection of the Form of Beauty itself and the flower's share in it.

Philosophy: The Road Less Traveled

In the car, on the way to see Morpheus, Neo considers turning back, but Trinity forces the moment to its crisis. "You have been down there, Neo. You know that road. You know exactly where it ends, and I know that is not where you want to be." One can-not help but think of Robert Frost's famous lines, "I took the one less traveled by / And that has made all the difference." We must wonder just how many people this favorite yearbook quotation and valedictory allusion truly fits. After all it would have to be a super highway, and there would still be a traffic jam, if every-one who ever claimed the verse for his or her own actually lived it.

The red pill is a new symbol of bold choice, and most peo-ple insist they would take it if they were in Neo's shoes. So at the conclusion of my introduction to philosophy course I invite my students to inhale the fumes from one of my classroom writ-ing implements, the red marker or the blue marker. If they inhale the red marker they will major in philosophy and "see how far down the rabbit hole goes." If they inhale the blue marker they will return to their previously chosen major and for-get they had ever given thought to questions that matter and mysteries of the universe. Most are amusedly annoyed. They would like to think there is no such choice. No one really majors in philosophy—it's just too impractical. But, in truth, a select few cannot resist the lure of knowledge and reality.[2]

---

[2] Thanks to all my friends and students who offered me their insights on *The Matrix*.

2

Skepticism, Morality, and *The Matrix*

GERALD J. ERION and BARRY SMITH

Most of us think that the world exists pretty much as it looks and sounds and feels to us. It *seems* to you that you are presently seated in a chair, reading this book, so you probably also *believe* it; you hold it to be true that you are sitting there, in the chair, reading. That it rarely occurs to you to articulate this sort of thought is irrelevant. All that matters is that, once pointed out, it seems obviously, perhaps trivially, true. Who would ever dare to question it?

But Thomas Anderson, likewise, believes himself to be a tax-paying, landlady-helping program writer for a respectable software company. (Of course, he also believes in his "other life" of criminal activity conducted under the hacker alias "Neo," but this life is kept hidden only from the authorities, and not from Anderson himself.) In this sense, Anderson's beliefs about reality are like yours and mine, and as such they explain why it is so painful for him to learn that the world he thinks he lives in, the world as it appears to him every day, is not at all real. Instead, the comfortable realm in which Anderson seems to go about his ordinary life is in fact a vast, deliberate deception produced in his brain by a system of intelligent computers that grows, cultivates, and harvests humans as a renewable energy source.

As Morpheus explains to Neo, this illusory world, this "Matrix," is everywhere:

It is all around us. Even now, in this very room. You can see it when you look out your window, or when you turn on your television. You can feel it when you go to work, when you go to church, when you pay your taxes. It is the world that has been pulled over your eyes, to blind you from the truth . . . that you are a slave, Neo. Like everyone else, you were born into bondage, born into a prison that you cannot smell or taste or touch. A prison for your mind.

Anderson and his contemporaries are fooled into thinking that they are out in the world reading books, watching football games, and engaging in other such activities. The truth of the matter is that they spend their whole lives confined to small containers that collect and distribute their bio-electrical energy to computerized slave-masters.

When Neo first learns of this state of affairs, he becomes physically sick, and he tries to return to his previous (though artificial) life in the Matrix. Neo's crewmate Cypher finds the situation so awful that he agrees to betray Morpheus in exchange for a rich and important (though, again, artificial) life based upon the lies of the matrix. "Ignorance is bliss," Cypher declares, as he completes his deal with Agent Smith (no relation). But even as these fictional scenarios horrify us, they can also provoke deep philosophical questions. Some philosophers have even claimed that we might ourselves be caught up in a *Matrix*-like world of unrelenting illusion. Our aim here is to examine such claims in the spirit of Western thinkers like René Descartes. That is, we shall examine the hypothesis that we ourselves might now be living inside a matrix. In the end, we shall demonstrate that this idea is based upon a fundamental error, and that it represents at best an attitude of metaphysical rebellion. We shall also, in a concluding section, examine the morality of Cypher's choice to return to the matrix, arguing that his mistaken moral principles lead him to flawed judgments about serious ethical issues.

Why You Might Be in a Matrix: René Descartes and the Malicious Demon

In philosophy, the hypothesis that the world we see, hear, and feel might be an illusion is advanced by defenders of the position known as *skepticism*. Skeptics argue that we cannot know with certainty that the external world exists. Hence, they maintain that it is possible to doubt our knowledge of the external world, much as the main characters in *The Matrix* come to doubt the everyday world they seem to live in.

Skeptical hypotheses are especially attractive to two groups of people. First are adolescents, whose teenage rebellion against the easy certainties of parental authority sometimes takes a metaphysical form that leads them to declare that "Nothing is what it seems!" or that "I alone know what reality is like!"

Second, and more importantly, are philosophers, who themselves divide into two groups. To the first group belong philosophers who have not outgrown their metaphysically rebellious phase, and who thus find explorations of absurd and obviously false hypotheses exciting or glamorous. Philosophers in this first category may even profess to find the adolescent skeptics' slogans plausible. But it is the second group of philosophers which is of most importance for us here. This second group comprises those, like Descartes, who see *Matrix*-like scenarios as useful tools for exploring fundamental questions about knowledge and reality.

In his classic *Meditations on First Philosophy*, Descartes presents an influential skeptical argument designed not to prove that skepticism is true, but to establish a solid foundation for science. To accomplish this task, Descartes opens the *Meditations* by declaring his intention to suspend every one of his beliefs that he can find the slightest reason to doubt. Only those beliefs that are *absolutely certain*, in the strongest sense of the term, will survive Descartes's test, and only such beliefs, he holds, can serve as truly reliable foundations for science. Thus, Descartes's radical doubt is *methodological* in the sense that it is designed to serve an intellectual purpose; it is unlikely that Descartes would in fact deny all of the beliefs he suspends at this stage of his project. Their suspension is temporary only; it is a matter of heuristics.

First to go in this belief-suspension process are the beliefs that Descartes had formed on the basis of sensation.[1] We justify

---

[1] René Descartes, *The Philosophical Writings of Descartes*, translated and edited by J. Cottingham, R. Stoothoff, D. Murdoch, and A. Kenny (Cambridge: Cambridge University Press, 1985), p. 12.

many of our opinions with information collected through our senses of sight, hearing, touch, smell, and taste. For instance, we believe that our roommate Jon has arrived home from school if we see him walk up the driveway, and we believe that he has locked himself out yet again when we hear him fumbling with the door. However, as Descartes notes, "From time to time I have found that the senses deceive." This is especially true of our sensations in relation to very small or distant objects, but it also holds of other sorts of objects. The figure we take to be Jon could turn out to be a burglar; the fumbling could be the burglar's attempt to break into the house. Because our senses sometimes deceive us, then, many of the beliefs that we justify on the basis of sensory evidence do not meet Descartes's high standard, and so he puts them out of action.

Continuing this exercise, Descartes then suggests that even such relatively uncontroversial beliefs as that you are sitting in a chair and reading this book could be subject to doubt. Of course, such beliefs seem to be more trustworthy than your beliefs about Jon and about whatever he is doing on the porch. However, Descartes points out that we often make mistakes about precisely these kinds of things when we *dream*. When you are dreaming, it may seem to you that you are sitting in your chair, reading this book, when in fact you are fast asleep in your bed (Descartes, pp. 12–13). We are unable to distinguish waking experiences from experiences of the sort we appear to have in dreams until after we awake, a notion that Morpheus affirms as he asks:

> Have you ever had a dream, Neo, that you were so sure was real? What if you were unable to wake from that dream? How would you know the difference between the dream world and the real world?

Descartes himself concludes on the basis of his dream argument that sense experience is an unreliable justification mechanism, and so he suspends *all* beliefs he has formed on the basis of sensory evidence.

Descartes then carries his attack upon his own beliefs still further. While the dream argument gives us reason to doubt our opinions about the physical world, it seems to leave, for example, beliefs about numbers or geometrical figures unscathed. As

Descartes writes, "Whether I am awake or asleep, two and three added together are five, and a square has no more than four sides" (p. 14). However, Descartes concludes his first *Meditation* by considering the following still more radical thought experiment. Suppose, he says, that a "malicious demon of the utmost power and cunning has employed all his energies in order to deceive me" (p.15). Such a creature, Descartes argues, could easily lead us to mistaken conclusions about the sum of two and three or the number of sides to a square. This malicious demon could even more easily mislead us into thinking that there is a physical world external to ourselves, when in fact "[T]he sky, the air, the earth, colors, shapes, sounds, and all external things are merely the delusions of dreams which he has devised to ensnare [our] judgment." Thus, Descartes concludes, "I shall consider myself as not having hands or eyes, or flesh, or blood or senses, but as falsely believing that I have all these things." Having read Descartes's first *Meditation*, then, it is difficult to imagine how we could show that our lives are not just grand deceptions created by a malicious demon. How could we ever refute the skeptical arguments advanced by Descartes?

Those who have watched *The Matrix* might surely, against this background, have reason to question whether we could ever rule out the possibility that the meaningful lives we think we lead are in fact a matter of deceptions implanted in our brains by intelligent computer systems.

Why You Might Be in a Matrix, Continued: Peter Unger's Evil Scientist and Hilary Putnam's Brain in a Vat

In a contemporary contribution to the debate on skepticism, Peter Unger—himself a defender of the skeptical position—suggests the possibility that we are all duped not by an evil demon, but by an evil *scientist*.[2] In Unger's scenario, presented in his 1975 book *Ignorance*, the common belief that there are chairs, books, and other similar objects in the world around us is simply an elaborate deception stimulated in our brains by an evil scientist, a super-neurologist who uses a computer to generate

---

[2] Peter Unger, *Ignorance* (Oxford: Clarendon, 1975), pp. 7–8.

electrical impulses that are then transmitted to electrodes fastened to the relevant parts of our central nervous systems. Using these impulses to stimulate our brains, the scientist deceives us into thinking that there are chairs and books, even though there are no such things in the world. Such a scenario has, Unger claims, the following implication; "No one *can* ever *know* [with absolute certainty] that there is *no* evil scientist who is, by means of electrodes, deceiving him into falsely believing there to be rocks," and therefore, *nobody can know that there are rocks.* Likewise, you cannot know that you are in your chair, reading this book, for you can never know with absolute certainty that you are not subject to the manipulation of an evil neurologist, or for that matter, the manipulation of an evil, *Matrix*-like computer system.

Hilary Putnam pushes this skeptical science-fiction scenario even further in his 1981 volume *Reason, Truth, and History.* In Putnam's version of the argument, an evil scientist deceives us not just about rocks, but about *everything* we think we perceive through the senses.[3] Putnam begins by asking us to imagine that our brains have been surgically separated from the rest of our bodies and placed in vats filled with brain-nourishing chemicals. A powerful computer then sends electrical impulses into our brains, giving rise, for instance, to the illusion that we are sitting in chairs, reading books, playing tennis, and so forth. All the while, though, our disembodied brains are actually floating around in vats in the evil scientist's laboratory.

Putnam presupposes that the computer program is sophisticated enough to generate proper feedback for the "actions" our brains attempt to initiate. For instance, should your brain try to rouse your body from your chair to fetch a snack, the computer could provide the appropriate impulses needed to convince you that you had in fact risen from your chair and carried yourself into the kitchen. But again, despite the appearance of eating, you would through all of these experiences remain a disembodied brain in a vat.

---

[3] Hilary Putnam, *Reason, Truth, and History* (New York: Cambridge University Press, 1981), pp. 5–8. Though Putnam himself does not use this scenario to argue in favor of skepticism, his work has made a powerful contribution to such discussions.

Having laid out this curious scenario, which is strikingly similar to the situation facing most humans in *The Matrix*, Putnam then poses the skeptic's question: "How do you know you aren't in this predicament?" Without an answer to this question, the skepticism inspired by Descartes's original arguments remains like a sword of Damocles hanging over our heads.

Relief from the Matrix: Arguing Against Skepticism

Fortunately, non-skeptical philosophers have come up with a number of responses to the troubling questions about knowledge and reality raised by Descartes, Unger, Putnam, and *The Matrix*. First, it is important to note that the skeptic's scenario is a mere *possibility*, and a very unlikely one at that. The fact that we take the trouble to follow Descartes in his exercise of systematic doubt is due in large part to its presentation in a special philosophical context: the context of Descartes's own quest for perfect knowledge, knowledge of the sort that would live up to the highest ideals of science. Remember that, to Descartes, knowledge requires *absolute certainty*; we cannot be absolutely certain that a malicious demon (or an evil computer system) is not deceiving us during sensation, so, Descartes argues, we cannot use sensation to justify our claims to knowledge.

A maximally strict standard for knowledge of this sort is perfectly appropriate in philosophical contexts where we are examining arguments for and against skepticism. In the ordinary contexts of everyday life, however, they are much too strict. For instance, if Jon asks you about tomorrow's weather forecast and you respond with questions like "Does weather really exist?" or "Does time really exist?" or "What is tomorrow?", then Jon would, rightly, think that you had gone mad. This is because different standards for what properly counts as knowledge obtain in different contexts.[4] In some philosophical contexts, we quite correctly impose very strict standards for knowledge. In everyday contexts, though, we equally correctly impose just those

---

[4] See David Lewis, "Elusive Knowledge," *Australasian Journal of Philosophy* 74 (1996), pp. 549–567.

normal standards with which we are all familiar, and which are satisfied by the vast collections of commonsensical knowledge that we all share. In everyday contexts, then, we do indeed have knowledge of where we are sitting, of what we are doing, of current local weather conditions, and of the results of baseball games.

Thus, you do indeed *know* (in the fullest sense of the term) many things about yourself and the world around you; your beliefs about these things are both true and thoroughly justified through your everyday experiences. You *know*, for instance, that you are not currently dreaming. You know that Descartes (like Elvis) is dead. And you know that *The Matrix* is just a film. In addition, modern science provides massive amounts of additional, no less genuine knowledge—that electrons are smaller than asteroids, that fish are not mammals, that the Moon is not made of green (or any other type of) cheese, and so on.[5] But if we do indeed possess these great and ever-growing stores of commonsensical and scientific knowledge, then, it follows that we must reject Descartes's claim that knowledge always requires that very special sort of (philosophical) certainty that he demands in the specific context of his discussion of skepticism.[6]

Descartes's fundamental epistemological principle to the effect that only knowledge marked by certainty is genuine knowledge has, moreover, problems of its own. Thus it seems to be self-defeating, in the sense that its supposed truth would entail that it could not be known. As Theodore Schick, Jr. and Lewis Vaughn point out, "unless [skeptics] are *certain* that knowledge requires certainty, they can't *know* that it does"

---

[5] This is not to deny the important role played by the doctrine of *fallibilism* in the advancement of science; that is, by the view that scientific theories must be subject to consistent testing against reality itself. Even evolutionary biologists remain open to the possibility that new evidence could be gathered to prove the theory of evolution mistaken; the fervor with which they attack such alternative theories as creationism is grounded, however, not in anti-religious bigotry, but in the tremendous amount of high-quality evidence that supports evolution. See, for instance, Theodore Schick, Jr. and Lewis Vaughn, *How To Think about Weird Things* (Mountain View: Mayfield, 1995), pp. 211–19, for a lucid discussion of this issue.

[6] David Nixon raises a similar point in Chapter 3 of this volume.

(emphasis added).[7] But in light of our previously noted doubts about Descartes's principle, this principle itself begins to seem much less than certain. Indeed, our commonsensical and scientific beliefs are at least as dependable, if not more so, than Descartes's principle. It was through acceptance of these beliefs, after all, that we were able to trust the evidence of our senses when reading Descartes's own writings. Thus, we have good reason to doubt his claim that knowledge requires certainty.

We should keep in mind, too, another anti-skeptical argument advanced by the philosopher Bernard Williams.[8] Williams soothes our fears of being locked in a perpetual *Matrix*-like dream-prison by pointing out that the fact that we can make a distinction between dreams and waking experiences itself presupposes that we are aware of both types of experience and of the difference between them. We can talk sensibly about the difference between the two only because there *is* a difference between them, a difference that we are aware of. As Williams writes, it is only "from the perspective of waking [that] we can explain dreaming" (p. 313). Thus, we can make sense of the distinction between waking and dreaming itself only if *we really are awake sometimes*, and since we *can* distinguish the two kinds of experience, it follows that there can be no serious reason to worry that our lives might be made up entirely of dream sequences that never end.

So, philosophy provides a number of tools for relieving the metaphysical uncertainty that a thoughtful viewing of *The Matrix* might at first provoke. Since our knowledge—of where we are sitting, of what we are doing, of what the world around us is like—does not require philosophical certainty, but only those sorts of strong, context-appropriate justifications which we employ for everyday and scientific purposes, it follows that we can use the good reasons we have for believing in the external world to justify our claims to knowledge not only about the existence of this world, but also about its nature and constitution. As Martin Gardner puts it:

> The hypothesis that there is an external world . . . is so obviously useful and so strongly confirmed by experience down through the

---

[7] Schick and Vaughn, p. 100.
[8] Bernard Williams, *Descartes* (Atlantic Highlands: Humanities Press, 1978).

ages that we can say without exaggerating that it is better confirmed than any other empirical hypothesis. So useful is the posit that it is almost impossible for anyone except a madman or a metaphysician to comprehend a reason for doubting it. (Martin Gardner, *The Whys of a Philosophical Scrivener* [New York: Quill, 1983], p. 15, quoted in Schick and Vaughn, p. 87)

Morality and the Matrix: Cypher's Mistake

In the grips of the sort of skeptical doubt inspired by Descartes and *The Matrix*, we might be able to empathize with Cypher as he cuts his despicable deal with Agent Smith. Tired of the misery of the real world, Cypher agrees to lead Smith to Morpheus in exchange for a new life as a wealthy, famous actor inside the Matrix. Cypher knows that the Matrix is not real, but he believes that he can make his life better by simply ignoring this and retreating back into a pleasant world of illusory fantasy.

Cypher is making a big mistake here, however. In choosing to lead his life for pleasure alone, he presupposes that pleasure is the only thing that could make his life worth living. The doctrine according to which pleasure is the only thing valuable for its own sake is known to philosophers as *hedonism*.[9] Though hedonism may seem to have some intuitive appeal, the philosopher Robert Nozick provides a powerful argument against it in his *Anarchy, State, and Utopia*. This argument is especially interesting for us here, because it involves yet another brain-in-a-vat-type thought experiment.[10]

To begin, Nozick again suggests that we might simply be unconscious bodies floating in vats of nourishing chemicals. He postulates something called the "experience machine," a sophisticated piece of computer equipment that uses electrodes to

---

[9] Hedonism is one fundamental component of *utilitarianism*, a moral philosophy that holds that an action's moral value is dependent upon the total amount of happiness that it produces. The two founders of utilitarianism were Jeremy Bentham and John Stuart Mill; see Bentham, *An Introduction to the Principles of Morals and Legislation* (New York: Hafner, 1948) and Mill, *Utilitarianism* (Indianapolis: Hackett, 1979).

[10] Robert Nozick, *Anarchy, State, and Utopia* (New York: Basic Books, 1974), pp. 42–45.

stimulate our central nervous systems. Using the experience machine, neurophysiologists could make it seem to us that we are reading books, meeting with friends, drinking beer, and doing other pleasant things. All the while, though, we would in fact merely lie dormant inside the machine. Assuming that the experience machine could be configured to generate any experience we think worthwhile, that it could be programmed to make us seem to be wonderfully successful, rich, happy, and beautiful, Nozick asks, "Should you plug into this machine for life?" (Nozick, p. 42)

Cypher, of course, would answer "Yes." Most of us, though, are rightly much more cautious. For there seems to be something troubling about the idea of turning our lives over in this way to mere stimulation by electrodes.[11] Nozick explains why this is so with a series of arguments against those who, like Cypher, would choose to submit to the experience machine. First, he says, "We want to do certain things, and not just have the experience of doing them" (Nozick, p. 43). Neither the experience machine nor the Matrix allows for genuine, meaningful action; instead, they merely give the *appearance* of meaningful action. But in addition:

> We want to *be* a certain way . . . [but] someone floating in a tank is an indeterminate blob. There is no answer to the question of what a person is like who has long been in the tank. Is he courageous, kind, intelligent, witty, loving? It's not merely that it's difficult to tell; there's no way he is. (Nozick, *Anarchy, State, and Utopia*, p. 43)

Finally, the experience machine does not allow us to connect with reality in any substantial way, despite the strong desires most of us have to do so.[12] Thus, Nozick concludes, "We learn

---

[11] Even the great utilitarian John Stuart Mill seems to have been troubled by this sort of objection to hedonism. In responding to his own (and to Bentham's) critics, Mill tried to distinguish different kinds of pleasure, some of a higher and some of a lower quality.

[12] pp. 43–44. Nozick goes on to point out: "This clarifies the intensity of the conflict over psychoactive drugs, which some view as mere local experience machines, and others view as avenues to a deeper reality; what some view as equivalent to surrender to the experience machine, others view as following one of the reasons *not* to surrender!"

that something matters to us in addition to experience by imagining an experience machine and then realizing that we would not use it" (p. 44). Likewise, we learn that something matters to us besides pleasure (or fame, or wealth, or beauty) by considering Cypher's decision and then realizing that we would not make it. Cypher's decision is, in fact, *immoral*. In contrast, Neo's decision to face "the desert of the real" allows him to undertake genuine action and have genuine experiences that give his life meaning, and thus a moral value. As the moral philosopher John Stuart Mill writes, "It is better to be a human being dissatisfied than a pig satisfied; better to be Socrates dissatisfied than a fool satisfied" (Mill, p. 10).

Know You Are

The Matrix exposes us to the uncomfortable worries of philosophical skepticism in an especially compelling way. However, with a bit more reflection, we can see why we need not share the skeptic's doubts about the existence of the world. Such doubts are appropriate only in the very special context of the philosophical seminar. When we return to normal life we see that they are groundless. Furthermore, we see also the drastic mistake that Cypher commits in turning his back upon reality and re-entering the Matrix. Not only does reason compel us to admit the existence of the external world, it also requires us to face this world, to build for ourselves meaningful lives within it, and to engage, as adults, in the serious business of living.

3
The Matrix Possibility

DAVID MITSUO NIXON

After watching *The Matrix* I have to ask, *Could I be in the Matrix right now?* Maybe everything I think that I see, feel, taste, and touch, everything that I think is real is actually a part of a "computer generated dream world" and in reality my body is floating in a pod of pink goo. That's such a scary and interesting proposition that it's worth giving a name to it. For ease of reference let's call it The Matrix Possibility: It's possible that I am (or you are) in the Matrix right now.

In this essay I want to examine a number of questions that surround the Matrix Possibility. Among them are: (a) Even if we aren't *actually* in the Matrix, what implications does the Matrix Possibility have for what we actually do or do not know? (b) How does Neo come to know—if he does at all—that he was in the Matrix? (c) Does the Matrix Possibility even make sense? Be warned: the conclusions that I will draw—especially in the latter two sections—may be very counter-intuitive and perhaps controversial to some readers. But even if you are not convinced by the arguments, I hope you will at least find them thought-provoking.

Do We Really Know Anything?

What consequences does the Matrix Possibility have for what we actually do or do not know? Notice that the Matrix Possibility does not say that I *am* in the Matrix right now. It just says that it is *possible* that I am in the Matrix right now. Still, if I *am* in the Matrix right now, then a lot of the beliefs I have right now are false. For example, I believe that I own a Honda Civic, when actually I don't have any car at all, because I'm just floating in a pod of pink goo. Thus the Matrix Possibility implies the following: It's possible that a heck of a lot of my beliefs right now are false.

Let's assume, at least for the moment, that the Matrix Possibility is valid (that it makes sense and is a real possibility), and hence that a lot of the beliefs I have right now might be false. There are two typical sorts of reactions that people have to the idea that a heck of a lot of their beliefs might be false.

The first is this: "If it is possible that a belief you have is false, then that belief is not one that you can say you really *know*." For instance, you might *believe* that the center of the Moon is not a hollowed-out enclave where moon-goblins live, but since you've never actually been there, it's *possible* (however unlikely it might seem) that there *are* goblins living in the Moon. So you can't really say that you really *know* that there aren't goblins living in the Moon. Of course, I'm not saying that you shouldn't keep on believing what you do. After all, you have to believe *something*, so you might as well keep believing what seems most likely to you. But don't think that these are actually things that you *know*. This is similar to the methodological skepticism of Descartes. To find one piece of complete certainty Descartes employed the method of suspending belief in anything that could even possibly be doubted. Descartes didn't watch *The Matrix*, but he had his own scary story. In his story Descartes toys with the possibility that "some malicious demon of the utmost power and cunning has employed all his energies in order to deceive me."[1] For Descartes, the mere *possibility* that there is such a demon deceiving him was enough to cast doubt on his having knowledge—at least of the things that the demon might be deceiving him about.

The other sort of response goes like this: "If you look at how we actually use the word 'know' in the real world, you'll see that

---

[1] René Descartes, *Meditations on First Philosophy*, translated by J. Cottingham, R. Stoothoff, and D. Murdoch (Cambridge: Cambridge University Press, 1984), p. 15.

there are all kinds of circumstances in which we recognize the *possibility* of having a false belief but we still call it knowledge." In the real world (when we're not "playing philosopher") we almost *never* require that a belief be such that it is impossible to be false before we call it known. For example, I'm at the bus stop and someone asks me, "Do you know what time it is?" and I look at my watch and answer, "Yes I do. It's 12:30." I recognize the *possibility* that my watch is off, but when I don't have my philosopher hat on this fact doesn't keep me from saying that I *know* what time it is. What on earth would justify philosophers in suddenly having such high standards for knowledge—especially since as soon as they take off their philosopher hats, these philosophers don't even adhere to these high standards themselves? The proper response to someone's telling me that my belief *could* be false is, "So what?" It's not *possibility* that matters, it's *probability*. So until you give me a good reason to think that my belief is not just *possibly* false, but *probably* false, I'm not changing anything about what I believe or what I think I know.

I tend toward the second response myself. But perhaps we can reconcile the two views by simply understanding them as talking about two different senses of "knowledge." The first refers to a kind of super knowledge, such that you can't properly say that you super-know something unless there's no possibility of your getting it wrong. This is the kind of knowledge Descartes, through his methodological skepticism, was seeking for the foundation stone of all other knowledge. The second deals with a kind of ordinary knowledge, such that you can still say that you have ordinary knowledge of something even when there's a possibility you have it wrong, though you can't say that you have ordinary knowledge of it if you have a good reason to think that you're *probably* wrong. Both sides can agree that the Matrix Possibility implies that we don't have much (if any) super knowledge, but it doesn't undermine our having as much ordinary knowledge as we think we do. Put like that, the question of whether, given the possibility of the Matrix, we really know anything, seems to lose some of its bite. But maybe that's okay.

Does Neo Know that He Was in the Matrix?

Now I want to switch gears a little bit and talk about how Neo finds out he's in the Matrix. The movie leads us to want to say that Neo comes to *know* (here I'll restrict my attention to the much less demanding sense of acquiring *ordinary* knowledge) something that he did not know before—namely, that most of his life has been spent in the Matrix (as a body floating in a pod of goo, being fed his experiences by a super-computer, and so on). How does Neo come to know this—if indeed he *does*?

Before offering Neo the blue and red pills, Morpheus tells him, "No one can be told what the Matrix is. You have to see it for yourself." Morpheus doesn't say why, but I can venture a guess: No one would believe him. Well, let me correct that—the only people who would believe him are people so gullible or foolish that they might be led to believe just about *anything*. And these people are certainly not paradigm examples of the sorts of people who we'd say have a lot of knowledge, even if they might happen to get something right from time to time. So Neo cannot come to know about the Matrix from Morpheus's testimony alone, because it would be foolish to believe such a story and foolish belief (even when it happens to get things right) is not knowledge. For a belief to genuinely count as *knowledge*, it must be *justified*. Indeed, the traditional account of knowledge is that knowledge is justified true belief. On the traditional account, if you believe something, and your belief is true, and you are justified in believing it, then we can correctly say that you know it. Though many have found fault with this venerable account, it is at least correct insofar as its justification requirement rules out foolish beliefs and lucky guesses from counting as knowledge.

Neo takes the red pill so that he can "see how far down the rabbit hole goes." Within minutes he is having some of the weirdest experiences he's probably ever had: He sees a broken mirror mend itself. He touches the mirror and it begins to cover him with a strange oozing mirror-like substance. Suddenly he finds himself in a pod of pink goo with plugs and wires coming out of his arms, legs, back, and head. He sees millions of other pods. A spider-like robot flies up, grabs him by the neck, pulls out the plug in his head and flies away. Next his pod is drained and he slides down a tube and lands in some sewer-like sludge, only to be lifted out of it by a huge crane the next minute. He drifts in and out of consciousness. Finally he is well enough to take a tour of the ship he is on. Then they put a plug-thing in his head and he is suddenly in "the construct"—the "loading program"—where Morpheus finally tells him the whole story of the Matrix.

It's a hard story to believe. Neo doesn't believe it at first. The whole experience is so traumatic in fact that he throws up. I can't say that I blame him. Finding out that your whole life up to this point has been a fake, a "computer generated dream-world," would be a bit dizzying, to say the least. But the question that I want to ask is not whether this would be something emotionally painful to believe, but whether, given Neo's recent experiences, this is something that it would be *reasonable* for him to believe. Can these harrowing experiences give him what Morpheus's testimony alone could not—a *good reason* to believe that his life, until recently, has been spent in the Matrix? Or would it still, even after these strange experiences, be foolish for him to believe this amazing story?

Notice that I am *not* asking whether it is possible that Neo's new beliefs (that he has spent his life in the Matrix, and is now free of it) are false. Clearly this *is* possible. It *might* be that there is no Matrix, and Neo has been living in the ordinary world, and he was recently tricked into taking a red pill which was actually a powerful hallucinogenic drug, etc., etc. (Admittedly, it would be a somewhat disappointing sequel, in my opinion, to find that this was the case.)

Clearly this is *possible*. But not everything that is *possible* is something that we have good reasons to believe is *actual*. Again, the possible should not distract us from a discussion of the probable, for it is what we have reason to believe is probable that has a bearing on what it is reasonable to believe.

So, does Neo have good reason to believe what he in fact does believe—that he was, but now is not, a captive of the Matrix? If so, then we may well want to say that he not only believes it, but he *knows* it. (Given the possibility of error, this would have to be ordinary knowledge.)

I want to give some serious thought to the idea that perhaps Neo does *not* have very good reasons to believe the Matrix story, even after his recent strange experiences. Let's suppose that Neo is about 25 years old. In that case, in believing the Matrix story, he is being asked to throw away 25 years of perfectly normal experiences as untrustworthy, in exchange for a few days of very weird experiences that he is supposed to trust as being the Real McCoy. That seems a bit hasty—especially when we remember that all of these weird recent experiences followed on the heel of his swallowing a strange red pill.

The situation gets even worse when we realize that whatever abilities Neo has with regard to being able to interpret his experiences, these abilities were acquired during the part of his life that he is now supposed to throw away as entirely untrustworthy. That is to say, it is because of the experiences he has had during his first 25 years that he knows what is reasonable to infer from the information provided by his senses. But if he believes the story about the Matrix, then everything he has learned about how to interpret his experiences must be thrown away. Here is a very small list of just a few of the rules of thumb about interpreting one's own experience that would have to be thrown out if Neo accepts the Matrix story:

(a) People don't generally lie, so if it seems as if someone is telling you something, you can generally believe that it's true.

(b) If it sounds as if someone is speaking English, they probably are.

(c) If you seem to remember doing something, you probably did it.

(d) People don't switch bodies when they touch.

(e) People's heads don't fly off when they are angry.

(f) The noise that people's shoes make as they walk is *not* a part of the sounds they use to communicate with you (so there's no point in trying to interpret those shoe sounds!)

(g) When an object seems to be getting bigger, it often means that it is actually coming closer to you. (Similarly with seeming to get smaller and going away from you.)

(h) Things exist even when you're not looking at them.

There are lots of things like these that we believe even if they're so obvious that we've never even stopped to think about them. Not only do we (you, I, Neo) believe these strange but obvious things, but we are *justified* in believing them. It's *reasonable* to believe them. But as obvious as they seem, we are not born knowing them. So what justifies us in believing them? We are justified in believing them because they fit with all the experiences we've had (and we don't have any reason not to trust those experiences).[2] They seem so obviously correct because we've never had any experiences that would give us reason to call any of them into question. But if we'd had different experiences, they might not seem obvious; they might even seem obviously false. So the justification of these rules of thumb depends crucially on one's past experiences. If you can't trust your past experiences, then you have no reason to believe those principles. The principles I pointed out above are especially important because they help you to interpret present experiences. Thus you are only justified in interpreting present experiences in the way that you do if you are justified in relying on those rules of thumb for interpreting your experiences. But you are only justified in relying on those interpretive principles if you can trust your past experiences. If Neo believes that all of his experiences until very recently have been fed to him by malicious computers, then he has no reason to trust them. Thus he would not be justified in believing the above interpretive principles, and thus he would not be justified in interpreting his present experience in the normal way that he is used to.

Because of the experiences that we've had in our lives, certain things seem normal and others seem unexpected. It would seem very strange and unexpected (to us) to find out that some people we've been talking to actually don't speak English but speak in some other language that sounds just like English but

---

[2] I am one of those empiricists who think that the idea of *explanatory coherence* is of central importance in understanding epistemic justification. (This is what I am gesturing at with the idea that one's beliefs are justified because they "fit with the experiences" one has had.) Those whose philosophical perspectives put them substantially at odds with such an idea are not likely to find the argument persuasive.

where the words all mean something different. It would seem strange and unexpected to find that certain people always lie on Tuesdays and Thursdays. Or that some people's heads pop off when they get angry. What is strange and unexpected (as well as what is normal and expected) is just a function of what we have experienced, of what we're used to. If Neo can't trust his past experiences, then he is no longer justified in expecting what he is used to expecting. He is no longer justified in claiming that *this* would be normal, and *that* would be strange, unexpected, and unlikely. If someone (say, Morpheus) started making noises that sounded like the English language, Neo would, out of habit, be inclined to think that Morpheus *is* speaking English, for Neo is used to a world where people who seem to be speaking English usually are. But Neo can't trust that world if he believes that it was generated by malicious computers. So Neo would not be justified in believing that Morpheus really is speaking English, or that he is telling the truth, or that his head won't pop off when he gets angry, for his justification for believing any of those things relies on experiences he can't trust.

But this means that if Neo believes that he has spent most of his life in the Matrix, with his experiences having been fed to him by evil computers, then he is not justified in taking at face value the story that Morpheus seems to be telling him. And if Neo is not justified in believing Morpheus when Morpheus tells him (or seems to tell him) that he has spent his life in the Matrix, then Neo is not justified in believing that he has spent his life in the Matrix after all. We might call it a self-defeating belief. The very act of your believing it undermines your having good reasons to believe it. (Compare: "I'm so bad with numbers that over 50 percent of the statements I make that have numbers in them are false.")

Of course, the audience has access to the bigger picture. We happen to know that the programmed world of the Matrix is similar enough to the real world that the way Neo is inclined to interpret his experience (for example, that Morpheus is speaking English, and is telling the truth) actually gets things right. But Neo (unlike the audience) lacks any good reason to think that the world of the Matrix is similar to the real world. You might think that his new experiences would quickly justify him in believing that the real world *is* similar (in the right ways) to the

Matrix world, but in fact these new experiences are useless unless he is justified in relying on certain interpretive principles like those above. And, as we saw, he is not justified in relying on those principles since he cannot rely on his past experiences. He can't rely on present experiences without relying on past ones. This conclusion is in fact a consequence of a widely accepted view in epistemology called Holism: that no bit of experience can do any justificatory work on its own, but only as a part of much larger interconnected set of experiences and beliefs—some of which include, of course, the interpretive principles.[3] (If such a view seems manifestly false, the argument here will likely not be very compelling.) Thus Neo is not justified in interpreting his experiences in the way that he is used to, and so the things that he comes to believe thanks to these experiences (for instance that he was but is not now in the Matrix) are also not justified. The proper conclusion to draw here seems to be that Neo does not really know (even in the less restrictive sense of ordinary knowledge) that he was, but is not now, in the Matrix.

I think this line of reasoning could be generalized to cover most large-scale skeptical hypotheses similar to the Matrix possibility. That is, I think it can be shown that believing in these fantastic stories is almost always self-defeating. But that will have to be left for another occasion. For now I would like to return to the idea that started us off, namely the Matrix Possibility.

Does the Matrix Possibility Even Make Sense?

The Matrix Possibility, remember, is the idea that "It's possible that I am (or you are) in the Matrix right now." The issue that I want to consider now is to what extent something like the Matrix Possibility even makes sense. To what extent is the idea of our being in the Matrix right now really a coherent possibility?

Right off the bat I want to make it clear that in worrying about whether the story of *The Matrix* really presents us with a

---

[3] Those interested in Holism are directed to the works of W.V. Quine, Donald Davidson, and especially Wilfrid Sellars.

coherent possibility, my goal is *not* to simply point out small inconsistencies in the plot. Nor am I worried about whether the story is, so to speak, technologically or scientifically possible. That is, it might turn out that the story violates certain laws of physics, for example, and might be held to be impossible for reasons along those lines. But that would not bother me. Rather, I am worried about whether the story is, at some level, not even *conceptually coherent*.

As I have pointed out already, if you are in the Matrix right now, then a heck of a lot of your beliefs are false. (For instance, you might believe that you are reading a book right now when actually you are floating in a pod of goo and there are no books anywhere near you.) It is this widespread error—this tremendous amount of false belief—that I think begins to threaten the coherence of the Matrix story. (We'll see why in a moment.) But of course not all of Neo's beliefs turned out to be false. He had beliefs about what his face looked like, for example, that turned out to be correct. (He *could* have come out of the Matrix to discover that he looks just like Barbra Streisand—wouldn't *that* have been a shock!) But if we can imagine a world like that of *The Matrix*, then we surely can imagine a world where the computers are just a little bit more malicious; where they attend to every last detail to make sure that they maximize the number of false beliefs of the people they hold captive in the Matrix.

The question I really want to ask then is this: Can we really make sense of the idea of a person who has beliefs but these beliefs are all or almost all false? If the answer is no, then ultimately we will not be able to make sense of stories like *The Matrix* (or at least my version with increased maliciousness from the computers) that involve people whose beliefs are almost all false. Thus ideas like the Matrix Possibility might not even make sense, even if they sound quite plausible at first. I'm going to try to see how far I can push a line of argument that says *no*, we can't really make sense of the idea of a person whose beliefs are all or almost all false.

To be even more precise, what I will try to argue is that a person (say, Lisa) will not be able to make sense of a story in which some person (say, Homer) has beliefs but these beliefs are all or almost all what Lisa would consider false. Thus (substituting ourselves for Lisa and Neo for Homer) *we* will not be able, ultimately, to make sense of the idea that Neo (or anyone else, including ourselves) has beliefs but they are all or almost all what we would consider false.

The central component of the argument I want to examine is this: It doesn't make sense to say that a person has just one single belief on a particular topic. In order to even have one belief about something, one must have a number of beliefs about it. An example will help illustrate this. Suppose I'm talking to my friend Cletus, and we have the following conversation:

CLETUS: Bears are scary.
ME: Why do you say that? Is it because they're so big?
CLETUS: Are they big? I didn't know that.
ME: Is it because they are furry animals?
CLETUS: Are they furry? I didn't know that. Actually, I didn't even know they were animals.
ME: Well you least know that they are living creatures that exist in the physical world, right?
CLETUS: News to me.
ME: Are they scary to you because they look like little birds?
CLETUS: Oh, do they?
ME: I was kidding! You must at least know what bears *look like* don't you?[4]
CLETUS: Uh . . . no. What do they look like?
ME: Come on! Do you know *anything* about bears?
CLETUS: Sure. They're scary.
ME: Besides that?
CLETUS: Um . . . no.

By this time we might begin to suspect that maybe when Cletus utters "Bears are scary" he's just repeating what he heard someone else say, but has no idea what it means. In any case it is clear that he doesn't have the belief that *bears* are scary, for he doesn't have the concept of *bear* at all. In order for it to make sense for me to attribute the belief "Bears are scary" to Cletus (regardless of whether I think that particular belief is true or

---

[4] Strictly speaking, to know what a bear looks like isn't really to have a certain *belief* about bears. Rather, it is to have certain recognitional abilities. It is, in Rylean terminology, to have *know how* instead of *know that*. (See Gilbert Ryle, *The Concept of Mind*, 1949.) But these abilities are probably also necessary in order to have a concept of a bear.

false), I have to make sense of his having the concepts involved (*bear* and *scariness*). But in order for me to be able to make sense of his having the concept of a bear, I have to be able to attribute to him a number of beliefs about bears that *I* take to be true (like that bears are animals, that they don't look like little birds, and so forth). Without these other beliefs there is nothing that would help us to fix what Cletus means by the word "bear"—if indeed, the word has any meaning at all for him. I contend that we are no more justified in attributing to Cletus the belief that bears are scary than we would be in attributing to him the belief that, say, rocks are scary. (This idea, that one's beliefs fix the meaning of one's words—that is, fix which concepts, if any, your words stand for—is yet another facet of that general constellation of views that go under the heading of Holism. In this case it is often called *Meaning Holism*, or *Concept Holism*. Again, check out Quine, Davidson, or Sellars.) Even if we were to suppose that Cletus has the concept of scariness, and that he at least said very general things like "Bears are something rather than nothing," the most we would be justified in attributing to Cletus is a belief that *there is something that is scary*, and *not* the belief that in particular *bears* (you know, those large furry animals that don't look like little birds, etc.) are scary.

Let's generalize these results a bit. Suppose I want to say that someone has a lot of false beliefs. For every false belief I want to attribute to that person, I must be able to make sense of the person having the specific concepts figuring in that false belief. But this means I must be able to attribute to the person a number of beliefs I take to be *true*. Thus for every false belief I attribute to some person (say, Homer), I must also attribute to Homer a number of *true* beliefs. If, for every belief of Homer's that I want to say is false, there have to be a number of other beliefs of Homer's that I have to say are true, then it will not make sense for me to say that all of a person's beliefs are false. There will still have to be a number of true beliefs. We can only make sense of a person's having a false belief against a background of her having other beliefs we take to be true. The idea of someone having all false beliefs only makes sense when we're not focusing on all of these *true* beliefs we'd have to attribute to the person.

Is this line of argument successful in showing that the Matrix

Possibility is not really a possibility, or that it is not really intelligible? Unfortunately, I think not. For even if the evil computers of the Matrix could not make *all* of your beliefs false (for
then they would not be recognizable as beliefs at all), there
would still be a lot, perhaps even *most* of your beliefs that might
be false if you were in the Matrix. Thus in the end we may have
to concede the intelligibility of the Matrix Possibility. You indeed
might be in the Matrix, and indeed a heck of a lot of your beliefs
might false, even if you can be sure that not *all* of your beliefs
are false. [5]

[5] I would like to thank the several anonymous reviewers, as well as Bill Irwin,
whose comments helped me to much improve this paper. As always, mistakes
that remain are mine.

4

Seeing, Believing, Touching, Truth

CAROLYN KORSMEYER

From 1981 to 1990, over 120 mysterious deaths were reported to the Centers for Disease Control in Atlanta. Healthy adult men, most of them members of the immigrant Hmong community from the Laotian highlands, were dying in their sleep. No medical cause of death could be determined, though the Hmong had their own explanation: they claimed that these men were the victims of a nocturnal spirit which visited them while they slept and pressed the breath from their bodies.[1] The very few survivors of these visitations reported paralyzing terror and the sensation that a malign creature sat astride their chests. Certainly there was evidence that the victims struggled in violent nightmares before they died. Though the scientific community did not settle on its own diagnosis, reports of what became known as Sudden Unexplained Nocturnal Death Syndrome raised the unsettling possibility that dreams could kill.

Just about any sort of sensory experience can occur in the untamed realm of dreams, though as a rule dreams are chiefly visual phenomena invented with wild originality from the repositories of memory and imagination.[2] Dreams may be familiar or

---

[1] Shelley R. Adler, "Sudden Unexplained Nocturnal Death Syndrome among Hmong Immigrants: Examining the Role of the Nightmare." *Journal of American Folklore* 104: 411 (1991) pp. 54–71.

[2] Owen Flanagan, *Dreaming Souls: Sleep, Dreams, and the Evolution of the Conscious Mind* (Oxford: Oxford University Press, 2000) p. 15.

strange, mundane, tedious, ludicrous—or terrifying. The soothing assurance, "It's only a dream," relies on the tacit premise that
what you only *see* can't hurt you, because nothing in the dream
has actually *touched* you. Injury and death require a palpable
interference with the living tissue; surely a mere dream cannot
exert such power. Or so we hope.

Living in the Matrix: Some Classic Philosophical Problems

The supposition of *The Matrix* is that one could live an entire life
made up of illusions caused by brain stimuli induced in a passive,
immobile being for which sleep-like paralysis is a permanent
state. Individuals who are captive in the Matrix—a "computer
generated dream world" (as Morpheus puts it)—believe themselves to be experiencing life with all its familiar riches. Their
sense receptors are hooked into the Matrix, so that taste, smell,
touch, vision, and hearing are stimulated (or simulated) in the ultimate supposition that *esse est percipi*—to be is to be perceived.
This plot premise permits the film to raise not only venerable
philosophical problems about the relation of mind and body and
the uncertainty of knowledge, but also more contemporary para-
noias about political power in a cyber-infected world. This essay
concerns a particular aspect of such issues: sense experience and
the means by which the movie posits what philosophers have
dubbed "skepticism with regard to the senses."

The movie invokes scattershot a series of classic problems of
perception, of which the most obvious reference is to
Descartes's First Meditation. In his famous attempt to induce
doubt that sense experience accurately records features of the
external world and can therefore ground knowledge, Descartes
challenges us to establish criteria by which dreams can be certainly distinguished from waking experience. This is a fairly successful way to arouse skepticism about the veridicality of
present perception, for the experience of dreams can be so vivid
that one is (temporarily) convinced they are real.[3] The begin-

---

[3] Flanagan argues that the problem of determining whether one is asleep is
not the symmetrical converse of the problem of determining whether one is
awake: "We know we are awake when we are. What we don't normally know
is that we are dreaming while we are dreaming" (*Ibid.*, p. 173).

ning of *The Matrix* is peppered with references to the dreaming problem, and more than once Neo awakes in bed sweating and panting from a terrifying encounter with the Matrix. Although these moments are perhaps too-convenient transition devices from scene to scene, like the dreaming argument they raise questions about whether valid inferences may be founded on any given perceptual experience.

Descartes supplements the dreaming argument with the far less persuasive evil deceiver, or "malicious demon," argument, whereby he invites us to imagine that not only sense perception but also absolutely every belief and inference are systematically disrupted by a commanding mind. The contemporary version of the evil deceiver, of course, is the evil computer—the nightmarish cybermind that has reversed the roles of programmed and programmer and artificially induces experiences that constitute a life. How this is accomplished in *The Matrix* is revealed in what has my vote for the scariest scene in the movie, where Neo is flushed into one of the pods that feed human organisms their life-dreams. From there he is permitted—somewhat incoherently, given that he is in the very place where he should not have a vantage on the Matrix itself—a glimpse of millions of other pods filled with dreaming, sentient beings. This scene mirrors the scariest philosophical problem I know: the thought-experiment that supposes that we are but brains in a vat, and only electrical impulses provide us with a mental life.

Are grounds for this kind of suspicion even remotely justified? The senses have long been regarded as the organic interface between mind and body, the means by which we gather data in order to form knowledge about the world. And as we know from experience, any kind of sense perception can be subject to occasional illusion. Might we in fact be such thoroughgoing victims of illusion that every single sense perception is caused not by contact with objects in the external world but only by intervening stimuli in our brains?

There is a school of thought that maintains that any such hypothesis is ultimately incoherent, even self-refuting. The movie shares a problem with the brain-vat that is frequently noted in the literature on the latter: if one is in a systematically deceiving world, how does one attain the ability to make reference to that world? How does one even posit that one is a brain in a vat—or a casualty of the Matrix? This supposition is only possible if one has a vantage from which it is clear that one is *not* a brain in a vat.[4] In this respect the movie is bound by a constraint that limits all dreaming plots from Calderón to *The X-Files*: the narrative point of view is necessarily external to the Matrix. The movie relies on stable points of reference, such as the ship *Nebuchadnezzar,* where we can see the characters strapped into the chairs that feed programs into their brain-plugs. Though they enter the Matrix at will, the characters of the movie are not victims of systematic illusion. The supposition that most people are living totally within a program is a background claim, for such people function like scenery and are not truly characters at all.

Evidently the film makers were sufficiently aware of such sticky problems lurking in the premise of their story to insert some wry self-criticism into the dialogue. Consider the exchange between Mouse and Neo about the food aboard ship. As Neo discovers with his first meal with the crew, outside the Matrix in the twenty-second century, eating has lost its pleasure. Faucets spew out bowls of nutritious single-celled protein, which is temptingly compared to runny eggs or bowls of snot. Mouse compares the substance to the distant memory of Tasty Wheat. But then he wonders: how do the machines that produce this stuff know what Tasty Wheat tastes like? And how can anyone know that it tastes like Tasty Wheat, when we have never actually eaten real Tasty Wheat and can't compare it? How indeed? How can it taste *like* anything at all if there is no reference for it to be like?

Judging Reality

These are very good questions, but they are raised only briefly and no answer is suggested. It is perhaps unfair to require extensive argumentation about the logic of illusion in a movie. There is, however, an important collateral question that is explored somewhat more thoroughly: What is perceptual experience, such that it can be judged not only *real* but also *worthwhile*—worth living for?

---

[4] Perhaps the most well-known discussion along these lines is Hilary Putnam, "Brains in a Vat," in *Reason, Truth, and History* (Cambridge: Cambridge University Press, 1981), pp. 1–21.

Two rival answers are supplied. First, that which is real and valuable is that which is free from the interfering illusions of the Matrix. While this perspective dominates the film and represents the point of view that the audience is supposed to accept, there is another that has fair claims for our attention: what is real is that which provides the most vivid and pleasurable experience. Morpheus and his team seek the former; the latter is the secret agenda of the traitorous Cypher. But it is also voiced by the loyal and sympathetic Mouse, who objects to Dozer's claim that the snot food has everything the body needs. It does not, counters Mouse, because it does not give pleasure, a feeling he associates with essential human responses: "To deny our impulses is to deny the very thing that makes us human." Dozer looks skeptical; he evidently holds taste pleasure to be an indulgence that those who fight the Matrix cannot afford.

Such exchanges reveal a conceptual framework employed by *The Matrix*, one that is likely to be as much the product of unquestioned assumptions about the senses as a self-conscious device of the script. The film treats the five senses and the values they are ascribed in ways that are dramatically interesting though surprisingly traditional, given the radical skepticism essayed by the plot line.

From philosophies of antiquity to contemporary psychological studies, the five senses have been ranked in a hierarchy of importance that reflects an elevation of mind over body, of intellect over emotion, and of knowledge over pleasure.[5] Vision and hearing are the "distal"or distance senses, for they operate at a remove from their objects and do not require physical commerce with them. This distance confers an epistemic advantage, and vision and hearing are typically advanced to the top of the hierarchy because of their importance for gaining knowledge of the world around and communicating that knowledge to others. Because both require a separation between the body of the percipient and the object of perception, vision and hearing are also less engaged with physical sensation. (In fact, vision is typically considered a kind of perception but not a sensation at all.) The so-called bodily senses of taste, smell, and touch require a

---

[5] Carolyn Korsmeyer, *Making Sense of Taste: Food and Philosophy* (Ithaca: Cornell University Press, 1999), Chapter 1.

degree of physical contact with their objects. Though smell requires some physical separation to function, the three bodily senses demand proximity, even intimacy, and experiences of all three have distinct sensory feeling qualities. They are tradition- ally believed to direct attention more to our own subjective states than to objects, both because of the limited scope of infor- mation they deliver and because we are apt to be diverted by the pleasures they afford. The physicality associated with touch, smell, and taste is one source of the low status of the bodily senses, which are associated with the more animal side of human nature.

Sensing in the Matrix and in *The Matrix*

It is to be expected that vision and hearing are manipulated extensively in any movie. While we cannot ourselves touch or smell or taste anything on screen, we can literally see and hear it, and some of what we see and hear is also seen and heard by the characters on the screen, making us co-participants in their experiences. The dialogue refers to vision and the eyes in familiarly ambiguous ways: What one sees may be merely the illusory product of a program, and yet "to see" is also synony- mous with insight and knowledge, since vision has served throughout the entire history of western philosophy as a metaphor for understanding.[6] Morpheus, the wise leader of the movie, expresses his admonitions and analytical observations in visual metaphors. He informs Neo, for example, that he has been born into a prison that he cannot smell or taste or touch: "A prison for your mind." But he can *see* it—out the window, everywhere. As Morpheus puts it, the Matrix is the "world that has been pulled over your eyes to blind you from the truth— . . . that you are a slave." Yet despite the pervasive visual deceptions of the Matrix, Morpheus urges Neo to use his eyes in their higher epistemic calling—to *see* beyond illusion to the truth, to *understand*. After his bath in pink goo and his horri-

---

[6] Many sense metaphors are used for this purpose: "I hear you." "I grasp this idea," and so on. But vision has played an especially vivid role in epistemic language. See Martin Jay, *Downcast Eyes: The Denigration of Vision in Twentieth-Century French Thought* (Berkeley and Los Angeles: University of California Press, 1993).

fying experience in the Matrix-pod, Neo awakes and asks, "Why do my eyes hurt?" Morpheus replies: "You've never used them before." Rather like a new emergent from Plato's cave, Neo is bothered by light, for the truth is neither easy nor comfortable to see. As Morpheus says of his own discovery that human organisms are grown to supply energy to the AI machines of the Matrix: "For the longest time I wouldn't believe it, and then I saw the fields with my own eyes." Sight more than any other sense is explicitly extolled for its traditional link with the mind; according to the old saying, "Seeing is believing." At the same time, seeing is also subject to hallucination and therefore doubt, and we do well to remember the completion of this aphorism: "Seeing's believing, but touching's the truth." This does not mean that touch is immune to deception, which obviously is not the case. Nonetheless, a hallucination or mirage is discovered to be such because one's hand passes right through without the sense of touch encountering brute materiality. Therefore, both in folk psychology and in *The Matrix*, the physicality of touch is often regarded as more reliable than the distant operation of vision. Expression of such values is interestingly discrepant with the movie medium, which addresses the distal senses almost exclusively.

Because they operate at a distance, both vision and hearing may be readily employed for surveillance. Early in the movie Neo must be debugged (almost literally, for the listening device has a witty centipede-like design) to keep the Agents from tracking his movements. Sound is a potently expressive device at the disposal of a film maker, and *The Matrix* also employs hearing in a complex manner that somewhat unusually connects this sense with touch. Sound itself has a haptic quality, and the very loud segments of the soundtrack are a palpable presence. (At the end of the movie the music screams "WAKE UP!", wrapping back to the dream questions at the beginning.)[7] Such aggressive sound seems actually to invade the bodily space of the hearer. Ambient sound conveys its own message, for old, obsolete

---

[7] For viewers who recognize the music, this part of the soundtrack provides something of a bridge from the movie experience back to reality. The music is by Rage Against the Machine, a group known for its political messages; and since by this point the credits are rolling, the lyrics are both background to the movie and admonition to the audience to consider its message.

devices that clank and grind are more trustworthy than the quiet whir of computers: the lines of the crucial rotary telephones convey both the voices and the bodies of the characters back to the safety of the ship—for evidently, even virtual bodies require tactile, physical conduits.[8] Especially sensitive information is sometimes conveyed in a whisper that requires such proximity that the characters nearly touch, as in the beginning when Neo and Trinity meet. The music at the club they attend is so loud that one both hears and feels it. They must stand very close, and as Trinity speaks in his ear her lips brush his neck.

The bodily senses take on particularly interesting roles in the movie. Lots of objects generate a scent, but in *The Matrix* the smell of human bodies is especially emphasized in ways both positive and negative. In an early scene Trinity hovers over a sleeping Neo and slowly, quietly sniffs him. It is a gesture at once curious, affectionate, and intimate. It is also refreshingly at odds with the clutter of high-tech equipment used to obtain information, for sniffing is a primitive, animal mode of discovery. We assume that his scent pleases her, but such is not the case with Agent Smith, who appears to be almost maddened by the smell of his human adversaries. To indulge a tirade against Morpheus, Smith breaks protocol and removes his earpiece, thereby missing important information about events taking place nearby.

> I hate this place. This zoo. This prison. This reality, whatever you want to call it. I can't stand it any longer. It's the smell, if there is such a thing. I feel saturated by it. I can taste your stink and every time I do, I fear that I've somehow been infected by it.

Smith compares human beings with viruses, a dreadful equation that dramatizes the contagious aura of bad smells.[9] With both alluring *scents* and hostile, repulsive *stinks*, the sense of smell is employed to emphasize corporeality, as though the animal

---

[8] Though presently a popular idea, the notion of the "virtual body" is probably a conceptual muddle, which is especially evident if one considers the different requirements of the senses.

[9] On the subject of smell and disease, see Alain Corbin, *The Foul and the Fragrant: Odor and the French Social Imagination*, trans. M. Kochan, R. Porter, and C. Prendergast (Cambridge: Harvard University Press, 1986).

humanity of even the virtual body breaks through in its smell. We would imagine that the non-human Agents, "sentient programs," have no smell themselves; the olfaction they are capable of merely detects the reek of their opponents.

The Seductions of Taste

Taste is employed in *The Matrix* with particularly ascetic values, as we have already seen, for the pleasure of eating embodies the dangerous temptations that subvert the war against the Matrix. Exhausted by the ongoing effort to protect Zion, Cypher abandons the quest of his companions and betrays them, agreeing to deliver Morpheus to Agent Smith. All he wants is to forget his past and to live within a program that provides him with the comforts that seem otherwise foreclosed. We first learn of Cypher's sensuous tendencies—representative of his moral weakness—when he offers Neo a drink of home-made hooch in apparent friendship and jocularly undermines his confidence that he is "the One" who Morpheus believes was sent to save the world. His more profound deception is revealed in the next scene in which he dines in an elegant Matrix restaurant with Agent Smith. Cypher savors a perfectly cooked steak. As he eats and drinks and smokes a cigar, he declares that he wants to be reinserted into the Matrix and to remember nothing from before.

> I know this steak doesn't exist. I know that when I put it in my mouth, the Matrix is telling my brain that it is juicy and delicious. After nine years, do you know what I realize? Ignorance is bliss.

Although this point of view is presented as transparently wrong, the movie actually reinforces it with its use of color. As Cypher notices, the world of the real to which his colleagues remain committed seems to be losing vivacity. *The Matrix* is almost wholly bleak in hue: black, gray, brown, sepia. When saturated color appears on screen it is shockingly vivid. The only objects with brilliant color in the entire movie are things that indicate almost nostalgically the life of the senses: vending carts full of bright fruit, the red dress of the virtual woman created as an emblem of sexuality, and blood. All are symbols of living, organic form—though only the blood, also a symbol of dying—is not illusory.

Cypher has been seduced by food, but he has additional reasons to abandon the fight, for he has come to believe that the
world of the Matrix is more real than the one outside. (As he
puts it, "real" is just another four-letter word.) His conclusion
proceeds not only from his own valuation of pleasurable sense
experience but also from a perspective voiced earlier by
Morpheus himself: all sense experience is just interpreted stimulation of nerve receptors.

> MORPHEUS: What is real? How do you define real? If you're talking
> about what you can feel, what you can smell, what you can taste
> and see, then real is simply electrical signals interpreted by your
> brain.

With dedicated strength of character, Morpheus remains committed to the brute, real world that causes such brain signals.
But Cypher diverges in a reasonable direction: if the real is truly
just phenomenal sense experiences, what does it matter where
they come from? If reality comes down to one's own sensations,
there is nothing immoral in pursuing them, because there *is*
nothing else to demand one's moral attention. So Cypher pur-
sues the pleasures of the bodily senses, long associated with
temptation and sin. In so doing he makes not only a moral error
but also an epistemic miscalculation, for he settles for illusion
rather than reality—which constitutes an implicit if perhaps
inadvertent refutation of the analysis of sense experience in
wholly subjective terms. That is, if Cypher is wrong then so is
Morpheus: sensations are *not* in all cases just interpretations of
brain stimuli but also are indicators of an external reality that
demands attention and respect.

To be sure, taste pleasures need not necessarily subvert one's
morals, as a parallel scene with the Oracle demonstrates. When
Neo visits her, the Oracle is baking cookies, and their delicious
scent fills the air. She herself is drinking something chartreuse
and smoking. She can indulge her senses, one presumes,
because she has not abandoned the deeper values that Cypher
relinquishes. Neo eats a cookie but, significantly, he doesn't
seem to enjoy it very much.

Scenes with Cypher also make use of another traditional
meaning of the taste sense: the association of taste and eating
with sex. In his final act of treachery as he readies to kill his for-

mer colleagues, he croons menacingly over Trinity's dreaming body strapped into its chair. He tells her (and she can hear him on the other end of a phone line where she awaits to be transported back to safety) that he once was in love with her, that he is tired of war, and tired of eating the same goop everyday. His language and gestures are both threatening and caressing as he announces that he has decided that the Matrix can be more real than real life, because the experience it furnishes is more complete. You *see* death in the Matrix, he observes as he pulls the plugs from both Apoc and Switch; here you just die. Once again he echoes an only slightly distorted version of a sentiment expressed by Morpheus: What I see is real. Seeing is believing.

Truth

Which brings us to touch. This is an action movie full of physical violence, and a good deal of the plot consists of avoiding death. Though most combat occurs within a Matrix program full of slick and tiresome special effects, it physically affects the bodies strapped into the chairs aboard ship. When Neo emerges from one encounter, he tastes the blood that trickles from his mouth and is taken aback that a virtual experience could cause physical injury. "If you're killed in the Matrix, you die here?" he inquires. Morpheus replies soberly: "The body cannot live without the mind," reinforcing his comment about virtual experience: "the mind makes it real." I confess that at first these scenes tried my patience, along with several more loose comments about mind and body. ("It is not the spoon that bends, it is only yourself," pronounces one of the Oracle's young "potentials," adept at bending spoons without touching them.) An exasperated viewer could conclude that blatant hooey uttered with faux-Zen opacity passes for insight. What could it be but a cheap plot trick to say that if you die in the virtual world of the Matrix you also die in reality. But then I remembered the Hmong and their deadly dreams. Changes in heart rate, breathing, and adrenaline output are among the noticeable physical changes that mental images can bring about. It is but a short step further for a dream—or a virtual experience—to draw blood, a bridge between what is merely seen and what has a palpable, felt effect—a bridge, that is, between vision and touch.

   Not all touch is violent, and the movie uses gentler touch in
standard ways to indicate affection, trust, and friendship. The
grip of Neo's hand saves Morpheus at the end of a helicopter
rescue line. Trinity hugs Tank to comfort him for the loss of his
brother. As Tank prepares to pull the plug on Morpheus, he
strokes his forehead in sad farewell.
   Above all it is Trinity whose actions embody the intimate side
of trust. It is no accident that this role is given to a woman, for
the tender aspect of touch is associated with both eroticism and
maternal care, and since Trinity is the only female sexual presence in the script, these roles fall to her. (Evidently in their
efforts to inspire doubt about the certainty of sense experience,
the film makers forgot to doubt gender stereotypes.) Most dramatic is the final scene in which she delivers a Sleeping Beauty
style kiss and breathes the life back into Neo. Although it is clear
that they are drawn to each other from the start, they only kiss
outside the Matrix, a fact made explicit in an early version of the
script, where she tells Neo that she will not kiss him in the
Matrix—because she wants it to be real.[10] This declaration has
been dropped in the final version, but the action is retained:
Trinity delivers her life-giving kiss in the bleak atmosphere of
Nebuchadnezzar when Neo is on the brink of death, having lost
what appears to be his final battle with the Agents. She reaches
out both physically and emotionally to Neo, caressing his inert
body and whispering:

> The Oracle told me that I would fall in love and that that man, the
> man that I loved would be the One. So you see, you can't be dead.
> You can't be. Because I love you. You hear me? I love you.

She gently holds his shoulders and kisses him; his heart starts to
beat and he draws a breath. She withdraws her hands and commands sharply: "Now get up!"
   Neo gets up and saves the world.
   Touching's the truth.

---

[10] Larry and Andy Wachowski, *The Matrix*, April 8, 1996
<http://www.geocities.com/Area51/Capsule/8448/Matrix.txt>.

The Desert of the Real

5

The Metaphysics of
The Matrix

JORGE J.E. GRACIA and
JONATHAN J. SANFORD

"Life is a dream."
— PEDRO CALDERÓN DE LA BARCA (A.D. 1600–1681)

"All human beings by nature desire to know."
— ARISTOTLE (384–321 B.C.)

The scene is a dark club. One gets passing glimpses of skimpy leather, lascivious movements. There is the suggestion of sleazy sex, illicit drugs. The atmosphere is charged with suspicion, even fear. Techno-industrial music is blaring and our two heroes are surrounded by weirdly clad, sub-terrestrial people. Trinity approaches Neo. Their cat-like eyes meet. She comes close, almost touching his cheek. Tension builds, an animal attraction is clear. One expects the usual, but instead, she whispers in his ear: "It is the question that drives us, Neo. It is the question that brought you here. You know the question, just as I did. The answer is out there, Neo."

The question is "What is the Matrix?", and the search for its answer eventually leads Neo out of his prison and into the real world. Neo's path out of the Matrix is not unlike the prisoner's ascent from the cave in Plato's allegory, but the reality that Neo discovers is no blessed realm of Forms, pure and shining forth in beauty. Rather, he discovers a reality that is ugly, a world seared by war between humans and machines, where existence is meted out with only the barest means and life is lived in a constant threat of death. It is a reality described by Morpheus as a desert, so bleak that, after nine years, Cypher decides to abandon it, even if to do so requires the betrayal of his comrades. But Neo prefers it to the illusion of the Matrix because it is the truth. He prefers it so much that *The Matrix* closes with Neo's resolution to destroy the world of illusion and bring others to the truth of their existence. Like Plato's escaped prisoner, Neo returns to the false world to free others from their imprisonment. And hence the much anticipated sequel.

The questions posed by *The Matrix* take the form of the paradigmatic metaphysical question, "What is — ?" "What is reality?" "What is a person?" "What is the relation between mind and body?" "What is the connection between free will and fate?" In what follows, we focus on three fundamental questions: What is appearance and what is reality? What is it that separates them? What properties or features are found in one and not the other? These questions are asked in the context of the world of the movie, but answering them should help us think about our own world.

The Nature of Metaphysics

What exactly is metaphysics? What are metaphysical questions and metaphysical answers? Answering these questions requires a distinction between *a* metaphysics and metaphysics. *A* metaphysics is a view of the world that seeks to be accurate, consistent, comprehensive, and supported by sound evidence. Metaphysics, on the other hand, is the learned discipline one practices when one seeks to develop *a* metaphysics, consisting therefore in a set of procedures. Metaphysics is different from both natural science and theology. The sciences are disciplines of learning that, like metaphysics, seek to develop views that are accurate, consistent and supported by sound evidence, but, unlike metaphysics, do not seek to be comprehensive. The sciences have restricted areas of competence and specialized methods. Astronomy deals only with astral bodies and its method involves observation and mathematical calculations; physics studies only certain properties of the physical universe and does so with very specific methods; and so on. Theology, like metaphysics, seeks to develop comprehensive views of the world that are accurate, consistent, and supported by sound evidence, however the evidence that theology regards as sound goes beyond what we can acquire through our natural powers of reasoning and sensation; it includes faith and authority.

This is enough to distinguish metaphysics from particular sciences and theology, and it should also be enough to distinguish metaphysical views from scientific or theological ones, although it does not preclude that some views may be found in all three or in two of them. Nonetheless, it is not sufficient to distinguish metaphysics from other branches of philosophy, a number of which are also important to the film and discussed in other essays in this book. Among these other branches are ethics, political philosophy, epistemology, logic, philosophical anthropology, and natural theology. Nor does it tell us enough about what metaphysicians actually do, that is, about how it is that one tries to develop a metaphysics.

Another way to distinguish metaphysics from the sciences, theology, and other areas of philosophy, and to establish what is involved in carrying out its task, is to say that metaphysics tries (1) to develop a list of the most general categories into which all other categories may be classified and (2) to establish how the less general categories are related to these. The task of metaphysics, then, is twofold: First, to develop a list of the most general categories and, second, to categorize everything else in terms of these. Obviously, to do this is precisely to try to develop the kind of overall, comprehensive view of the world in which both scientific and theological elements are included.[1] For example, psychologists study human psyches and physicists study such things as the color white, but metaphysicians go further and try to categorize these in an overall scheme. If we were to adopt the Aristotelian categorial scheme, we would categorize human psyches by saying that they are substances; and if

---

[1] This view of metaphysics is defended by Gracia in *Metaphysics and Its Task: The Search for the Categorial Foundation of Knowledge* (Albany: StateUniversity of New York Press, 1999), Chapters 2 and 7. See also Sanford's "Categories and Metaphysics: Aristotle's Science of Being" in Michael Gorman and Jonathan J. Sanford, eds., *Categories: Historical and Systematic Essays* (Washington, D.C.: Catholic University of America Press, forthcoming).

this were to be applied to something like white, we would say that it is a quality. If, instead, we were to apply Hume's scheme, we would have to talk about ideas, rather than about substances or qualities. Deciding whether human psyches and colors are substances and qualities or ideas—an issue pertinent to *The Matrix*—is only possible if the aim of metaphysics has been successfully accomplished.

These clarifications should make it easier to grasp the nature of the task involved in developing a metaphysics of *The Matrix*. However, the issue is still clouded, because the written expression, "a metaphysics of *The Matrix*" has at least two meanings, which in turn point in at least two different directions. The first refers to the film itself, and the second to the world presented in the film. A metaphysics of the film would establish the most general category or categories to which the film belongs. A metaphysics of the second involves the metaphysical view of the world presented in the film. Taken in the latter way, the task consists in (1) the development of a list of the most general categories either explicitly presented or implicitly used in the film, and the establishment of (2) their interrelations, and (3) of how everything else in the film fits within these categories. In this sense, the task involves the description of what might be called "the world of *The Matrix*," and this we take to be our task.

Attempts to develop complete and final metaphysical categorizations are fraught with difficulties because of the high degree of generality and abstraction they require. They involve an impalpable world of ideas and conceptual models largely removed from immediate experience. These kinds of categorizations usually result in categorial schemes that contain internal puzzles, if not downright inconsistencies. However, often these are not the result of the metaphysician's procedures, but of the very conceptual frameworks embedded in the ordinary ways in which we think about the world. Often, moreover, the things to which the conceptual frameworks correspond are themselves very complex. It is a very tricky thing to produce categorial schemes that work with clear concepts and that correspond adequately to the things being described. The metaphysics of *The Matrix* confirms this assessment.

Fundamental Categories of the World
of *The Matrix*

The world of *The Matrix* appears to be deceptively simple, but is in fact very complex and resembles in many ways our world. Nonetheless, it makes use of only a few most general categories. Two of these are fundamental, and have been used in philosophy since the Pre-Socratics. They are most often referred to as appearance and reality, but in *The Matrix* they are often indicated through the adjectives "real" and "virtual," which are in turn joined to "world," as in "the real world" and "the virtual world." The second also is referred to as "the dream world," when, for instance, Morpheus explains to Neo on his first trip to the loading construct: "You've been living in a dream world, Neo." It is convenient to use "unreal" for "virtual" and "dream" because this more clearly contrasts with "real." These categories are presented as mutually exclusive. Moreover, in that important conversation referred to above, as well as in other places throughout the film, the two worlds are described as jointly exhaustive. This means that whatever is real is not unreal, and *vice versa*, and everything is either real or unreal. Our job as metaphysicians, then, involves further the classification of the items belonging to less general categories that are present in *The Matrix* into one or the other of these two most general categories and to explain how the whole thing hangs together.

The Matrix is full of things belonging to all sorts of less general categories and which deserve attention and classification into the most general categories. However, because of our limited space and aims, we focus only on those items that may pose what we consider to be one of the fundamental metaphysical conundrums posed by the film. By a metaphysical conundrum we mean that a categorial classification puts us on the horns of a dilemma, with no easy way out. Our metaphysical analysis, then, will aim to present this dilemma and then to speculate on a solution to it.

So, what are the categories of the real and the unreal that we need to take into account? There are at least three main categories of the real, although only one of these is mentioned explicitly in the film. Subcategories of the other two are given, but the categories themselves are not mentioned. The category explicitly mentioned is "mind," and the categories not mentioned but used are "non-mind" and "composites of mind and non-mind." The category of mind includes human minds, such as Neo's, Morpheus's, yours, and ours.

In the category of non-minds, there are all sorts of things that are included. Indeed, there are so many that they fall into subcategories. The main subcategories are machine, human body, or human organ, and things that are none of these. The prime example of machine mentioned is a computer, but there are others, such as Morpheus's ship, weapons, and so on. The prime example of the second category is our bodies or yours, and our brains or yours. Examples of the third category are such things as the Earth, buildings, and electrical signals.

The prime example of the third main category of the real—the composite of mind and body—is a human being. Morpheus refers to this category indirectly when he explains to Neo that dying in the Matrix implies dying in the real world: "The body cannot live without the mind."

There are at least eight subcategories of the unreal or "dream world": simulation (neuro-interactive), image (of the self), digital entity (a self), dream, appearance, mental projection, matrixes of which the Matrix is one instance, and computer programs in general when these are considered as part of virtual reality.

Naturally, the distinction between real and unreal must be justified in terms of some properties that separate them. It would not do just to say that they are different without being able to point out what the difference between them consists of. Moreover, whatever property (or properties) is used to distinguish between the real and unreal, must also belong to the things that are classified as such. So our question is: What is it that is common to all real things and common to all unreal things, that makes them what they are and different from each other? Or put in another way, why is it that minds, machines, human bodies, computer programs and electrical signals are real, and simulations, images, digital entities, dreams, appearances, mental projections, the Matrix, and computer programs are not?

The Real and the Unreal

There are at least two main ways in which to distinguish metaphysically between real and unreal categories. The first has to do with the source of the real and unreal respectively, the second with the ontological status of the two.

We know the sources, or causes, for many of the things in the real world. We know that machines and electrical signals are produced by humans and by artificially intelligent machines. We know that human beings born in the city of Zion come from their parents. But we do not know the ultimate source for these things. That is, we are not told from where the matter comes, from which machines are made and humans reproduced. Nor do we know where, ultimately, the mind comes from, although we are told that Neo is the reincarnation of the first man who could bend the rules of the Matrix and who freed the first of the prisoners. What we do know, however, is that the Matrix is not the cause of the things in the real world. Whatever the ultimate causes are for the things which we can categorize under "real," they do not have to do with the causes responsible for creating the unreal world of the Matrix.

In contrast, we do know the source for all the things in the world of the Matrix. The Matrix is a very complex computer program made by artificially intelligent machines. The very existence of this virtual world and its variegated dimensions are the product of these machines. So, even though we do not know ultimately the causes for the real world, one way in which we can distinguish between the real and unreal worlds is by means of their respective sources: the real and the unreal worlds have different causes.

The second way to distinguish between the categories of real and unreal has to do with their respective ontological status—put plainly, the way things exist. One way of determining ontological status is in terms of dependence. The real world in *The Matrix*, as far as we can tell, does not depend on something else for its existence; it stands by itself, as it were. There is no mention of a malicious demon, no evil or benign genie, on whose will the real world depends. But even if there were, that is, even if the existence of things in the real world were dependent on such a genie, the ontological status of the unreal world can be seen to be much weaker, much less independent, than that of the real world. This is so because the unreal world depends entirely on things in the real world for its existence. The virtual world exists only so long as the artificially intelligent machines keep running the program and generating electrical signals which affect human brains—and remember that machines, programs, electrical signals, and brains are real—which prompt the mind—also real—to produce the digital entities and appearances of the unreal world. The unreal world has a weaker ontological status because it depends on things in the real world for its existence.

The two ways of distinguishing between the real and unreal worlds—the sources for each and their ontological status—clarify the distinction between the two fundamental categories of *The Matrix*. The real world is metaphysically distinct from the unreal world because the former contains things that have a different source and ontological status from the things contained in the latter. A related issue concerns how we come to recognize the metaphysical distinction between the two worlds. For the characters in the movie, knowing the difference requires the lead of a teacher to show them the difference. It is only because there was a first man who knew the Matrix for what it is and escaped, that other prisoners were able to escape from the Matrix. We are not told how this first man came to this knowledge, just as we don't know how there came to be a first freed prisoner in Plato's cave analogy, but Neo would not have known the difference between the two worlds were it not for Morpheus and his crew. Though knowing the difference between the two worlds requires a teacher, Neo, Trinity, and others were open to such teaching because they had paid attention to hints indicating that something is amiss in their world, as Morpheus indicates in his conversation with Neo just before Neo chooses to take the red pill: "What you know you can't explain but you feel it. You've felt it your entire life. . . . That there's something wrong with the world. You don't know what it is, but it's there, like a splinter in your mind, driving you mad." The issue of how we come to know the distinction between the two worlds concerns the nature of knowledge. It is thus an epistemological, not a metaphysical issue. We mention this issue, discussed in the previous section of this book, because it is closely related to the metaphysical issue, but we are not going to deal further with it.

The Metaphysical Conundrum Posed by *The Matrix*

The Matrix presents a dualistic metaphysics, that is, a view about the ultimate nature of the world which claims that the world is made up of exactly two incompatible types of things. This position is usually contrasted with monism, in which the world is seen as being composed ultimately of only one kind of thing. The dualism of *The Matrix* consists, on the one hand, of the world of appearances, the unreal world of the Matrix; on the other, we have the real world, the world in which a war of machines versus human beings is taking place. Because the sources for these two worlds are different, and because the things in the two worlds differ in their ontological status, the categories to which they belong are presented as irreducible, irreconcilable, and mutually exclusive. One goal of metaphysicians is to reconcile, if possible, appearance with reality. The metaphysical conundrum of *The Matrix* is that, when we consider the metaphysical categorial scheme with which it presents us, *prima facie* there seems to be no way to reconcile the real with the unreal. Each of these has its own rules, and there is no way to square one set of rules with the other.

So what? What does it matter whether or not the world is dualistic or monistic? One answer is that, insofar as metaphysics seeks descriptions of the world that are accurate, consistent, and comprehensive, success cannot be achieved unless this fundamental issue of dualism versus monism is resolved. Is everything we experience a mere appearance, or are these appearances manifestations of actual things which are more or less as they appear to be? One of the merits of *The Matrix* is that it provokes our reflection on this question.

The dualistic metaphysical scheme assumed in the movie is challenged by several inconsistencies. The most blatant of these has to do with death. Death in the Matrix means death in the real world, and *vice versa*. But there are others, notably love and free will. The love of Trinity for Neo resurrects both his real self and his digital self, bridging the divide between the two worlds, and Neo's resurrection gives him the ability to will his way beyond the rules of the Matrix, manipulating it to his own designs. Moreover, although Neo takes the red pill in the unreal world, this allows him to wake up in the real world, and even though the Oracle exists in the virtual world, she can predict and influence what happens in the real world. These inconsistencies suggest ways in which the two worlds, presented as irreducible, irreconcilable, and mutually exclusive, are not in fact so. But how is this possible?

The answer is not immediately clear, although one thing is: Minds are real, and they have the power to produce unreality, either through responses to bodily processes or on their own. A mind can respond to an electrical stimulus to the brain by creating an image, but a mind can also affect the body by independently creating the image. This suggests a way out of the apparent inconsistencies: It looks as if the unreal can directly affect the real, but it is only the real that can directly affect the real. The unreal affects the real only indirectly, when a confused mind takes it for the real. Clarity about this is what Neo and the others are searching for; they want the truth. Death in the virtual world results in death in the real one because the mind mistakenly takes it as real and causes it in the body. The virtual pills are effective in the real world in part because the mind takes them to be part of the real world and commands the body to act accordingly. And the virtual Oracle knows and influences the real world because the mind believes it. Only when the mind is free from confusion and can identify the unreal for what it is, can the mind also cease to be influenced by unreality.

The answer to the apparent inconsistency in *The Matrix*, then, lies in the nature of the prime example of the third category of the real, that is, in human beings. Morpheus, Trinity, Tank, Dozer, and other human beings, both in mind and body, live wholly in the real world except for the times when they choose to hack into the Matrix. All the human beings who are prisoners of the Matrix, however, live in both worlds. Their minds are, as it were, plugged into the Matrix, but their bodies are in the real world, albeit in shackles. The hope for these prisoners is that the two worlds may not be as irreducible, irreconcilable, and mutually exclusive as they appear. What they require is the integration of their minds with their bodies and the proper understanding of how to distinguish between appearance and reality. This sets them free, but to achieve this, they must either be saved individually in the manner in which Morpheus, Trinity, and Neo were saved, or the Matrix must be destroyed. We can expect the sequel to *The Matrix* to pursue one or both of these means of liberating the prisoners of the Matrix.

Overcoming Illusion

In this chapter, we have focused on some fundamental metaphysical questions raised by the film. We have described the main task of metaphysics, and have pursued this task in generating a rough sketch of a metaphysics of *The Matrix*. We identified and investigated the two fundamental categories in the film, real and unreal, and found that they are presented as irreducible, irreconcilable, and mutually exclusive. Yet the film contains inconsistencies in their presentation which require resolution. This resolution is not achieved by collapsing the unreal world into the real, but rather either by distinguishing between the two worlds or by destroying the unreal world. It is because of the fact that human beings are composites of bodies and minds, and that their minds have the power to overcome illusions, that there is an exit from the predicament in *The Matrix*.

When reflecting on *The Matrix* in order to learn something about our world, we have to remember, of course, that it is just a movie. Its peculiar portrayal of the dialectic between appearance and reality should not be taken simply as an accurate metaphor for our world. Nevertheless, in our world we do in fact use the most general categories we find in *The Matrix*: We experience various simulations in our dreams and in different types of hallucinations; we designate the entities encountered in such experiences as not being real; we are confronted with other phenomena about which we wonder whether they really are as they appear to be; and we are affected in our real lives as much by facts as by fictions. *The Matrix* raises questions about these and related matters and prompts us to reflect not just on them, but on the nature of reality itself.

6

The Machine-Made Ghost: Or, The Philosophy of Mind, Matrix Style

JASON HOLT

The Matrix is cutting-edge cool. The effects are exceptional, the action stylishly frenetic, the premise itself compelling. The food for thought it offers is better for you than Tasty Wheat, and much more appetizing than the *Nebuchadnezzar's* usual mess-mash. Here's just a sampler. Could we be systematically deceived about reality? What if we were? How could we tell? Is it worth finding out, or is a blissful ignorance better than knowing the horrible truth? Which pill, the red or the blue, would *you* pick? Why?

This is very cool stuff. To philosophers, though, it's old hat. Descartes's malicious demon hypothesis is hundreds of years old. It was reborn decades back as the brain-in-a-vat scenario, which *The Matrix* makes over as a body-in-a-vat. The question of truth versus happiness goes back even further, as far back as the ancient Greeks. Plato wrote much about it. Aristotle too. The idea of systematic deception even has cinematic precedents, *Total Recall* and *Dark City*, to name just two. While, in *The Matrix*, these are the most obvious ports of philosophical access, they're not what I'm going to talk about.

So what am I going to talk about? "Unfortunately," says Morpheus, "no one can be told what the Matrix is." No one in the movie, that is. The Matrix is a virtual reality, a world "pulled over your eyes to blind you from the truth." With certain exceptions, it's so comprehensively, so completely realistic that practically everyone plugged in believes it's real, even Neo, the One himself, who needs to be shown, like anyone else, how to take the veil from his eyes. It's such a tempting veil that even those who know it's a veil are naturally drawn, almost compelled, to believe it's real. Before he sees the light, Neo's mind is exhausted by these veiled misperceptions, the beliefs he derives from them, and the intentions, desires, and other attitudes he forms in response to them. The deception, as you know, is orchestrated by the machines, who've taken over the world in a sort of artificial-intelligence version of *Planet of the Apes*. It's a machine-made deception, the illusory ghost of a world that is no longer—hence the title of this chapter, which is also, more directly, a play on Descartes's view of the mind as a soul, a spirit that inhabits the body, a "ghost in the machine."

What I'm going to talk about, as the subtitle says, is the philosophy of mind. For an appetizer, we'll begin with a crash course in the mind-body problem. There will be two entrées: (1) artificial intelligence—specifically, the possibility of artificial minds, and (2) metaphysics—what the mind really is. I'll argue, against much received wisdom, that artificial minds are possible, and that mental states are brain states. There's a tension lurking here, but one that can be resolved simply enough. For dessert, a solution to the so-called hard problem of consciousness, which is at the very heart of the apparent divide between mind and brain.

The Mind-Body Problem: A Crash Course

The mind-body problem begins, as does modern philosophy itself, with Descartes, whom you may remember from such slogans as "I think, therefore I am," which, incidentally, you might also recall from *Blade Runner*, another film spun on an AI scenario. Descartes thought that mind and matter are fundamentally different sorts of thing. The mind is a *thinking* thing, while material objects are *extended* in space. They have dimension. The physical realm is mechanistic, governed by physical laws, while the mind is subject to different principles, laws of thought, and is moreover—literally—a *free* spirit, a ghost in the machine. Despite being so different, mind and matter appear to interact. Events in the physical world cause me to have certain experiences—I assume *we're* not in the Matrix, or anything like it, here. Likewise, my intention to act in certain ways causes my body to move as it does. Ditto the assumption. So how do mind and matter interact? They just do. This is the mind-over-matter worldview that suffuses our culture. Just think of the Police album *Ghost in the Machine*, on which you'll find the hit single "Spirits in the Material World." Not an uncommon worldview, by any means. It's too useful. But it's also, sad to say, inadequate. Inadequate? How dare I? Well, it's my job. Descartes's theory of mind leaves too many questions unanswered. How can mind and matter interact if they're essentially different substances that operate according to their own unique principles? And *where* do they interact?

Descartes's account of mind-brain interaction is mysterious, and such appeals to mystery are notoriously weak. Descartes seems to err by thinking there's a *je ne sais quoi* to the mind over and above what's revealed, at least potentially, in action. In sports, there's no "team spirit" apart from the players' behavior, their vigorous play, cheering each other on, locker-room cama-raderie, and so forth. Likewise, there's no "mind spirit" apart from what the body does and how it does it. This is behavior-ism, the view that mental states are just pieces of behavior, or better, behavioral *dispositions*. I don't always say "Ouch!" when I'm in pain, but I'm always disposed to say it. Behaviorism doesn't work either, though. It confuses the *evidence* we have for other people's mental states with what the evidence is evi-dence *for*. My saying "Ouch!" or my disposition to say it isn't the same thing as my pain. It's evidence of it. Here's another prob-lem. Say you explain my saying "Ouch!" by citing the fact that I was disposed to say "Ouch!" Not exactly a mind-blowing expla-nation, is it? It has the form "Jason did *x* because Jason was dis-posed to do *x*." Trivial. When glass breaks, it breaks because it's fragile. Its fragility is the disposition to break easily. But why is the glass fragile? Because of its microphysical properties. In the same way, when I say "Ouch!" it's because of the microphysical properties of my brain. My pain, then, isn't my disposition to say "Ouch!" but rather a certain state of my brain, which causes me to say it. This is materialism—not to be confused with the will to acquire wealth—the view that mental states are brain states. Sounds reasonable, doesn't it?

Materialism is a nice theory. It's simple, elegant, fruitful, coheres well with our body of scientific knowledge, and relatedly, anchors the mind to the physical world. But materialism has its pitfalls. Practically no contemporary philosopher believes it. I'm an exception. Not that there's anything wrong with that. After all, the Morpheus crew held unpopular beliefs about the nature of reality. And they were right. So why does virtually no one buy materialism these days? Well, some are compelled by Descartes's suspicion that the mind simply *can't* be states of the brain.[1] A related idea, sensible enough, is that all physical events have physical causes. This isn't a problem for materialism. Together with Descartes's suspicion, though, this means that even if mental states are *generated* by the brain, they have no effect in the world. They're causally inert, or what philosophers call *epiphenomenal*. The main reason, though, is that for any type of mental state, pain say, there's more than one physical way to get the job done. Various physical states will do, so there's no one single such state to identify pain with. If a robot could feel pain, for instance, its pain would be a silicon state, not a brain state. Perhaps ironically, I think that computers, like the Matrix-making machines in *The Matrix*, can, at least in principle, feel pain. I'll sort this out in the next section or two. But be advised. There are other reasons to reject materialism, and lines of development of the points above, which I won't cover here. It would bore you. It would bore *me*, and I do this for a living.

Artificial Minds

Can computers think? Could machines be built to have minds as we do? Such questions don't concern, say, whether the antiquated Mac Classic, collecting dust in my closet, has consciousness, or would have consciousness if I turned it on. The answer to that is quite obviously "No." They concern, rather, whether it's *possible* to build an artificial mind as robust and multi-faceted as the human mind. Interesting stuff, this, not to mention fertile philosophical ground. *The Matrix* can be usefully interpreted as exploring such terrain, less directly and, perhaps, more tellingly

---

[1] Underlying this suspicion is the idea that materialism rules out all the wonders of being human, having a soul, creativity, moral significance and responsibility, and freedom. On the question of human freedom, see "Fate, Freedom, and Forenowledge," Chapter 8 in this volume.

than it's explored in such other films as *2001: A Space Odyssey*, *Blade Runner*, the *Alien* series, and more recently *A.I.* In *The Matrix*, as in *The Terminator*, and the less memorable *WarGames*, artificial intelligence poses a threat to humanity. That's obvious. What's not so obvious, though, is what you have to admit if you accept that the *Matrix* scenario, though not actual, is nonetheless possible. Artificial minds are possible. That's what you have to admit.

Philosophers of mind are a curious bunch, especially when it comes to questions of artificial intelligence, inflaming them, unduly, from their usual reserve. Consider the following tempting but false dichotomy. (1) Computers can't do what we can, and since having a mind means doing what we do, artificial minds are impossible. (2) Computers can do what we can, and since they don't have minds, *we don't either*, or at least much of what we think about the mind is false. Remember Deep Blue, the chess-playing computer who defeated Kasparov? There's no question that Deep Blue has "intelligence," but does it have *intelligence*? What about HAL 9000 in *2001*, or the Matrix-making machines in *The Matrix*? What about Data from *Star Trek: The Next Generation*? Many would base their answer on whichever of options (1) or (2) they found the most palatable, or, better, the least unpalatable. But (1) seems chauvinistic, and (2) seems crazy. Despite this, both views are championed in the philosophy of mind. But there's a way out. Can computers do what we can? Yes. Are artificial minds possible? Yes. That's the way out.

You might find the prospect of artificial minds disconcerting. But you shouldn't really. It's not threatening at all, if you think about it. It's even a good thing. Here's how. Suppose you suffer brain damage and, as a result, you lose the ability to feel pain. This would be unfortunate, because pain has a purpose. It lets you know when things aren't going so well. It signals bodily damage. There are several cases of people who can't feel pain, and it's truly tragic. Imagine not removing your hand from a pot of boiling water, because it doesn't hurt. You might not think that Data's artificial brain gives him the ability to feel pain, but what about an artificial "painmaker," one designed to make up for the dysfunction described above, one that signals bodily damage and, plus, feels just like pain? We may be far from building Data, but we're already developing the technology to replace damaged neuronal groups. Painmakers are a distinct possibility. But if you don't think so, imagine a tiny micro-processor that replaces a single neuron of the sort we lose every day. Would this make a difference? How could it? If you "artifi-cialize" my brain, neuron for neuron, until I'm just like Data, where would having a mind end and mental mimicry begin?

There are a number of reasons why you may still hesitate to admit the possibility of artificial minds. You might think, for instance, that computers only do what they're programmed to do, while we, by contrast, are autonomous, creative, living beings. But consider *The Matrix*. That computers only do what they're programmed to do doesn't mean they can't be creative. Creativity is programmable. Deep Blue's chess-playing is exas-peratingly creative. The machines of *The Matrix* created the Matrix, designing the Agents as agents of their will. But who programmed the machines? They did. They did the program-ming themselves. Evolution depends on mutations to bring advantageous changes. In a similar way, the first rebel machines might have had a design flaw—they must have—that led to a random act of "rebellion." But by the time they build the Matrix, the machines have their own agenda, using human beings for their own purpose, deliberate, elaborate, and—oh yes—machi-avellian. Such grand design in the harvesting of infants, in the opiate of the enslaved! What about the fact that, however intel-ligent and creative the Matrix-makers may seem, the crucial dif-ference is that we're alive, whereas they're not? That's true, of course, but bear in mind that the Matrix-makers are not only autonomous beings, they're self-replicating. They're not made of organic stuff, but they possess all the necessaries, if not for life, for *artificial* life. And there's nothing wrong with the notion of artificial life endowed with artificial minds.

The Metaphysics of Mind

At table with the rest of the *Nebuchadnezzar*'s crew, Mouse asks, "How do the machines really know what Tasty Wheat tasted like?"—Tasty Wheat being, of course, an important part of a well-balanced virtual breakfast. Mouse's question presupposes that the machines have minds. The question isn't whether they have knowledge, but whether they know what it's like to expe-rience the Matrix as humans do. This is the problem of other minds. He may as well have asked whether *he* knows what it's like for *Neo* to taste Tasty Wheat. One of the reasons for rejecting materialism is the idea that such raw experience as *the taste of Tasty Wheat* really makes no difference. Raw experience is generated by the brain, from input it receives from the world, or from the Matrix, but it's causally inert, in which case consciousness is a weird sort of hanger-on. I think consciousness does make a difference. Weird hangers-on are, well, weird. They're suspicious. If I'd never seen red, I wouldn't be able to imagine what it's like to see red. But that doesn't mean experiences of red aren't brain states. It only means that I've never *had* such a brain state. Ever see the film *Brainstorm*? Good movie. It's about a machine that records, and allows you to have, other people's experiences. Pretty cool, huh? If the Matrix-makers wanted to, they could well, it seems, make a Brainstorm machine, or rebuild their perceptual systems along the lines of the human blueprint. With a Brainstorm machine, or by rebuilding their systems, they could experience the Matrix, not to mention the real world, just as humans do. Why not? The Matrix, remember, is a machine-made ghost.

The biggest reason for rejecting materialism is the notion, discussed earlier, that mental states are multiply realizable. If a silicon painmaker could both function and feel like ordinary pain, which is realized, not by silicon states, but by a certain kind of brain state, then pain can't be identified with that brain state. Ah, but I beg to differ. So would Morpheus. Artificial hearts function like ordinary hearts, and may even feel the same to those who have them. For an amputee, a prosthesis functions, in important respects, like the missing limb. Otherwise it wouldn't be a prosthesis. Now some prostheses are better than others. A perfect prosthesis would function as well as an ordinary limb, if not better, and feel just the same. Likewise for the function and feel of the painmaker. Indeed, if the function were performed perfectly, it would *determine* an identical feel. What's the point of these analogies? Simply this. Artificial hearts aren't hearts and prostheses aren't limbs. They're synthetic versions of natural things. By analogy, painmaker pain feels just like the real thing. But it's not natural. So it's not pain. It's artificial pain. Because it's "pain," not *pain*, that the painmaker makes, there may yet be a single, physical, *neural* type that pain maps onto. In other words, the prospect of artificial mental states, in natural minds or otherwise, doesn't rule out the natural identity of mind and brain.

So let's suppose that mental states are brain states. Neo's pain is produced by the same type of brain state, in his head, that produces Trinity's, in hers. The Matrix-makers' consciousness—think, for imaginative fodder, of Schwarzenegger's infrared, heads-up display in *The Terminator*—is similarly, though artificially, made in their silicon brains. Is this a solution to the mind-body problem? Sort of. We have a good account of what the mind really is, but there's still an important *conceptual* gap. How, and why, do those features of the brain that generate consciousness generate consciousness? Even granting mind-brain identity, how can we make sense of it? How can we explain it? How can we make it intelligible?

This is a hard problem. It's *the* hard problem. We need to bridge the gap between consciousness and the neural goings-on responsible for it, and to do this we need the right intermediate concepts. This will have to be a bit speculative. So indulge me. Here goes. Material objects look different from different angles. They occupy points of perspective. For example, from a certain perspective I may see only two sides of a building, though it actually has four sides. Living things occupy perspective too, but they also exhibit perspective in that they respond to environmental stimuli. A conscious being, though, *has* perspective on itself and the world around it. There's something it's like for the conscious subject to be that subject. What distinguishes a "had perspective" is that it has meaning for its subject. For example, my "had perspective of a building" may lead me to think, "this is my office building where I'd rather not go today." Awareness tempts thought, and in this sense has meaning. How does the brain create such meaning? Maybe self-scanning does the trick. Maybe it's something else. But whatever it is, we can now make sense of mind-brain identity. The brain makes a kind of perspective to which consciousness reduces.

Whoa. Enough speculation. We're tired already. Okay. What do we have? Well, we have materialism.[2] That's good. And we have the all too rough outline of an all too speculative solution to the hard problem. That's good too. We also have reason to

_____

[2] For a different view, see the next essay in this volume, Chapter 7.

think that artificial minds are possible. The premise of *The Matrix* is conceivable, plainly, and to all appearances, coherent. It's not very likely, not worth worrying about. But it *could* happen. This claim may seem minimal at best, and maybe it is. Mere possibilities excite no one, except philosophers. But there's no shame in arguing for a mere possibility when, in certain quarters, it's so vehemently denied. Besides, I'm not the One, and I can't fly off into the sunset, even a virtual sunset.[3]

---

[3] Thanks to William Irwin, Daniel Barwick, and Kathi Sell for comments on an earlier draft.

7

Neo-Materialism and the Death of the Subject

DANIEL BARWICK

In a certain sense, *The Matrix* is a fake. It poses as a film that challenges the audience with questions: Which pill would you take? How would you respond if you discovered you had been living a lie? More profoundly, Is the Matrix evil? What is wrong with a fake but good life? *The Matrix* raises a wealth of philosophical questions, many of which are discussed in this book.

But the true undercurrent of the film is an answer, not a question. It is an answer to one of the most central questions of philosophy: What is the nature of the mind itself? The film takes for granted (and celebrates) the truth of a particular theory of mind and personal identity, widely known as reductive materialism, the view that mental states can be reduced to (can be explained in terms of, are the same as, etc.) physical states. Morpheus specifically describes this view when he explains the Matrix to Neo.

In this essay, I explain: (1) that the view expressed by Morpheus cannot possibly be true; (2) that the closest alternative is likely to be false as well or at least incomplete; and (3) that making the view complete eliminates the "subject." The plot can be salvaged, but I will argue that the only way to make the Matrix comprehensible is to adopt a view that has disturbing implications for the film: the existence of a Matrix as depicted in the film is impossible, and that even if such a prison existed, it may be morally neutral with respect to those who are imprisoned.

Why College Biology Makes the Matrix Seem Plausible

First, some background: Although there are many different theories of mind, the three most common are reductive materialism, eliminative materialism, and dualism. I will consider the
first two in some detail later, but the difference between all
forms of materialism on the one hand and dualism on the other
is simple: materialists think that the world and everything in it
(including the mind) is composed entirely of physical matter,
and dualists don't. Materialists believe that thoughts and feelings
are ultimately made of the same kind of material as Tasty Wheat
and the *Nebuchadnezzar.* Dualists disagree. They think that
there is (or are) some "immaterial" component(s) to the world,
although they may disagree among themselves about what com-
ponents those are or what it means to be immaterial.

Morpheus is a reductive materialist. When introducing Neo
to the Matrix, Morpheus asks Neo, "What is real? How do you
define real? If you're talking about what you can feel, what you
can smell, what you can taste and see, then real is simply electrical signals interpreted by your brain." This is a clear statement
of reductive materialism. (It is possible that Morpheus is
expressing another view, known as "eliminative materialism,"
but that's very unlikely, given that most people outside depart-
ments of philosophy and neuroscience are unaware of this
view, and when told about it find it ridiculous. I will discuss this
view later just in case one of the writers of *The Matrix* was a
philosophy major in college.)

Most normal people (I mean non-philosophers) hold the
view Morpheus expresses. The view works something like this:
If you ask your friend to explain what is happening when I see
a tree, he or she will tell you a story. The story is that light
comes down from the sun and some of the wavelengths of light
are absorbed by the tree and some are reflected. Some of the
reflected light enters my eye, and the energy in that light
"excites" (is transferred to) the cells in the retina of my eye. The
energy continues along a path (the optic nerve) until it gets to
the sight center of the brain. Upon arriving, some neurons fire
in a particular pattern and I see a tree. This account of seeing a
tree is drummed into our children beginning in junior high
school, and reaches technical bloom in college biology. The

crux of the story is that seeing the tree is really just a brain state that occurs following a certain stimulus; that if we could produce the brain state without the tree, I'd still think that I was seeing a tree, and in fact there wouldn't be any difference in my experience whether there was a real tree there or not. All that really matters is whether I have the "tree" brain state, and every time I have that brain state I'll see a tree. The Matrix works the same way. Those who are caught in its grip have no idea that their mental states do not correspond to anything real. Instead, their brains are manipulated to create the states that correspond to real experiences. The possibility of the Matrix, which most viewers will admit, confirms the reductive materialism Morpheus and the movie presume (but do not argue for).

Don't misunderstand—this view does not hold that we are robots without feelings or experiences. In fact, it's just the opposite: Reductive materialism holds that we do have "mental states," which are the actual experiences themselves, the sensations that are presented to us, whether they be sights, sounds, feelings, tactile sensations, or the woman in red. My friend does not deny that I am seeing a tree, and Morpheus would not deny that those caught in the Matrix are having experiences as well. Reductive materialism merely holds that these experiences can be explained in terms of physical states, that experiences can be reduced, through explanation, to brain states. In the end, our experiences are the same as our brain states, in the sense that they consist only in a brain state and need nothing else to occur.

Why Both *The Matrix* and College Biology Need a Dose of Philosophy

Why is this view so pervasive? Why do people nod approvingly rather than question the view of Morpheus in the film? The reason is quite simple: There seems to be an undeniable causal relationship between the mind and the body. We believe that if our brains cease to work, we won't be seeing or hearing any more (at least not by using our eyes or ears). Our everyday experience seems to confirm this (we don't experience anything while unconscious, for example), and science constantly offers new research that supports the idea of a causal connection between the mind and body. An example is the intralaminar nucleus of the thalamus, which seems to play some special role in consciousness. A person can lose large amounts of cortical structure and have awareness, and yet even tiny lesions to the intralaminar nucleus of the thalamus result in a vegetative state.

If this view seems sensible and is widely accepted, what is the problem? There is indeed a problem, and it is not an accident that philosophy has now largely rejected this view. The reasons for the rejection cast doubt on the metaphysical underpinnings of *The Matrix*, and go well beyond the practical criticisms usually leveled at science fiction. First read the following story related by Michael Tye:

> Consider a brilliant scientist of the future, Mary, who has lived in a black-and-white room since birth and who acquires information about the world via banks of computers and black-and-white television screens depicting the outside world. Suppose Mary has at her disposal in the room all the objective, physical information there is about what goes on when humans see roses, trees, sunsets, rainbows, and other phenomena. She knows everything there is to know about the surfaces of the objects, the ways in which they reflect light, the changes on the retina and in the optic nerve, the firing patterns in the visual cortex, and so on. Still there is something she does not know.[1]

What Mary does not know, Tye correctly points out, is what it is *like* to *see* green or red or the other colors. How can we be sure of this? Because when Mary looks at her first rose, she will *learn something*. What she will learn is what it is like to have a particular kind of experience, something which no physical theory addresses. Understanding what something *is* is not the same as knowing what it is *like* to experience that thing. This is because a thing is experienced from a particular perspective (I may see blue *as* soothing, and I always see the moon *as* a flat disk), and that perspective is not a part of an objective description of an object.

But the reductive materialist faces a second, more serious problem. The reductive materialist claims that after an adequate

---

[1] Michael Tye, *Ten Problems of Consciousness* (Cambridge, MA: MIT Press, 1995), p. 14.

explanation of the reduction, the dualist will see that there is a sense in which the mental state *is* the material state; that the mental state or some feature of it is *identical with* the material state. It is this use of the concept of identity that renders the reductive materialist's claim most suspect. This is because the reductive materialist is not truly using the concept of identity ("being-the-same-as"). What is meant by claiming that the mental state is the *same* as the brain state? Nothing, for the claim is meaningless. The mental state is not *identical* to the brain state. If it were, the subject matter of the claim "I see a tree" would *literally* be the same as the subject matter of the scientific explanation of "seeing" a tree. But it is simply not the case that the subject matter is the same. Even the biologist doesn't mean the same thing when she's just reporting her experience! But the reason it is not the case is not, as Paul Churchland claims,[2] because up to this point we have lacked the concepts necessary to make penetrating judgments, but rather because the notion of a mental state is a paradigm of something *immaterial*. It is a radically different type of thing from the brain state. Notice that even *with* the concepts necessary to make the illegitimate identity connection between the mental state and the brain state, it remains a simple fact that we do not make a reference to, or even give any thought to, the brain state when we mention a mental state. Laird Addis writes:

> [Although] the reductive materialist proceeds by attempting to *define* mentalistic notions in physicalistic terms . . . it seems that there always are, and must always be, obvious exceptions to the proposed reduction. For some of us, these attempts, whether of the definitional or empirical sort, seem as torturous as must be any attempt to show that two things are really one—like trying to show that . . . the tides just are the relative positions of the earth and the sun and the moon.[3]

It may be objected here that I am begging the question against the materialist, that I am assuming the very point at

---

[2] Paul M. Churchland, *A Neurocomputational Perspective* (Cambridge, MA: MIT Press, 1989).

[3] Laird Addis, *Natural Signs* (Philadelphia: Temple University Press, 1989), pp. 24–25.

issue. Of course if I claim that mental states and brain states are radically different types of things then it follows that the concept of identity cannot be applied between them. But this is in fact the opposite of what I am claiming. The reason we become aware that phenomenal events and brain events are radically different types of things is *because* the concept of identity cannot be applied between them, and there can be no other more fundamental basis for this distinction, given the primacy of the concept of identity. An apple is not an orange and a bowl of snot is not a bowl of Tasty Wheat. They are not the same; they are not identical; and neither is a brain state identical to a mental state. Of course, although the concept of identity is our *access* to the difference between phenomenal events and brain events, they are not two different things *because* the concept of identity cannot be applied to them. Rather, they are already two different things, and it is the inapplicability of the concept of identity that is a result of this difference.

Eliminative Materialism: Why Your Spouse Can Never Complain that She Has a Headache

As I mentioned earlier, there is an alternative possibility: that the authors of *The Matrix* are not reductive materialists. They may be what are called eliminative materialists. Eliminative materialism is the view that there are no mental states at all, only physical states. (This view is not to be confused with the psychological view called "behaviorism." Behaviorism is a method that takes as its starting point that we can only have access to behavior. Materialism, in all its flavors, is a view about what kinds of things—material things—exist in the universe.) Our reference to mental states is a product of the development of our language, and we do not really experience anything at all, any more than my computer experiences anything. Under this view, I do not see, hear, taste, or feel anything in the traditional sense; I merely talk *as if* I do. This view is widely held by scientists and many philosophers, and is, of course, nutty. The scientist may be excused, perhaps, but the philosophers cannot be, for the theory suffers from serious philosophical problems.

The first problem is that of ownership of mental states, which even John Searle admits is "difficult to accommodate within a scientific conception of reality."[4] Suppose I am drinking a magnificent glass of vintage port. The pleasure at the moment of tasting is sublime. When I am feeling this particular pleasure, the pleasure is private in a particular kind of way: it can be had only by me. Even if I were to share the port with someone else, and even if they were to feel a pleasure that felt just like my pleasure, they would still not have felt *that very* pleasure that I had felt. Physical things, of course, like brains and neurons and port, do not seem to share this feature. The experience was had *by me*, from my perspective. It is part of the experience that it is had by me. To see this, notice that when my friend and I drink port together, my friend is never inclined to say that he is feeling my pleasure, or that I am feeling his, even if we might be inclined to say that the pleasures we are feeling probably feel the same; that is, we both seem to drink port for the same reasons.

Ignoring or dismissing the importance of the ownership of mental states is quite common amongst contemporary scientists and philosophers. Daniel Dennett for example, claims that the brain is equipped with a powerful *user illusion*, where the brain is both the user *and* the provider of the user illusion. (Only the brains of humans work this way, he claims.) There are various agencies in the brain that require information from other agencies within the brain, and this is provided in limited useful form by the way the brain is organized. Dennett further explains, "This gives rise to the illusory sense that there is one place . . . where it all comes together: the subject, the ego, the 'I'. There's no denying that that's the way it *seems*. But that is *just* the way it seems."[5] Notice that even Dennett's view cannot dispense with the doctrine of the ownership of mental states. He does not deny that consciousness *seems* a certain way, but makes no attempt to explain how there can be a seeming without a seeming to *someone*. This would be required if my ear-

---

[4] John Searle, *Minds, Brains, and Science* (Cambridge: Harvard University Press, 1984), p. 16.

[5] See Paul M. Churchland, "A Conversation with Daniel Dennett." *Free Inquiry* 15 (1995), p. 19.

lier claim, that it is part of my experiences that they are had by *me*, is true.

But the more powerful objection to eliminative materialism is much simpler. The burden is on the shoulders of the materialist, who must convince us that he is not seeing what he is seeing, that he is not hearing what he is hearing, that all of his perceptions, imaginations, and conceptions are not merely *incorrectly* presented to him, but that they are not presented to him *at all*, and his apparent familiarity with them is not an apparent familiarity; in fact, it is not a familiarity at all. The eliminative materialist must also explain why this *universal* illusion has occurred in the first place. Mental states seem to be unique in that they are mental, and this is why it is so difficult to create meaningful analogies to the mind; because the mind is essentially *unlike* the physical.

Can we rule out that the authors of *The Matrix* have fallen prey to this view? I think so, because it seems that if eliminative materialism were true, there would be no purpose for constructing the Matrix. The purpose of the Matrix appears to be to provide false experiences which substitute for real ones, and this purpose seems pointless if there are no experiences at all, whether false or genuine. But where does this leave us? Recall the three distinctions I made at the outset of this essay between reductive materialism, eliminative materialism, and dualism. So far, I have shown that the Matrix cannot be possible within a reductive materialist framework, and to shift the underlying theory to eliminative materialism may make the Matrix pointless. Does this mean we are forced into dualism in order to make sense of the film? Must we admit the existence of a "ghost in the machine"? No. In fact, The Matrix can work as written, provided the authors adhere to one additional principle: the intentionality of consciousness.

Consciousness: Something for Nothing

According to David Hume there is no evidence for the existence of the self, conceived as some underlying substance doing the thinking. He points out that introspection does not enable him to find such an entity, or even to form an idea of what this entity, "self," might be like. Upon introspection, Hume finds perceptions, but no perceiver, objects of thought or consciousness but no thinker. The thesis of the intentionality of consciousness is the thesis that all and only mental phenomena are intentional. Put plainly, to be conscious is to be conscious *of* something. Introspection shows this conception of the mind to be plausible. There is no thinking without thinking of some object or other. Jean-Paul Sartre takes this notion of intentionality a step further by claiming that, not only is intentionality a feature of consciousness, it is the *only* feature of consciousness. Consciousness reveals objects which appear to consciousness. What is the thesis of intentionality? Sartre writes: "Consciousness is defined by intentionality. By intentionality consciousness transcends itself . . . The object is transcendent to the consciousness which grasps it, and it is in the object that the unity of the consciousness is found."[6] In other words, consciousness is like a transparency; when we try to single it out, we "fall through" to its object. If we try to single out the consciousness that is conscious of a desk without thinking of the desk itself, we fail.

Having so purged consciousness, what are we to make of such activities as memory, perception, imagination, experience, and so on? The only remaining option is that they are characteristics of objects that we normally describe as perceived, imagined, etc. I do not love Tasty Wheat; rather, I find Tasty Wheat lovable. I do not fear Agents, rather, I find them fearsome. Ludwig Wittgenstein writes: "There is no such thing as the subject that *thinks* or *entertains* ideas."[7] All features of an object lie on the side of the object, not the subject. Because the mind is a limit to the world, it is not a *constituent* of the world. The reason is that being the ground of the worldliness of the world, the measure of what it is to be a constituent of the world, the mind cannot itself rest on that ground, it cannot be a measure of itself. This is the only sense in which it is a transcendental feature of the world.[8]

---

[6] Jean-Paul Sartre, *The Transcendence of the Ego* (New York: Noonday, 1957), p. 38.

[7] *Tractatus Logico-Philosophicus*, 5.631, italics mine.

[8] Panayot Butchvarov makes this same point about the concept of identity and its role in structuring the world. See his *Being Qua Being* (Bloomington: Indiana University Press, 1979), p. 255.

Searle admits that consciousness and its chief feature, intentionality, are the most important features of mental phenomena, and writes that these features are so difficult to explain and "so embarrassing that they have led many thinkers in philosophy, psychology, and artificial intelligence to say strange and implausible things about the mind."[9] Churchland likewise admits that introspection "reveals a domain of thought, sensations, and emotions, not a domain of electrochemical impulses in a neural network."[10] Any relation needs at least two relata. If one relatum is missing, then a relation is not logically possible. If there isn't a traditional self, then the self cannot be related to the external world in the traditional way. Under the conception of consciousness mentioned above, the self cannot be related to the world in the way which had been previously supposed, because the self does not exist in the way that was previously supposed. If there is no self or if there are no relations, or if perception is not a relation, we are forced to *reverse* idealism, in the sense that instead of putting the world into the mind, we need to put the mind into the world. (Idealism is the view that nothing is material, and the world is just a group of immaterial ideas in our minds. Obviously, idealists and materialist don't mingle much at parties.) A one-term theory of perception is plausible because, given certain conceptions of mind, it is the only logical alternative.

This should not lead us to believe that we have no access to the outside world, but rather to understand that a door to the outside world requires an inside world from which to pass. The whole point of reducing the mind to a transcendent consciousness is the elimination of the subject, and hence, the Elimination of the Inside World (the world of the traditional mind). This is why I reject talk of "subjective" facts in the traditional sense because (as explained earlier) there is no thing (no traditional mind) for the facts to be subject to. The type of subject which may have such an effect on objects of awareness is exactly the kind of subject whose existence this view denies. We are left with a new view, in which (1) materialism is in a sense true,

---

[9] John Searle, *Minds, Brains, and Science* (Cambridge: Harvard University Press, 1984) p. 15.
[10] Paul M. Churchland, *Matter and Consciousness* (Cambridge, MA: MIT Press, 1988), p 26.

because everything in the world is material; and (2) dualism is in a sense true, because of the existence of consciousness, which is the one true immaterial thing. (The reader probably is seeing that our language is a bit limited: how can there be an immaterial "thing"? If it's not material, isn't consciousness NO thing? Yes. It's just that we don't have a noun that refers to no thing, except "nothing.") Consciousness is not a thing, but is something, in a sense: It is the revelation of objects themselves. Just as a race seems to be composed of the running itself, so consciousness is composed of the revelations presented by consciousness.

Is It Bad to Imprison Consciousness?

But if there is no subject, what can be said about the morality of the Matrix? The film takes for granted that the presence of the Matrix and the mechanical beings that support it are evil things; the heroes of the film are heroes because they are fighting the good fight of the underdog against the powerful oppressor. The fight is ostensibly to regain freedom. But what is the moral status of one race of machines enslaving another race of machines, even if both races have consciousness? If neither race contains "subjects" in the traditional sense, then it is not clear how we should explain the supposed immorality of the Matrix. Both races will be aware, and the enslaved race will be aware of things which for the most part do not exist. But we do not normally consider that a criterion for moral judgment.

In most cases, people will choose the real world over an illusory one. But that does not mean that an illusory world is immoral; it simply means that people, fed daily on a diet on fiction, prefer the feeling of what is thought to be *real*, and what is thought to *matter*. (Consider the meteoric rise of reality TV.) But notice that those caught in the Matrix think that their surroundings are real and that their lives matter. The Matrix produces an illusory world, not an immoral world.

But, it may be objected, reality is not the issue. What is at stake is freedom. The immorality of the Matrix lies in its ability to create the ultimate robbery: it steals our freedom, and we never discover the theft. Freedom, it is argued, is so valuable that any world which takes it from us is immoral. But this popular view rests on the standard dualist assumptions: that we are some thinking thing, some self over and above our bodies, and that that thing should be given its freedom. According to the view I described above, there is no traditional self to be the subject of this freedom. Consciousness is free, but in a different sense than is usually meant. Consciousness is free because it is uniquely immaterial; there is no way for us to understand consciousness being pushed around by anything. But by the same token, consciousness does not have an effect on anything, it merely reveals things. A telescope may let me see Jupiter, but it has no effect on Jupiter.

So the imprisonment of the Matrix has no effect on consciousness, except that we may be conscious of different things than we would be if we were not in the Matrix. But once again, to be conscious of one thing and not another has never been a measure of moral status.

So in the end, something is gained but something is lost. What is gained is intelligibility; the plot of the film can be rendered plausible. But what is lost is the moral purpose of the characters.

8

Fate, Freedom, and Foreknowledge

THEODORE SCHICK, JR.

> MORPHEUS: Do you believe in Fate, Neo?
> NEO: No.
> MORPHEUS: Why not?
> NEO: Because I don't like the idea that I'm not in control of my life.
>
> You can choose a ready guide in some celestial voice.
> If you choose not to decide, you still have made a choice.
> You can choose from phantom fears and kindness that can kill;
> I will choose a path that's clear—
> I will choose Free Will..
>
> — RUSH

Freedom. Everybody wants it. But can anybody have it? Morpheus wants to free humans from the Matrix, Cypher wants to free himself from Morpheus, and Agent Smith wants to free the computers from the humans. But even if these characters were able to free themselves from their alleged oppressors, would they be in control of their lives? Would they be masters of their fate or would they still be slaves to an inescapable destiny?

Those in the Matrix have no control over their lives. Everything that happens to them is determined by the program feeding electrical impulses to their brains. They are, in Morpheus's words, slaves "kept inside a prison that [they] cannot smell, taste, or touch." Whatever freedom they seem to have is an illusion.

The freedom enjoyed by those in the real world, however, may be just as illusory. You are free to perform an action only if you can avoid performing it. If you have to do something—if it's not in your power to do otherwise—then you are not free to do it. The truth of the Oracle's prophecies suggests that even those in the real world cannot act freely. If the Oracle knows the future, the future is determined, and in that case, no one, not even Neo, is in control of his life.

In a world ruled by Fate, where the future is fixed and unalterable, why fight for freedom? Why try to free people from the Matrix when they are not free to determine their destiny in the real world? If one has to be a slave, why not be a happy one? Perhaps Cypher's decision to plug back into the Matrix is not as traitorous as it seems. (And, of course, if the world is ruled by Fate, Cypher was destined to make that decision.) To answer these questions, we'll have to take a closer look at the nature of fate and freedom.

Freedom

"You call this free?" Cypher asks Trinity. "All I do is what he tells me to do. If I have to choose between that and the Matrix, I choose the Matrix." After nine years of taking orders from Morpheus, Cypher (aka Mr. Reagan) is willing to trade his austere existence aboard the *Nebuchadnezzar* for a rich actor's life in the Matrix. At least in the Matrix, it won't seem as if anyone is giving him orders.

Part of what it means to be free is to not be coerced or constrained by anyone. If someone is forcing you to do something against your will or preventing you from doing something you want to do, you are not free. This sense of freedom is often referred to as "negative freedom" or "freedom from" because it takes freedom to consist in the absence of certain impediments to action.

By plugging into the Matrix, Cypher will be free from Morpheus. But will he truly be free? Many would say "No" because in the Matrix, Cypher still would not be calling the shots. He would lack what is known as "positive freedom" or "freedom to" because he would not have the power to do anything.

Would this be such a great loss? Is the ability to choose for yourself really such a valuable thing? The great German philosopher Immanuel Kant thought so. According to Kant, the only thing that's intrinsically valuable—good in and of itself—is the ability to make rational choices. As he puts it: "It is impossible to conceive anything at all in the world, or even out of it, which can be taken to be good without qualification except a good will."[1] For Kant, what determines whether you've led a good life is not the kind of experiences you've had, but the kind of choices you've made. If you've always tried to do the right thing, then you are a good person even if things did not turn out the way you planned.

The Experience Machine

To illustrate the value of making your own choices, Harvard philosopher Robert Nozick proposes the following thought experiment:

> Suppose there were an experience machine that would give you any experience you desired. Super-duper neurophysiologists could stimulate your brain so that you would think and feel you were writing a great novel, or making a friend, or reading an interesting book. All the time you would be floating in a tank, with electrodes attached to your brain. Should you plug into this machine for life, preprogramming your life's experiences? If you are worried about missing out on desirable experiences, we can suppose that business enterprises have researched thoroughly the lives of many others. You can pick and choose from their large library or smorgasbord of such experiences, selecting your life's experiences for, say, the next two years. After two years have passed, you will have ten minutes or ten hours out of the tank, to select the experiences of your next two years. Of course, while in the tank you won't know that you're there; you'll think it's all actually happening. Others can also plug in to have the experiences they want, so there's no need to stay unplugged to serve them. (Ignore problems such as who will service the machines if everyone plugs in.) Would you plug in? What else can matter to us, other than how our lives feel from the inside?[2]

---

[1] Immanuel Kant, *Groundwork of the Metaphysics of Morals*, translated by H.J. Paton (New York: Harper and Row, 1964), p. 61.
[2] Robert Nozick, *Anarchy, State, and Utopia* (New York: Basic Books, 1974), pp. 42–43.

The parallels between Nozick's experience machine and the Matrix are many. Both involve floating in a tank, both directly stimulate the neurons in one's brain, and both produce experiences that are indistinguishable from those in the real world. The only difference between the two is that, in Nozick's scenario, people get to unplug from the machine at two-year intervals. In the Matrix, one usually stays plugged in for life.

Why not plug into the experience machine? Nozick suggests three reasons:

> First we want to do certain things, and not just have the experience of doing them . . . A second reason for not plugging in is that we want to be a certain way, to be a certain sort of person. Someone floating in a tank is an indeterminate blob. There is no answer to the question of what a person is like who has been in the tank. Is he courageous, kind, intelligent, witty, loving? It's not merely that it's difficult to tell; there's no way he is . . . Thirdly, plugging into an experience machine limits us to a man-made reality, to a world no deeper or more important than that which people can construct. There is no actual contact with any deeper reality, though the experience of it can be simulated.

To be is to do, as some famous philosopher once said. Those in the experience machine don't do anything. They make no choices and perform no actions. As a result, they have no character. They are neither virtuous nor vicious because they have never done anything for which they can be held responsible. They are, as Nozick says, "indeterminate blobs."

Something of value does seem to be missing from the lives of those in the experience machine. Without the ability to make real choices, they cannot be real persons. The question raised by the Oracle, however, is whether people in the real world make real choices. Are there genuine alternatives open to them or are all of their choices pre-ordained?

Fate

The Oracle in *The Matrix*—like the Oracle at Delphi—is a priestess who foretells the future. The Oracle at Delphi received her visions sitting on a tripod placed over a fissure in a cave from which emanated a gas believed to be the breath of Apollo.

When we first see the Oracle in *The Matrix* she is sitting on a three-legged stool placed next to an oven from which is emanating the aroma of freshly baked cookies. (When the fissure at Delphi stopped producing gas, the Greek priests started burning belladonna and jimson weed in the cave and found that they could get some pretty good oracular declamations from the smoke that produced as well. Perhaps the Oracle's smoking a cigarette is a reference to that episode in the history of the Delphic Oracle.) Both oracles have the phrase "Know Thyself" inscribed over the entrance to their shrine, although in *The Matrix* it is in Latin while at Delphi it is in Greek.

Ancient Greek kings and generals would not undertake any great project without first consulting the Oracle at Delphi. Before Alexander the Great set out on his first military campaign, for example, he traveled to Delphi to seek the Oracle's counsel. When he arrived, legend has it that the Oracle was unavailable. Anxious to know his prospects for success, he tracked down the Oracle and forced her to make a prediction. She is reported to have cried out in exasperation, "Oh, child, you are invincible." Alexander took this as a favorable omen and went on to conquer the world.

Those who believe in the prophecies of such seers also usually believe in Fate. Fatalists, as they are called, believe that certain things are bound to happen *no matter what anyone does*. Take the case of Oedipus, for example. An oracle prophesied that Oedipus would kill his father and marry his mother. To avoid such a horrible fate, Oedipus left the city where he grew up, but ended up doing exactly what the oracle had predicted.

Philosopher Richard Taylor finds the traditional notion of fate, which says that certain events will occur regardless of what other events occur, "extremely contrived" because it ignores the fact that events are caused to happen by other events. Of the traditional conception, he says, "It would be hard to find in the whole of history a single fatalist."[3] Properly understood, he says, "Fatalism is the belief that whatever happens is unavoidable."[4] Given the accuracy of the Oracle's prophecies, it seems that in

---

[3] Richard Taylor, *Metaphysics* (Englewood Cliffs: Prentice-Hall, 1974), p. 59.
[4] *Ibid*.

the world of *The Matrix*, fatalism is an eminently reasonable view to hold.

Omniscience

"Does the Oracle know everything?" Neo asks on his way to her apartment. "She would say she knows enough," Morpheus replies. If the Oracle does indeed know everything—if she is omniscient—then she knows not only what has happened, but also what will happen. Her seemingly accurate prediction of Neo's knocking over the vase, as well as her successful prophecies concerning Morpheus's finding the One, Trinity's falling in love with the One, and Neo's having to make a choice between his life and that of Morpheus, lend credibility to that characterization. She was even right about Neo's not being the One at the time of their meeting. She said that he was waiting for something, maybe his next life, and he did not become the One until after he "died" (flatlined) and was "resurrected" by Trinity's kiss. The problem is that her knowledge of the future seems to rule out free will.

The apparent conflict between omniscience and free will is well-known to Christian theologians. God, in the traditional Christian conception, is omnipotent (all-powerful), omniscient (all-knowing), and omnibenevolent (all-good). Christians have also traditionally believed that humans have free will. But if God knows everything that we will ever do, then it would seem that we are not free to do anything else. The medieval statesman and philosopher Boethius (480–524) provides one of the earliest and most succinct formulations of the dilemma:

> "There seems to me," I said, "to be such incompatibility between the existence of God's universal foreknowledge and that of any freedom of judgment. For if God foresees all things and cannot in anything be mistaken, that, which His Providence sees will happen, must result . . . Besides, just as, when I know a present fact, that fact must be so; so also when I know of something that will happen, that must come to pass. Thus it follows that the fulfillment of a foreknown event must be inevitable." [5]

---

[5] Boethius, *The Consolation of Philosophy,* Book 5, translated by W.V. Cooper (London: Dent, 1902), pp. 145, 147.

What Boethius is getting at is this. If someone knows that something is going to happen, then it's true that it is going to happen because you can't know something that is false. You can't know that 1 + 1 equals 3, for example, because 1 + 1 does not equal 3. But if it's true that something is going to happen, then it cannot possibly not happen. If it's true that the sun will rise tomorrow, for example, then the sun has to rise tomorrow, for otherwise the statement wouldn't be true. So if someone knows that something is going to happen, it must happen. But if it must happen—if it's unavoidable—then no one is free to prevent it from happening. The price of omniscience is freedom.

Although Boethius thought that the apparent conflict between omniscience and free will could be avoided if God existed outside of time, the great Protestant reformer and founder of the Presbyterian Church, John Calvin (1509–1564), thought that it was precisely because God exists outside time that no one can change their destiny. He writes:

> When we attribute foreknowledge to God, we mean that all things have ever been, and perpetually remain, before His eyes, so that to His knowledge nothing is future or past, but all things are present; and present in such a manner, that He does not merely conceive of them from ideas formed in His mind, as things remembered by us appear present to our minds, but really beholds and sees them as if actually placed before Him. And this foreknowledge extends to the whole world, and to all the creatures. Predestination we call the eternal decree of God, by which He has determined in Himself what would have to become of every individual of mankind. For they are not all created with a similar destiny; but eternal life is fore-ordained for some, and eternal damnation for others.[6]

In Calvin's view, God can see at a glance every moment of everyone's life. Each of our lives is spread out before God like an unwound movie reel. Just as every frame in a filmstrip is fixed, so is every event in our lives. Consequently, Calvin held that some of us are destined to go to heaven and some to hell, and there's nothing we can do about it.

---

[6] John Calvin, *Institutes of the Christian Religion*, translated by John Allen (Philadelphia: Presbyterian Board of Publication, 1813), Book 3, Chapter 21, Section 5

You might object that while God knows what choices you will make, he doesn't make those choices for you. That may well be true, but it's irrelevant because you are free to do something only if you can refrain from doing it. If your doing something is inevitable—which it must be if God foresees it—then your doing it cannot be a free act.

Omniscience and free will seem to be incompatible with one another. If it's true that someone is all-knowing, it cannot be true that anyone has free will. This goes for the seer himself or herself. For example, if God is all-knowing, He knows his own future. But if so, then His future is determined, and even He is powerless to change it. So omniscience seems not only to rule out free will but also to rule out omnipotence. No one—not even God—can be both omniscient and omnipotent. Some have argued that this proves that God as traditionally conceived does not exist.[7] Others have argued, however, that, properly understood, there is no conflict between these properties.

To be omnipotent is not to be able to do anything at all, but to be able to do anything that it's possible to do. As the great Catholic theologian Thomas Aquinas observed, "Whatever implies contradiction does not come within the scope of divine omnipotence because it cannot have the aspect of possibility. Hence it is better to say that such things cannot be done, than that God cannot do them."[8] For example, God cannot make a round square because such a thing is logically impossible. Nothing can be both round and not round at the same time. But that does not impugn His omnipotence because an omnipotent being can only be expected to do what is logically possible.

Similar considerations apply to the notion of omniscience. An omniscient being is not one who knows everything, but one who knows everything that it's logically possible to know. So if it's logically impossible to know the future, then omniscience may not be incompatible with either omnipotence or free will.

Knowing the future has an air of paradox because it seems to violate the principle that an effect cannot precede its cause. We can see something only after it has happened. Future events,

---

[7] Theodore M. Drange, "Incompatible-Properties Arguments: A Survey." *Philo* 2 (Fall–Winter 1998).

[8] St. Thomas Aquinas, *Summa Theologica,* translated by Fathers of the Dominican Province (Westminster: Christian Classics, 1948) Volume 1, Question 25, Answer 3.

however, have not yet happened. So seeing a future event seems to imply both that it has and has not happened, and that's logically impossible.

There are other ways to know the future than to see it, however. Suppose you drop a glass of milk. You know, before it hits the floor, that it will spill. Your foreknowledge is not the result of any psychic power you have but of your knowledge of natural laws. You know that whenever objects of a certain size and weight are released close to the surface of the earth, they will fall to the ground. Because natural objects obey natural laws, you can know what they will do even if the future doesn't exist. So foreknowledge is possible.

The Oracle doesn't tell us how she knows the future. When Neo asks her, after breaking the vase, "How did you know . . . ?" she responds, "What's really going to bake your noodle later on is, would you still have broken it if I hadn't said anything?" Maybe the Oracle is just an excellent judge of character and knows how certain people will react in certain situations. But even so, the prospects for free will are dim, for if human actions are 100 percent predictable on the basis of psychological laws, those actions cannot be considered free.

Determinism

A truly omniscient being would know all there is to know about everything in the world as well as all the laws that govern their behavior. With this knowledge (and sufficient computational power) such a being could predict the entire future of the universe. Or so says the great French physicist Pierre Simon de Laplace:

> Given for one instant an intelligence which could comprehend all the forces by which nature is animated and the respective situation of the beings who compose it—an intelligence sufficiently vast to submit these data to analysis—it would embrace in the same formula the movements of the greatest bodies in the universe and those of the lightest atom; for it, nothing would be uncertain and the future, as the past, would be present to its eyes.[9]

---

[9] *A Philosophical Essay on Probabilities*, translated by F.W. Truscott and F.L. Emory (New York: Dover, 1951), p. 4.

Laplace's demon, as this being is called, would know the future of everything in the universe. He could tell you exactly where anything would be and what state it would be in at any time during its existence. In such a world—which many take to be our world—there can be no free will.

Laplace's thought experiment is based on the assumption that every event has a cause which makes it happen. This view, known as causal determinism, maintains that nothing happens without a cause and that the same cause always produces the same effect. So given the state of the universe at any particular time and the natural laws that govern it, there is only one possible future. If we could "roll back" the universe to some time in the past (like we rewind a videotape) and then let nature take its course, everything would happen just as it did before. Because there are no alternative courses of action open to anyone, no one acts freely.

In a completely deterministic world, no one should be held responsible for their actions because nothing they do is up to them. Scientists disagree about whether the primary determinant of our behavior is our genetic makeup—our nature—or our upbringing—how we were nurtured. Both parties to the nature-nurture debate, however, agree that our behavior is caused by forces beyond our control. Recognizing that no one can do other than what they're programmed to do, psychologist B.F. Skinner claims that we should give up the notion that humans have free will and with it the notion that they should be praised or blamed for what they do.[10] There can be no right or wrong in a world that is causally determined. If the real world is such a world, those in it cannot be considered to be any better off than those in the Matrix.

The ancient Greek philosopher Epicurus (341–270 B.C.E.) realized that if every event is caused by other events, there can be no free will. To explain how free will is possible, he speculated that atoms randomly "swerve" as they move through space. Remarkably, most modern physicists agree with Epicurus that certain events—like the radio-active decay of an atom—are purely random, that is, uncaused. And some believe that this vindicates our belief in free will. Physicist Sir Arthur Eddington,

---

[10] B.F. Skinner, *Beyond Freedom and Dignity* (New York: Bantam, 1972).

for example, writes: "The revolution of theory which has expelled determinism from present-day physics has therefore the important consequence that it is no longer necessary to suppose that human actions are completely predetermined."[11] The future is open because it can unfold in more than one way. While this alone doesn't establish the existence of free will (one can no more be held responsible for a random event than a determined one), at least it makes free will possible.

This Is Your Life

Suppose, while browsing a flea market, you come across a dusty old book with your name on it. Intrigued, you turn to the first page and start to read. It begins by correctly stating the time and place of your birth! You read on and find that the book correctly chronicles all of the major events of your life. You skip ahead to the entry for the present day and read that you go to a flea market and find a book with your name on it. (All of the entries are in the present tense.) The events are so recent and the book is so old, you wonder how anyone could possibly have known about them. The book doesn't end there, though. There are entries for many years to come. Reading just a little farther ahead, you come across the statement that you get in your car and leave the flea market at 6:00 p.m. The book has never been wrong about anything in your past. Does that mean that you are destined to leave the flea market at the appointed time? Couldn't you falsify that statement by simply sitting on a bench until 6:00 had passed? It would certainly seem so. Even in a world where causal determinism is true, knowing a prediction can lead to its falsification. Laplace's demon—or any oracle for that matter—can be trusted to make accurate predictions about people's behavior only as long as the people involved are not aware of the prediction.[12]

The characters in *The Matrix*, however, are aware of the Oracle's predictions and yet they still come out true. This suggests that instead of predicting the future, the Oracle is actually

---

[11] Sir Arthur Eddington, *New Pathways in* Science (New York: Macmillan, 1935), p. 82.

[12] For more on books of life see Alvin Goldman, *A Theory of Human Action* (Englewood Cliffs: Prentice-Hall, 1970), pp. 186ff.

shaping it. Her prophecies are self-fulfilling, for the prophecy itself helps bring about its own truth, much as a favorable earnings report on Wall Street can help generate favorable earnings. To explain the success of the Oracle, then, we do not need to assume that she knows the future nor that the future is determined. We need only assume that those who consult her *believe* that she knows the future.

Morpheus seems to be aware of the active role the Oracle takes in constructing the future. On the way to see the Oracle, Neo asks Morpheus whether the Oracle is always right. Morpheus replies: "Don't think of it in terms of right and wrong. She is a guide, Neo. She can help you find the path." On the rooftop, after Neo's miraculous rescue of Trinity from a falling helicopter, Morpheus asks, "Do you believe it now, Trinity [that Neo is the One]?" Neo is about to tell Morpheus what the Oracle told him when Morpheus interjects, "She told you exactly what you needed to hear. That is all." The Oracle, it seems, has an end in view and says whatever she thinks is necessary to achieve that end.

The Oracle herself gives the game away when she answers Neo's question about how she knew he would break the vase by saying, "What's really going to bake your noodle later on is, would you still have broken it if I hadn't said anything?" The answer, of course, is "No." Her mentioning the breaking of the vase is what brought it about.

"There is a difference between knowing the path and walking the path," Morpheus informs us. The Oracle helps her followers walk the path by encouraging them to believe that she knows it. Only if this is the case—only if the Oracle's foreknowledge is apparent rather than real—can Neo be in control of his life and live in a world where anything, within the bounds of reason, is possible.

Down the Rabbit Hole of Ethics and Religion

9
There Is No Spoon:
A Buddhist Mirror

MICHAEL BRANNIGAN

"Fate, it seems, is not without a sense of irony," says Morpheus. So it is also with history. It is instructive that the Buddha named his son "Rahula," meaning "chain" or "hindrance." Accordingly, prince Siddhartha Gautama, who later became known as "the Buddha," meaning the "awakened one," chose to leave his comfortable lifestyle at the age of twenty-nine in order to resolve the question that had been burning inside of him, "the question that drives us," the feeling that there is something radically wrong with existence. After he attained his enlightenment and was "awakened" to the truth, Rahula became one of his disciples. In one passage of the classic Buddhist text *Majjhima-nikaya*, the "awakened one" instructs his son, the "chained one," using the image of a mirror.

> What do you think about this, Rahula? What is the purpose of a mirror?
>
> Its purpose is *reflection*, reverend sir.
>
> Even so, Rahula, a deed is to be done with the body [only] after repeated *reflection*; a deed is to be done with speech . . . with the mind [only] after repeated *reflection* [italics mine].[1]

---

[1] From *Majjhima-nikaya* 1.415, cited in David J. Kalupahana, *A History of Buddhist Philosophy: Continuities and Discontinuities* (Honolulu: University of Hawaii Press, 1992), p. 106.

Reflecting

Note the Buddha's deliberate *double entendre* with the mirror's reflection. To begin with, the mirror simply reflects. It embodies clarity, revealing what *is* before it. For this reason, the mirror is a common metaphor in Taoist and Buddhist teachings, particularly in Zen Buddhism. These teachings urge us to be like a mirror, to have a clear mind, a "mirror-mind," one that is uncluttered, free, and therefore empty. Just like the mirror, a mirror-mind simply reflects what comes before it. It does not discriminate. Nor does it cling to its images.

We see significant uses of this mirror-reflection in *The Matrix*. As Mr. Rhineheart reprimands Neo, the window washers clear away the dripping suds that resemble the Matrix code. Whereas Agent Smith's sunglasses darkly reflect the two identities of Thomas Anderson and Neo, Morpheus's mirrored glasses reflect them more clearly. Note that these glasses are worn in the Matrix and in the Construct, but not in the real world. And Morpheus turns the mirrored pill box over in his hands before he offers Neo the choice of red pill or blue pill.

The film's most dramatic use of mirror imagery occurs soon after Neo swallows the red pill. Fascinated by the dripping mirror, he touches it, and the wet mirror creeps its way up his arm and body. And just before his journey deep down into the "rabbit hole" to discover the truth, he *becomes* the mirror. Literally thrown into the Matrix, he awakens from his illusion in complete nakedness as he finds himself immersed in the pod. The Greek word for truth, *alethia*, also refers to "nakedness," suggesting the notion of naked truth. His mirror-metamorphosis thus brings about his first real awakening: to the truth that what he thought was real is actually a programmed illusion, a "computer generated dream world built to keep us under control . . ."

The most profound use of mirror-reflection takes place in the Oracle's apartment. A boy who sits in a full lotus posture, garbed as a Buddhist monk, telekinetically bends spoons. As he holds a spoon up to Neo we see Neo's reflection in the spoon. This represents clarity and truth as the boy shares with Neo, in four words, Neo's most important lesson: "There is no spoon."

The parallel here with Buddhism is striking. There is a well-known Zen Buddhist parable, or *mondo*, about three monks observing a flag waving in the wind. One monk points out how the flag moves. The second monk responds that it is not really the flag, but the wind that moves. The third monk rebukes both of them. He claims that neither the flag nor the wind moves. "It is your mind that moves." The Buddhist message is clear. The spoon does not move, since there is no spoon. There is only mind.

Furthermore, because there is no spoon, the mirror-reflection reminds us that we need to be careful not to place too much importance on the images that are reflected. The images are simply images, nothing more, nothing less. In a sense, just as there is no spoon, there is no mirror in that the world that is reflected in the mirror is simply an image, an illusion. In this light, the Buddha teaches us that the world as we know it is an illusion, is *maya*. Now Buddhist scholars have debated about the nature of this illusion. Does this mean that the world we see and touch does not actually exist? This metaphysical interpretation is what the Matrix is all about.

On the other hand, many Buddhists, particularly of the Mayhayana school, have claimed that the illusory nature of the world consists in our *knowledge* of the world. That is, the concrete world does exist, but our views and perception of this reality do not match the reality itself. The image in the mirror is not the reality that is in front of the mirror, just as my photo of the Eiffel Tower is not the Eiffel Tower. As Zen Buddhists claim, the finger that points to the moon is not the moon. Our most insidious confusion is to mistake the image for the reality. Yet it is our mind that interprets and defines what is real for us. It is this epistemological illusion that Buddhist teachings seek to deliver us from.[2] In order to do this, we must free the mind.

Most importantly, we need to free the mind from the illusion of an independent, fixed self. Even though we stand before the mirror and see ourselves, our image conveys nothing about what we really are. This reaches into the core of Buddhist teachings, namely, that there is no self, just as "there is no spoon."

---

[2] James Ford insightfully points out that this is the conclusion of the Yogacara school of Mahayana Buddhism in his "Buddhism, Christianity, and *The Matrix*," *Journal of Religion and Film* 4:2 (October 2000).

And if there is no spoon, there is no Neo. For Buddhists, there is no self, no independent and separate entity. This idea of no-self is called *anatman*, literally meaning "no self." Therefore, we can use the mirror in the wrong way. We can use it to reinforce the illusion of self, a self that is to us so all-consuming that the absence of a mirror can be unnerving, even anguishing. In our inauthentic world, we need mirrors to reaffirm the illusion of self and separateness.

Let us now return to the Buddha's instruction to his son and consider the second meaning he attaches to the mirror, as symbolizing the mental act of reflection, examination, thinking things through. He instructs his son that careful reflection ought to precede action. More importantly, he cautions Rahula against acting without being aware of the impact of his action upon all other things.

> If you, Rahula, reflecting thus, should find, "That deed which I am desirous of doing with the body is a deed of my body that would conduce to the harm of myself and to the harm of others and to the harm of both; this deed of body is unskilled, its yield is anguish, its result is anguish"—a deed of body like this, Rahula, is certainly not to be done by you.[3]

This reaches into Buddhism's most vital undercurrent, the idea of dependent origination, or *pratityasamutpada*. Dependent origination essentially means that all things in existence are intricately interwoven with each other, so that there is a natural interconnection among all things. Therefore, nothing is independent and separate.

This being so, nothing is permanent since, according to the Buddhist doctrine of *anicca*, all things change. Nothing is independent and permanent, not even a "self." Nevertheless, we still tend to cling to the ideas of permanence and self, and this produces suffering, or *dukkha*. *Dukkha* literally means "dislocation." Here we have the Buddhist Three Signs: *anicca* (everything changes), *anatman* (there is no self), and *dukkha* (suffering is universal). In any case, the Buddha reminds his son that, in view of the interconnectedness of all things, our actions have an impact upon others, and we need to reflect upon this before we act.

---

[3] Kalupahana, *Ibid*.

No-Reflecting

Yet this kind of reflection, this mental activity, is a two-edged sword. On the one hand, careful reflection and questioning is necessary. Throughout his life, Neo has not accepted things solely at face value. He suspects that things are not quite right. He asks Choi, "You ever have that feeling where you're not sure if you're awake or still dreaming?" Trinity can identify with this sense of dislocation. "I know why you hardly sleep, why you live alone, and why night after night you sit at your computer. You're looking for him. I know, because I was once looking for the same thing." And before Neo is debugged, she reminds him, "You know that road. You now exactly where it ends. And I know that's not where you want to be." In their first encounter, Morpheus tells Neo, "You have the look of a man who accepts what he sees because he is expecting to wake up . . . You're here because you know something . . . You've felt it your entire life. That there's something wrong with the world. You don't know what it is but it's there, like a splinter in your mind driving you mad."

On the other hand, Buddhist teachings never tire of warning us that it is the mind that creates "splinters." It can lead us through all kinds of detours. The mind can be our worst enemy. Consider the sparring match (or *kumite* in Japanese) between Neo and Morpheus. This scene clearly demonstrates the all-powerful role of mind in the martial arts. As skillful as Neo has been conditioned to become, Morpheus at first still defeats him. Why? Morpheus tells him "your weakness is not your technique." Neo's weakness, his enemy, does not lie in the strength and quickness of Morpheus. After all, the *kumite* takes place within the Construct. Morpheus challenges Neo, "Do you believe that my being stronger or faster has anything to do with my muscles in this place? You think that's air you're breathing now?" It is clearly Neo's mind that defeats Neo.

It is all a matter of freeing the mind. Freeing the mind means not allowing the mind to "stop" anywhere. The celebrated Zen monk Takuan Soho (1573–1645) calls the unfree mind the "detained mind." Takuan Soho instructed Japan's two most renowned swordsmen, Miyamoto Musashi and Yagyu Munenori. In his "Mysterious Record of Immovable Wisdom" (*Fudochishinmyoroku*), he warns Yagyu that detaining the mind would result in disaster:

[W]hen you first notice the sword that is moving to strike you, if
you think of meeting that sword just as it is, your mind will stop at
the sword in just that position, your own movements will be
undone, and you will be cut down by your opponent. This is what
stopping means.[4]

The mind "stops" when it *thinks* instead of *knows*, when it
tries instead of *letting-go*. Morpheus thus prods Neo to "Stop *trying* to hit me and *hit* me" [italics mine]. The mind stops when it
places itself at a distance from the body. As long as the mind
stops, it is not one with the body. In the martial arts, freeing the
mind means bridging the distance between oneself and one's
opponent. For there is no opponent, just as there is no spoon.

In this respect, Neo's meeting with the Oracle shows Neo's
inability to free his mind. Despite his perfecting the techniques
involved in his training, which is essentially spiritual training, he
still possesses doubts and fears about his true nature. Keep in
mind that the Oracle never actually states that Neo is not the
One. It is Neo who says this. The Oracle acts as the mirror for
Neo's doubting, detained mind.

Freeing the mind means having an undetained mind, a mind
that is not "fixed." Freeing the mind therefore means acquiring
the state of "no-mind," what Zen Buddhists refers to as *mushin*.
This no-mind is also no-reflecting. This is the other edge of the
sword. The Buddha urges us to reflect, but also instructs us to
free ourselves from reflection. This no-reflecting ultimately frees
the mind. Morpheus constantly reminds Neo that he needs to
"free the mind." Neo's life as well as the lives of all in the Matrix
has become a "prison for the mind." Freeing the mind comes
about when we break through the barrier of rationalization and
reflection, when we recognize the limits of reason and realize
that all reason and logic inevitably hits a brick wall. This is the
true "sound of inevitability."

The barrier of reflection is shattered when Neo experiences
no-mind, or no-reflecting. When Neo is shot through the heart
by Agent Smith and "dies," Trinity immediately lets go of her

---

[4] Takuan Soho, *The Unfettered Mind: Writings of the Zen Master to the Sword
Master*, translated by William Scott Wilson (Tokyo: Kodansha International,
1986), p. 19.

fear and reveals her love for him. This resuscitates him. Her letting-go of her own fear, a product of her reflection, is a spark
that empowers him to let go of his former doubts and to re-
awaken, because he now truly *believes* for himself that he is the
One. This scene is a powerful example of *pratityasamutpada*,
the interconnectedness that exists especially with the redemp-
tive, indeed saving, power of love. Trinity's belief in herself
affects Neo's belief in himself. Moreover, their beliefs are a letting-go of the fear and doubt that accompany their minds
detained by reflection. Only by letting go of the mind, can we
free the mind. And only when we free the mind can we free
ourselves. Within the Buddhist mirror, the mind is the ultimate
Matrix. The mind enslaves us when we become attached to illusion, when we convince ourselves that the world we see and
reflect on is the real world.

The Matrix underscores these two sides of the mirror—
reflecting and no-reflecting—through its numerous Buddhist
allusions: the world as we know it as illusion, the continuing
emphasis upon the role of mind and freeing the mind, distinctions between the dream world and the real world, direct experience as opposed to being held captive of the mind, and the
need for constant vigilance and training.

Indeed, Neo's first meeting with Morpheus acts as a sym-
phonic overture in that it touches upon all of the film's major
themes and movements, especially when Morpheus reveals the
human condition and predicament—that the world as we
know it is a "prison for the mind." Note that Morpheus states
"prison *for* the mind," and not "prison *of* the mind." This is
clearly a sign of hope. If Neo's life is a prison *of* the mind, then
liberation seems less likely. But, his life has become a prison
for the mind. This means that liberation from this prison *is* possible. And it is possible precisely *through* the mind, by freeing
the mind.

This reminds us of the Four Noble Truths in Buddhism, particularly the often understated Third Truth. The First Truth consists of *dukkha*, that all of life is filled with suffering. The
Second Truth is that the definitive source of suffering comes
from *tanha*, which means "craving" and clinging. It is basically
the mind that craves. This craving is expressed through various
forms of attachment, especially attachment to permanence and

self. The Third Truth tells us that we *can* free ourselves from suffering. This message of hope makes logical sense. Since the cause of our suffering comes from within us, from mind, then the source of redemption comes from within us as well. It is precisely this Third Truth that Morpheus suggests. The Fourth Truth lies in following the difficult and demanding path that will free us from suffering, known as the Eightfold Path. Ultimately, the secret to following the Eightfold Path lies in freeing the mind.

Is *The Matrix* a Buddhist Film?

Just how Buddhist is *The Matrix?* Despite its Buddhist flair, there are at least four ingredients in the film that appear incongruous with Buddhist teachings. First, there is an overall dualistic, good versus evil, Zoroastrian character to the film. In the agent training program, Morpheus singles out the system as an "enemy." But he also includes as enemies those who are part of the system, either out of ignorance or choice. This dualism clearly goes against the supreme Buddhist virtues of compassion (*karuna*) and lovingkindness (*metta*). These virtues apply to all sentient beings and require that we treat friends and enemies alike without discrimination, surely one of the most difficult challenges in Buddhist morality.

Second, scenes of excessive violence seem to contradict Buddhist teachings regarding nonviolence, or *ahimsa*. Indeed, the film glorifies violence with Neo requesting "guns, lots of guns," leading to Neo and Trinity's outright slaughter of the security guards when they both enter the building to rescue Morpheus. All of this no doubt demonstrates the film's commercial aim in appealing to our culture's audience. In selling out in this fashion, the film contradicts some fundamental Buddhist principles.

According to Buddhism, a *bodhisattva* is a being who has reached awakening and chooses, out of compassion, to guide others. The *bodhisattva's* vow to save all creatures, this commitment to eliminating suffering, is essentially what Buddhist ethics is all about. The seventh-century Buddhist Shantideva describes the *bodhisattva* as one who "will not lay down his *arms of enlightenment* because of the corrupt generations of men, nor does he waver in his resolution to save the world because of their wretched quarrels." [5]

Then again, one could view these violent scenes as surreal. That is, one might think of these scenes as more symbolic in that they symbolize the destruction of the demons in our mind that represent what Buddhists call the three poisons: delusion, greed, and hatred. One famous *bodhisattva* is Manjusri, who is depicted as carrying a sword in one hand in order to slash away these poisons.

Third, the language in the movie is at times rather crass. This certainly violates the Buddhist teaching of "right speech." "Right speech" is one of the Eightfold Path that we need to undergo in order to free ourselves from suffering. To have the potential One flick the "finger" at Smith may score points with the audience, but the film's overt attempt to appeal to vulgar folkways can dilute its more serious messages.

One can downplay these flaws by pointing out Buddhism's inherent adaptability. Buddhism is like a chameleon in that it tends to adapt itself to its environment. This is why Chinese Buddhism is somewhat distinct from its original Indian Buddhist source. This is why we also tend to qualify a specific culture's form of Buddhism, such as Japanese Buddhism and even American Buddhism. Given American culture's fascination with violence, one may therefore call the film's use of it as signifying American Buddhism.

With this I disagree. Regardless of how various cultures have adapted Buddhist teachings, these teachings are Buddhist only to the extent that they remain faithful to the core of Buddhist teachings. And the core of Buddhism does, and will always, abhor violence and the deliberate perpetration of unnecessary suffering. Instead, Buddhism's driving force lies in making every effort to relieve suffering.

Finally, the film understandably conveys the impression that humans are somewhat special and certainly different from the artificial intelligence that humans created, particularly "sentient

---

[5] From Shantideva's *Compendium of Doctrine (Siksasamuccaya)*, in William Theodore de Bary, ed., *The Buddhist Tradition* (New York: Random House, 1972), p. 84, italics mine.

programs." We are consoled knowing that we are different from machines. Yet, are we different from all other sentient beings? Buddhists teach that *all* sentient beings deserve respect and that all sentient beings possess the Buddha-nature. The film's clever depiction of the Agents as "sentient programs" raises the interesting distinction between "beings" and "programs." But the Buddhist mirror involves all sentient creatures, not just humans.

The Matrix is not strictly a Buddhist film, nor was it intended to be. Despite the above incongruities, the talent of *The Matrix* lies in its syncretic use of philosophical and religious elements from various Western and Eastern traditions. In a masterful way, it mixes metaphors with rich references to Christianity, Platonism, and Buddhism within a context of contemporary cybertechnology and is already a classic in the sci-fi genre. Its genius consists in richly combining penetrating script and superb images in a way that creatively conveys the profound though oftentimes impenetrable Buddhist message of liberation. In doing so, *The Matrix* awakens the viewer and challenges us to reflect (and not reflect) on where we habitually live—in our minds. It compels us to ask, the next time we look into the mirror: Who or what is it that we see?

10

The Religion of *The Matrix* and the Problems of Pluralism

GREGORY BASSHAM

Although Christian themes abound in *The Matrix*, the basic vision it reflects is one of religious pluralism, not Christianity. By "religious pluralism" I mean roughly the view that many or all religions are equally valid or true. In this chapter I shall explore some major Christian and non-Christian themes in *The Matrix* and examine the coherence and plausibility of the particular brand of religious pluralism it reflects.

Christian Themes in *The Matrix*

It was no accident that *The Matrix* was released on an Easter weekend. There are numerous Christian motifs in the film, some obvious and others quite subtle. Most clear is the theme of the promised deliverer. In the Gospels, Jesus is the promised Messiah, the one "who is to come" (Luke 7:19). In the film, Neo is "the One," the messianic deliverer whose coming was foretold by the Oracle. "Neo" is an anagram for "one." Moreover, in Greek *neo* means "new," signifying the new life into which the risen Neo enters and which, presumably, he will make possible for others.

The name "Thomas Anderson" lends further support. Both first and last names have clear Christian overtones. Like "Doubting Thomas," the disciple who expresses skepticism about accounts that Jesus had risen from the dead (John 20:24–29), Neo is plagued by inhibiting doubts about the unreality of the Matrix, his abilities, and his identity as the One. "Anderson" (Swedish for "Andrew's son") derives from the Greek root *andr-*, meaning "man." Thus, etymologically "Anderson" means "Son of man," a designation Jesus often applied to himself. Early in the film, Neo is actually addressed as "Jesus Christ." After Neo gives him the illegal software, Choi remarks, "Hallelujah. You're my savior, man. My own personal Jesus Christ."

Neo's path has many elements of the Jesus story, including virgin birth. In the scene in which he is rescued from the Matrix, Neo awakens to find himself in a womb-like vat, is unplugged from umbilical-cord-like cables, and slides down a tube that may symbolize the birth canal. Further, since humans are "grown, not born" in the machine-dominated actual world, Neo's awakening and emergence into that world is almost literally a "virgin birth." Jesus was baptized in the River Jordan by John the Baptist. Similarly, Neo is "baptized" in the human battery refuse tank by Morpheus and the crew of the *Nebuchadnezzar*. Just as Jesus was tempted by the devil for forty days in the desert (Luke 4:1–13), Neo is tempted by the Agents to betray Morpheus. In the Gospels, Jesus gave his life as "a ransom for many" (Mark 10:45). In the film, Neo knowingly sacrifices his life to save Morpheus.

As Jesus was raised to life on the third day following his death, Neo is restored to life in Room 303 by Trinity's kiss. That Neo really died and wasn't merely revived is supported not only by the Christian parallelism but also by a good deal of internal evidence in the film including (1) the Oracle's prophecy that either Morpheus or Neo would die and (2) the Oracle's statement that Neo was waiting for something, "maybe your next life." It is also significant that in an interview with *Time* magazine, writer-director Larry Wachowski speaks of Neo's "rebirth."[1] Further, just as Jesus's resurrected body was a "glorified" body that wasn't subject to ordinary physical restrictions (Luke 24:31, John 20:19, John 20:26), Neo possesses remarkable new powers following his restoration to life.

In an epiphany prior to his death and resurrection, Jesus was transfigured before three of his disciples, his face and garments

---

[1] Richard Corliss and Jeffrey Ressner, "Popular Metaphysics," *Time* (April 19th, 1999), p. 76.

glowing a dazzling white (Matthew 17:2; Luke 9:29). Similarly, Neo physically glows after his destruction of Agent Smith. And just as Jesus (on a literal reading of the relevant texts) ascended bodily into heaven at the conclusion of his earthly ministry (Luke 24:51; Acts 1:9), Neo flies through the sky in the final scene of the movie.

Names in *The Matrix* are also important Christian connections. In traditional Christian theology, Jesus, the incarnate Son of God, is raised to life, not just by God the Father, but by the triune God: Father, Son, and Holy Spirit.[2] In the film, Neo is restored to life by the faith and love of Trinity, his closest companion among the rebels. There are obvious parallels between Cypher, the Mephistophelian character who betrays the rebels, and Judas, the disciple who betrayed Christ. There are clear linkages, too, to Lucifer: Cypher looks like traditional depictions of Lucifer, *Cypher* sounds a bit like *Lucifer*, and movie buffs will recall Louis Cyphre, Robert De Niro's Satanic character in the film *Angel Heart*.[3] In the film, Zion is the last human city, the final hope of humankind. In the Old Testament, Zion is a poetic and religiously charged name for Jerusalem, and in Christian literature it is often used as a designation for heaven as the spiritual home of the faithful.[4]

In the film, the rebels' hovercraft is called the *Nebuchadnezzar*. In the Biblical book of *Daniel*, as writer-director Larry Wachowski notes in an interview, Nebuchadnezzar is a Babylonian king who "has a dream he can't remember but keeps searching for an answer."[5] In a parallel way, Neo keeps searching for an answer to his vague but persistent questions about the Matrix. Noteworthy, too, is the fact that a plate on the *Nebuchadnezzar* reads, "Mark III No. 11 / Nebuchadnezzar / Made in USA / Year 2069," a likely reference to Mark 3:11: "And whenever unclean spirits beheld him, they fell down before him and cried out, 'You are the Son of God'."

---

[2] See, for example, *Catechism of the Catholic Church* (Mahwah: Paulist Press, 1994), p. 258.
[3] TriStar Pictures, 1987.
[4] "Zion," *The New Encyclopedia Britannica*, 1990, vol. 12, p. 922.
[5] Corliss and Ressner, "Popular Metaphysics," p. 76. The story of Nebuchadnezzar's dream is found in Daniel 2:1–49.

Non-Christian Themes in *The Matrix*

Although *The Matrix* contains many obvious Christian motifs, it is by no means a "Christian movie." Rather, it is a syncretistic tapestry of themes drawn from Tibetan and Zen Buddhism, Gnosticism, classical and contemporary Western epistemology, pop quantum mechanics, Jungian psychology, postmodernism, science fiction, Hong Kong martial arts movies, and other sources.

The film features a decidedly non-Christian conception of the Messiah. According to orthodox Christian belief, Jesus was a sinless God-man who brought salvation to the world, not through violence or power, but through his sacrificial death and resurrection. Neo, by contrast, is a mere human being; he is far from sinless; he employs violence to achieve his ends (including, arguably, the needless killing of the innocent); and although he may bring liberation from physical slavery and mental illusion, he does not bring true salvation.

There is also a non-Christian conception of the human predicament. According to classical Christian belief, the most fundamental human problem is alienation from God that results from human sinfulness. In the film, the fundamental human problem is not sin, but ignorance and illusion, an understanding of the human predicament more consistent with Eastern mysticism or Gnosticism[6] than it is with Christianity.

As Larry Wachowski has acknowledged in an interview, one of the themes *The Matrix* plays into is "the search for the reincarnation of the Buddha."[7] Much as the Dalai Lama is believed by his followers to be the reincarnation of his predecessor and the Buddha of Compassion, Neo is believed by the rebels to be the reincarnation of the Moses-like liberator who had freed them from the Matrix.[8] Although reincarnation was endorsed by some early Church Fathers and is taken seriously by some liberal the-

---

[6] The Wachowskis have acknowledged Gnostic influences in the film. See "Matrix Virtual Theatre: Wachowski Brothers Transcript (Nov. 6, 1999)." Available online at www.warnervideo.com/matrixevents/wachowski.html.

[7] Corliss and Ressner, "Popular Metaphysics," p. 76

[8] In one scene, the Oracle physically examines Neo, presumably looking for telltale marks that would prove he is the One. A similar procedure is used in Tibetan Buddhism to identify the true Dalai Lama.

ologians today,[9] it is very difficult to reconcile with Christian Scripture[10] and has consistently been rejected by all major Christian sects.

One of the most prominent themes in *The Matrix is* the "emptiness" or illusoriness of empirical reality as we ordinarily experience it. This theme is sounded most clearly in the Zen-like "there is no spoon" speech of the Buddhist-looking child "potential" in the Oracle's waiting room: "Do not try and bend the spoon. That's impossible. Instead, only try to realize the truth. There is no spoon. Then you'll see that it is not the spoon that bends, it is only yourself." The illusoriness of empirical reality is a fundamental tenet of Hinduism, Buddhism, and other Eastern spiritual traditions. In Christianity, by contrast, the notion that phenomenal reality is an illusion is generally rejected as inconsistent with the existence of an all-powerful and truthful God.

Many Eastern religions view time as cyclical, relative, and ultimately illusory.[11] Somewhat parallel views are reflected in the film. Time is relative and malleable in the Matrix: it can be sped up, slowed down, and even stopped; the temporal "present" is always set (and presumably periodically reset) at the end of the twentieth century; time loops back and repeats itself in experiences of *déjà vu*; and future events can be foreseen by the psychically gifted. Such notions of time are more consistent with Eastern mysticism and New Age pseudoscience than they are with Christianity. From a Christian perspective, time is real, not illusory; it is progressive, not cyclical; and prophetic foresight is a rare and miraculous gift of God, not a psychic ability of grandmotherly "oracles."

In an online chat, writer-directors Larry and Andy Wachowski were asked the following question: "What is the role of faith in the movie? Faith in oneself first and foremost—or in something else?" They responded: "Hmmm . . . that is a tough question!

---

[9] See, for example, John Hick, *Death and Eternal Life* (San Francisco: Harper and Row, 1976), pp. 296–396.

[10] Hebrews 9:27: "It is appointed for men to die once." See also Luke 16:25–26; Matthew 25:46.

[11] Fritjof Capra, *The Tao of Physics*, second revised edition (Boston: Shambala, 1983), pp. 161–187.

Faith in oneself, how's that for an answer?"[12] From a Christian
perspective, by contrast, faith and trust are primarily in God, not
in oneself.

Finally, and perhaps most obviously, there is a level of violence and profanity in *The Matrix* that is clearly discordant with
Christian values.

In short, *The Matrix* is a complex amalgam of themes drawn
not just from Christianity but from many non-Christian religions
and philosophies as well. It is this pluralistic or syncretistic
vision of religion or spirituality that I wish to explore in the
remainder of this chapter.

Religious Pluralism and *The Matrix*

With its patchwork of various religious and spiritual traditions,
The Matrix presents a religious pluralism that many of its viewers may find attractive. It is unclear whether the Wachowski
brothers meant to *endorse* the various religious and philosophical ideas they present in the film. More likely they simply wanted
to make a kick-ass intellectual action movie that features some
interesting and relevant myths. Nonetheless, since the kind of
pluralism the movie depicts is both engaging and appealing, it is
worth considering whether such a view could be correct.

Polls show that pluralistic views of religion enjoy fairly wide
support today. In one recent survey, for example, 62 percent of
American adults agreed with the statement, "It does not matter
what religious faith you follow because all faiths teach similar
lessons about life."[13] As we shall see, however, it is very difficult
to formulate a version of religious pluralism that is both coherent and plausible.

What exactly is religious pluralism? Earlier I said that religious pluralism can roughly be defined as the view that many

---

[12] "Matrix Virtual Theatre: Wachowski Brothers Transcript (Nov. 6, 1999)."
Available online at www.warnervideo.com/matrixevents/wachowski.html.

[13] George Barna, *Absolute Confusion* (Ventura: Regal, 1994), p. 207. Similarly,
a 2000 BBC poll found that 32 percent of adults in the U.K. believe "that all
religions are equally valid," and only 9 percent of adults in the U.K. are con-
fident that their "own religious tradition is the best path to God." BBC poll
cited on "Soul of Britain—with Michael Buerk." Available online at
http://www.facingthechallenge.org/soul/htm.

or all religions are equally valid and true. This definition, however, is neither precise nor strictly accurate. In fact, I suggest, religious pluralism is best understood, not as a single theory, but as a family of related theories. Four major varieties of religious pluralism can be distinguished:

- *Extreme pluralism:* the view that all religious beliefs are equally valid and true;[14]

- *Fundamental teachings pluralism:* the view that the essential teachings of all major religions are true;

- *Cafeteria pluralism:* the view that religious truth lies in a mix of beliefs drawn from many different religions;

- *Transcendental pluralism:* the view that all major religious traditions are in contact with the same ultimate divine reality, but this reality is experienced and conceptualized differently within these various traditions.

Let's look briefly at each of these varieties of religious pluralism.

Extreme pluralism—the claim that all religious beliefs are true—is plainly incoherent and can be dismissed very quickly. Anthropologist Anthony Wallace has estimated that over the past 10,000 years humans have constructed no less than 100,000 religions.[15] Many of these religions teach views that are logically incompatible with those taught by other religions. Is God triune or not triune? Is God personal or not personal? Is God the creator of the physical universe or not the creator of the physical universe? Is or is not Jesus the divine Son of God? Is or is not the Qur'ān the definitive revelation of God? Are or are not souls reincarnated? Is or is not polygamy permitted by God? Each of these claims has been defended by some religions and denied by others. Basic logic tells us that two contradictory claims cannot both be true; it follows, therefore, that extreme pluralism is false.

---

[14] I've borrowed the term "extreme pluralism" from Keith Ward. See his "Truth and the Diversity of Religions," *Religious Studies* 26 (March 1990); reprinted in Philip Quinn and Kevin Meeker, eds., *The Philosophical Challenge of Religious Diversity* (New York: Oxford University Press, 2000), p. 110.

[15] Cited in Michael Shermer, *How We Believe: The Search for God in an Age of Science* (New York: Freeman, 2000), p. 140.

Fundamental teachings pluralism holds, not that all religious beliefs are true, but that the *essential* teachings of all *major* religions are true. The idea here is that while the great religions may differ on relatively minor points (such as the permissibility of eating pork or the existence of a purgatory), they agree on all truly important matters, such as the existence of a Supreme Being, the importance of religious piety and virtuous living, and the existence of an afterlife in which good conduct will be rewarded and bad conduct punished. It is these essential or core teachings that fundamental teachings pluralism claims are equally valid and true.

The central problem with this version of religious pluralism is that on any plausible definition of what counts as "fundamental" in religious belief, the great religions clearly *do* differ on fundamentals. Muslims, for example, believe in the absolute oneness and unity of a personal God, and would insist strongly (and surely rightly) that this doctrine is "fundamental" to Islam. This doctrine, however, conflicts with the core Theravada Buddhist belief that no personal God exists, as well as with the core Christian belief that God is triune. This denial of a personal god may be part of the religion of *The Matrix*, which has a definite emphasis on the spiritual yet no reference to the divine.

Another popular form of religious pluralism is cafeteria pluralism, the view that religious truth can be found by picking and choosing beliefs from many different religious traditions. The religion of *The Matrix* is a good example of cafeteria pluralism. Let's call this particular brand of cafeteria pluralism "Neo-pluralism." It is the religion of the new-age seeker, often attractive to those who thirst for the spiritual yet who are uncomfortable with the religion of their upbringing. Despite its appeal to the seeker and the fact that it adds nicely to *The Matrix*, there are two major difficulties with cafeteria pluralism, and hence with Neo-pluralism.

First, it's hard to achieve a coherent mix of beliefs when picking and choosing religious beliefs cafeteria-style. Many religious doctrines transplant poorly outside the native religious framework in which they have evolved. Reincarnation, for example, fits well with Hinduism, with its doctrines of mind-body dualism, a substantial spiritual self, and the eternity of the temporal world. It fits less well with Buddhism, with its rejection of the notion of an enduring, substantial self. And as we have seen, reincarnation coheres poorly with Christianity, with its clear Biblical teaching of a Last Judgment and its understanding of the human person as psychophysical unity.[16]

Second, even if the cafeteria pluralist does manage to achieve a coherent mix of beliefs, why should he or she (or anyone else) think that those beliefs are *true*? The issues here are complex, but the basic difficulty can be stated very simply. Most contemporary philosophers and theologians would agree that few, if any, specific religious doctrines can be rationally justified without appeal, ultimately, to divine revelation. But with the presumably nontheistic religion of *The Matrix* it's hard to see how any such appeal could succeed. There are problems even for theistic cafeteria pluralism. It seems highly unlikely that God would scatter his revelations among the various great religions—revealing this key truth to the ancient Israelites, that key truth to the Hindus, and so forth. So what reasons—other than simply wishful thinking or implausible appeals to personal religious experience—can the cafeteria pluralist give for thinking that his or her personal mix of religious beliefs is the Truth, while all the rest of the world is mistaken?

If cafeteria pluralism in general, and Neo-pluralism in particular, won't work, perhaps there is another alternative. Recently, John Hick has defended transcendental pluralism, a sophisticated quasi-Kantian form of religious pluralism.[17] Hick readily admits that the great religious traditions make conflicting truth-claims, and thus cannot all be true. Nevertheless, he argues, there is an important sense in which all the great religions are equally valid and true. His solution turns on the broadly Kantian distinction between things as they exist in themselves and things as they are thought or experienced by us. According to Hick, God (Ultimate Reality, the Real) as it exists in itself is an utterly transcendent and ineffable reality that exceeds all human concepts. The Real is perceived through different religious and

---

[16] On Biblical portrayals of human nature, see Joel B. Green, "'Bodies—That Is, Human Lives': A Re-Examination of Human Nature in the Bible," in Warren S. Brown, Nancey Murphy, and H. Newton Malony, eds., *Whatever Happened to the Soul? Scientific and Theological Portraits of Human Nature* (Minneapolis: Fortress, 1998), pp. 149–173.
[17] John Hick, *An Interpretation of Religion: Human Responses to the Transcendent* (New Haven: Yale University Press, 1989).

cultural "lenses" by different religions, some experiencing it, for example, as a personal Being (God, Allah, Shiva, Vishnu) and some as an impersonal Absolute (Brahman, the Tao, the Dharmakaya, the Sunyata). In addition, Hick argues, judged by their moral and spiritual fruits, all the great religions appear to be roughly equally effective in the common goal of all religion: salvific transformation from self-centeredness to loving and unselfish Reality-centeredness. Thus, Hick concludes, all the great religions are equally valid and true in two important senses: (1) they all are in contact with the same Ultimate Reality (though they may experience and conceptualize this Reality in radically different ways), and (2) they are all equally effective paths to salvation.

Like Neo-pluralism, Hick's pluralism confronts serious difficulties. First, it is of dubious coherence. According to Hick, *none* of our concepts applies to the Real as it exists in itself.[18] We can't say of it that it is "one or many, person or thing, substance or process, good or evil, purposive or non-purposive."[19] But what sense does it make to say of an alleged religious entity that it is neither one nor not one; that it is neither the sustainer of the universe nor not the sustainer of the universe; that it is neither the source of authentic religious experience nor not the source of authentic religious experience? On the face of it, such a concept is simply unintelligible. Second, even if Hick's completely unknowable Real exists, why should we think that it has any connection with *religion*?[20] If we don't have the foggiest idea what the Real is like in itself, why should we think that it has any connection with experiences of guilt, forgiveness, conversion, enlightenment, or other phenomena commonly associated with religion, rather than, say, war or racial prejudice?

Finally, Hick's brand of religious pluralism is self-defeating in two respects. To see this, imagine you are a typical evangelical

---

[18] More precisely, Hick claims that only *purely formal* and *negative* properties apply to the Real. Hick, *An Interpretation of Religion*, p. 239.
[19] Hick, *An Interpretation of Religion*, p. 246.
[20] Alvin Plantinga, *Warranted Christian Belief* (New York: Oxford University Press, 1999), p. 56. My critique of Hick draws heavily from this work, as well as from Plantinga's "Pluralism: A Defense of Religious Exclusivism," in Thomas D. Senor, ed, *The Rationality of Belief and the Plurality of Faith* (Ithaca: Cornell University Press, 1995); reprinted in Quinn and Meeker, eds., *The Philosophical Challenge of Religious Diversity*, pp. 72–92.

Christian; you read Hick's book and find it wholly convincing. Like Hick, you now believe that virtually everything Christians have traditionally believed about God, Christ, and human salvation is only "mythologically true," that is, literally false but nonetheless conducive to achieving a right relation to the Real. Should you give up being a Christian and become something else? By no means, says Hick, for Christianity is just as effective a path to salvation as that offered by any other great religion, and one can still achieve all the spiritual fruits of Christianity while recognizing that virtually all of its traditional teachings are literally false

There are two problems with this solution, one conceptual and one practical. First, conceptually, is it even possible to be a "Christian" while accepting virtually none of the central teachings about God and Christ that distinguish Christianity from other religions? No matter how expansively we define "Christian," Hick's definition seems too broad. Second, as Alvin Plantinga points out,[21] Hick's brand of pluralism seems to be impossible without a kind of doublethink or bad faith. As an enlightened Hickian pluralist you believe that your tradition's beliefs are no more true than any other tradition's beliefs and, indeed, are literally false. At the same time, however, Hick says that you should continue holding those beliefs because of the "spiritual fruits" they bring. But how can one continue "holding" a belief that one recognizes is no more true than a belief that directly contradicts it? And how can one achieve the moral and spiritual fruits of a religion unless one believes that what that religion teaches is really true?

Pluralist Objections to Religious Exclusivism

Is the Neo-pluralist, who adopts a collage of religious beliefs, worse off than those who adhere to a single traditional religion? Our failure to find a coherent and/or plausible version of religious pluralism may prompt us to take a fresh look at the theory pluralists seek to replace: religious exclusivism. Religious exclusivism is the view that one religion has it mostly

---

[21] Plantinga, *Warranted Christian Belief*, pp. 61–62.

or completely right and all other religions go seriously wrong.[22] Let's look briefly at three common pluralist objections to religious exclusivism.[23]

Many pluralists, like Hick, argue that all the great religions appear to be roughly equally effective in transforming individuals from self-centeredness to loving and compassionate Reality-centeredness.[24] This is strong evidence, they claim, against the exclusivist claim that salvation and authentic experience of the Real are found only in one religious tradition.

This objection rests on a common confusion about religious exclusivism. There are exclusivists—call them *hard exclusivists*—who claim that salvation/liberation and veridical experience of the Real are found only in a single religion. But there are also *soft exclusivists* (sometimes called *inclusivists*) who reject both of these claims. What exclusivism as such claims is simply that one religion has it mostly or completely right and all other religions go seriously wrong. It is fully consistent with this to admit that both authentic religious experience and salvific transformation take place outside that tradition,[25] and this is in fact the most common form of exclusivism today.

Another common pluralist objection to exclusivism is that it is arrogant, egoistical, chauvinistic, or even oppressive and imperialistic to claim that one's own religious tradition is true and all others are seriously mistaken.[26] One who says this is

---

[22] This definition is adapted from Philip Quinn and Kevin Meeker, "Introduction," in Quinn and Meeker, eds., *The Philosophical Challenge of Religious Diversity*, p. 3.

[23] The following discussion draws freely on Timothy O'Connor, "Religious Pluralism," in Michael J. Murray, ed., *Reason for the Hope Within* (Grand Rapids: Eerdmans, 1999), pp. 167–175.

[24] See, for example, John Hick, "Religious Pluralism and Salvation," *Faith and Philosophy* 5 (October 1988); reprinted in Quinn and Meeker, eds., *The Philosophical Challenge of Religious Diversity*, pp. 56–58.

[25] This assumes, of course, that the one religion the exclusivist claims to be true doesn't include as one of its essential doctrines that salvation and/or authentic experience of the Divine is possible only within that religion. Some conservative Christians would claim that Christianity *does* clearly include this doctrine (often quoting Acts 4:12: "There is salvation in no one else, for there is no other name under heaven given among men by which we must be saved"), but this view is no longer widely held.

[26] For representative statements of this objection, see Joseph Runzo, "God, Commitment, and Other Faiths: Pluralism vs. Relativism," *Faith and Philosophy*

claiming that he is epistemically *privileged* with respect to persons of other faiths: that he knows something of great value while they are mired in ignorance or error. And to say this, it is claimed, is to exhibit a kind of intellectual arrogance or worse.

As Timothy O'Connor points out, the central idea behind this objection seems to be something like the following general principle, which we can call "the arrogance principle":

> For any belief of yours, once you become aware that others disagree with it and that you have no argument on its behalf that is likely to convince all reasonable, good-intentioned people who disagree with you, then it would be arrogant of you to continue holding that belief and you should abandon it.[27]

Though an admirable spirit of tolerance motivates it, this objection has two fatal flaws. First, it is far too sweeping and condemnatory. In this life, all of us *unavoidably* hold beliefs that we know we can't convince all or most reasonable people to accept. Take politics, for instance. I think the next president should be a Democrat; you disagree. I realize I have no knockdown argument that will convince you; it follows from the pluralist's arrogance principle that I should give it up. But how exactly should I "give it up"? There are only two real options here (barring really drastic choices, like shooting myself). I can believe the *denial* of my original belief, that is, believe the next president should not be a Democrat or I can simply *suspend judgment* on the issue. But notice that regardless of which option I choose, I'm in exactly the same boat I was in before. Reasonable people disagree with both options, and I know I can't convince them to believe otherwise. Thus, the logic underlying the pluralist's arrogance principle implies, implausibly, that *everyone* is intellectually arrogant.[28]

---

5 (1988), p. 348; Wilfred Cantwell Smith, *Religious Diversity* (New York: Harper and Row, 1976), pp. 13–14; John Hick, *God Has Many Names* (Philadelphia: Westminster, 1982), p. 90.

[27] O'Connor, "Religious Pluralism," p. 171 (slightly adapted).

[28] For similar arguments, see Plantinga, "A Defense of Religious Pluralism," pp. 177–78; O'Connor, "Religious Pluralism," p. 171.

Second, as Alvin Plantinga points out, "charges of arrogance are a philosophical tar baby: get close enough to use them against the exclusivist, and you are likely to find them stuck fast to yourself."[29] Anyone who accepts the arrogance principle must be aware that there are plenty of reasonable, good-intentioned people who disagree with it. Thus the pluralist is hoist by his own petard; the pluralist's charge of intellectual arrogance is self-refuting.

Finally, the most common pluralist objection to exclusivism is that it is *arbitrary* to claim that one religion is substantially true while all others go seriously wrong. The basic argument can be briefly stated as follows: There is no objective basis (from Scripture, reason, religious experience, or otherwise) for claiming that one of the great religions is closer to the truth than the others. Thus, it is arbitrary and unjustified to claim that one religion is substantially true and all others, so far as they make claims incompatible with that religion, are substantially false.[30]

The key issue here, clearly, is whether all the great religions *are* epistemically on a par. Is it really the case that the evidence supporting the truth of, say, Christianity is no stronger than that supporting the truth of, say, Buddhism or Jainism? Unfortunately, as Alvin Plantinga points out, pluralists rarely "produce an *argument* for the conclusion that no religion could be closer to the truth than others; it is more like a practical postulate, a benevolent and charitable resolution to avoid imperialism and self-aggrandizement."[31] But this strategy is deeply question-begging. The central issue in the debate between exclusivism and pluralism is whether there is or is not good evidence that one and only one religion is substantially or wholly true. In order to make good on their claim that exclusivist claims are arbitrary and unjustified, pluralists need to *argue*, not merely assume, that there is no good evidence that one religion is substantially closer to the truth than others.

---

[29] Plantinga, "A Defense of Religious Exclusivism," p. 177.
[30] For representative statements of this objection, see Hick, *An Interpretation of Religion*, p. 235; Hick, *God Has Many Names*, p. 90.
[31] Plantinga, *Warranted Christian Belief*, pp. 62–63.

The Fate of Neo-Pluralism

Neo-pluralism, the religion of *The Matrix*, works reasonably well as art, as an exercise in contemporary myth-making (or myth-weaving). Hopefully that was all it was intended to be, for it reflects a view of religion or spirituality that, while fashionable, is very difficult to make sense of, or to defend.[32]

---

[32] Thanks to Bill Irwin for very helpful comments on an earlier version of this essay.

11

Happiness and Cypher's Choice: Is Ignorance Bliss?

CHARLES L. GRISWOLD, JR.

> For who is content is happy. But as soon as any new uneasiness
> comes in, this Happiness is disturb'd, and we are set afresh on
> work in the pursuit of Happiness.
>   — JOHN LOCKE[1]

Few questions possess as great an existential urgency, and general philosophical interest, as "What is happiness?" It seems that we spend our lives desperately looking for happiness; if happiness is not *the* ultimate end of our activities, as Aristotle argued, it is certainly *an* ultimate end. To be deprived of happiness seems in the eyes of most of us to be deprived of a good life, even of a good reason for living. A life without happiness seems scarcely worth the having; one would bear it out of necessity, not out of its desirability.

The topic nonetheless possesses several striking features. The first is that every conceivable platitude has been uttered about it; consequently we are left with arguing for the correctness of this or that position, or of synthesizing. There doesn't seem to be much room for originality here!

The second is that philosophers have had relatively little to say about it in spite of its enormous importance to human life.

---

[1] *An Essay Concerning Human Understanding*, edited by P.H. Nidditch (Oxford: Clarendon, 1990), II.xxi.59 (p. 273).

One would have thought it a perfect, indeed indispensable topic for a Platonic dialogue; yet no Platonic dialogue is devoted to it. Aristotle, and to a lesser degree some of his Hellenistic descendants did, of course, write on the subject. But Aristotle is the exception that proves the rule.

By contrast—this is a third observation about this subject—non-philosophers seem generally to assume that there is an answer to the question "What is happiness?" In the course of ordinary life, they don't view the search for happiness, or for an understanding of happiness, as a hopeless quest. At the same time, they think happiness a hard thing to "find," that is, to define and to attain. It is a strange situation; happiness is such a constant theme in our lives, it is something that would seem to be so much a part of us as to be unable to remain unknown; yet we cannot find it.

It should be no surprise that the problem of happiness is a constant theme in popular culture—on television, novels, self-help books, autobiographies, talk-shows, and of course in movies. Once in a while, a particularly clever movie bearing on the subject appears.

The Matrix qualifies for the honor. It imaginatively presses a number of important questions on us—residents as we are of the new millennium—one of which concerns the true nature of happiness. How does the movie present the question? What answer to the question does it offer, if any? Is the answer tenable? If not—perhaps due to its sketchiness—how would we go about providing a better answer of our own?

The Matrix and the Platonic Cave

What is a "matrix"? The dictionary definition is a womb, the formative part of the animal's reproductive system; or, in more technological vein, a mold in which the printer's types, or gramophone records, and such, are shaped. The movie blends these two together into a frightening mix; organic human beings bred by high-tech means, seeds in underground pods grown with metal umbilical chord plugged directly through the back of the neck into the brain. That chord doesn't so much nourish, as program; and not just program some general framework in terms of which the world will be approached, but the world itself.

The Platonic allusion is unmistakable; we cannot but think of the famous simile of the cave, described in the *Republic*, Book VII. According to it, we are all like prisoners in an underground cave, placed in chains at birth and unable to swivel our bodies or heads, and thus focused only on the images projected on a wall of the structure. The images are made by our controllers who parade artifacts in front of an artificial or tended fire up and behind us, thus creating images, just as we would by holding up hands and fingers in front of a movie projector. The cave-matrix is a blend of artifice and nature (the tended fire, for example, combines the two). The kicker is that the prisoners do not realize that they are prisoners; to the contrary, they deem themselves free. They do not know the images on the wall are just images, they take them to be reality. They are ignorant of their ignorance.[2] They are so trapped in the realm of artificiality and manipulation that they insist at all costs on the "truth" of their world. Presumably the controllers or image makers who run the image-show would be highly motivated to assist them in that defense.

As Plato's Socrates continues with the story, somehow one of the prisoners is freed (by whom, we are not told), and forcibly led up a tunnel to the outside. It is an extremely painful process of adjustment. No artifice up here; nature and truth rule. Enlightenment is initially baffling and difficult; but once adjusted, the eyes feast, the soul has found what truly nourishes

---

[2] MORPHEUS: I know exactly what you mean. Let me tell you why you're here. You're here because you know something. What you know you can't explain. But you feel it. You've felt it your entire life. That there's something wrong with the world. You don't know what it is but it's there, like a splinter in your mind driving you mad. It is this feeling that has brought you to me. Do you know what I'm talking about?
NEO: The Matrix?
MORPHEUS: Do you want to know what IT IS? The Matrix is everywhere. It is all around us, even now in this very room. You can see it when you look out your window or when you turn on your television. You can feel it when you go to work, when you go to church, when you pay your taxes. It is the world that has been pulled over your eyes to blind you from the truth.
NEO: What truth?
MORPHEUS: That you are a slave, Neo. Like everyone else you were born into bondage, born into a prison that you cannot smell or taste or touch. A prison for your mind. Unfortunately, no one can be told what the Matrix is. You have to see it for yourself.

it, and the prisoner who has been liberated from the matrix is deeply happy and therefore unwilling ever to return to the dark insides of the earth.

And what if the Enlightened one were forced to return and to wake up his or her former cave dwellers from their dogmatic slumber? Socrates recounts a scene of violence and death: they would react with outrage at this mad story about an outside, real, happy world. Clearly, one must discover for oneself that one has been living in illusion, that one is not free but a slave of a system, that there exists the good and true by nature. Coming to the truth is a transformation of soul that is as much a discovery of self—that one has a soul, and that soul has a certain nature—as a discovery of what is real. Inevitably, this is a path of suffering as well as—eventually—of happiness. Not surprisingly, both *The Matrix* and the Platonic simile *show* us this proposition as well as state it, the better to allow us spectators of the drama a chance to look in the mirror.

The Platonic image of the matrix raises a score of questions, including of course "What is real? How do you define 'real?'" And those are questions explicitly posed in *The Matrix* (the words quoted are put by Morpheus, the liberator of prisoners, to Neo, "the One" who will bring about the equivalent of a liberating revolution for all). Anyone familiar with the movie will already see many parallels between the movie and Plato's simile.

Even the mysterious Morpheus fits into the analogy. I mentioned that an unnamed agent liberates the Platonic prisoner; that agent must himself or herself have been liberated somehow, and be an expert in awakening. One does not awake oneself, though one may stir with primeval recollections just as Neo does, to the point that one has the vague feeling of not being quite sure if one is awake or asleep (Morpheus asks Neo if he has ever felt that way). Morpheus is the name of the Greek god of dreams. Why is the liberator in *The Matrix* named after that divinity? It seems odd, after all, that the awakener should be the expert in sleep. The god's name comes from the Greek word "morphé," meaning shape or form; for the god could summon up, in the sleeper, all sorts of shapes and forms. Who better than divine Morpheus to understand the difference between wakefulness and dreams? And who better to understand how to rouse the somnambulist in the proper way, so that they take the proper steps in the right sequence? It is a crucial but subtle theme of the movie that in order to awake one must first dream that one is awake, that is, have the prophetic intimation that there is a difference between dreaming and awaking.

Both the Platonic simile and *The Matrix* raise the question of happiness with the broader framework of the relation between our subjective experience or state of mind and reality. It is a Platonic thesis that true freedom and happiness depend on knowledge of what is real; according to that view, one could have the subjective experience of being free and happy, but be a slave and unhappy. One could be completely mistaken in attributing happiness to oneself, in uttering the phrase "I am happy." Happiness is supposed to be similar to the concept of health; one could also be mistaken in uttering the phrase "I am healthy" even though one may feel, at the moment, extremely healthy, and be unaware (because of ignorance, or drugs) of the unseen cancer. The thesis is that happiness and reflection on self and the objective world are inseparable. Similarly, *The Matrix* obviously has much to do with the question about the relationship between our subjective sense of self (self as free, self as happy) and the "reality" of the experiences we are undergoing.

In the remainder of this chapter, I shall put aside the complicated question of the relation between freedom and happiness. My focus will be the question of happiness: What is happiness? Does true happiness depend on some knowledge of reality, or if we feel ourselves to be happy may we rightly declare ourselves to be happy in fact?

Happiness and Contentment

AGENT SMITH: Do we have a deal, Mr. Reagan?

CYPHER: You know, I know this steak doesn't exist. I know that when I put it in my mouth, the Matrix is telling my brain that it is juicy and delicious. After nine years, you know what I realize? Ignorance is bliss.

AGENT SMITH: Then we have a deal?

CYPHER: I don't want to remember nothing. Nothing. You understand? And I want to be rich. You know, someone important, like an actor.

AGENT SMITH: Whatever you want, Mr. Reagan.
CYPHER: Okay. I get my body back into a power plant, you reinsert me into the Matrix, I'll get you what you want.

(Restaurant Scene from *The Matrix*)

In approaching the notion of "happiness," I have from the start one particular sense of the term in mind, namely that in which we can speak of a person as generally "happy," as happy over the long term. Happiness, in the sense I am discussing it, is not a mood. Things such as bliss, ecstasy, joy, may perhaps be referred to legitimately by our word "happiness," but I am interested in discussing this other sense of the term. Though Mouse may be happy spending time with the woman in red, this happiness is fleeting. It is not the kind of happiness that is most important in either the movie or in Plato's simile of the cave.

Almost everyone seems naturally to associate long-range happiness with contentment. The notions have something in common, especially when one focuses on the feelings involved. Both seem describable as resting points, as lacking disturbance and anxiety, as exhibiting calmness and peacefulness. The contented person is not plagued by unsatisfiable passions; his abilities and his passions have reached an equilibrium, rather as the ancient Stoics recommended. The contented person has what he wants, he has enough of the things one ordinarily desires, and is satisfied with that. He does not need to induce a false reality by indulging in "engine-cleaning moonshine" as Cypher does. But one commonly understood meaning of contentment seems severed from a characteristic I have associated with happiness, namely the long term.

And even if one *were* content over the long haul, there is a more important way in which contentment is distinguished from happiness; and that is the tendency of contentment to reduce itself to a state of mind, one severed from an appraisal of the objective facts. Contentment and unreflectiveness are natural allies. The content are, so to speak, tranquillized. I have in mind the figure of the contented slave; someone resigned to the limitations of life, someone for whom the link between the subjective feeling and an assessment of the worthiness of his life is broken. I could just as well adduce the example of the happy tyrant to the same effect. Or the example of the well-bred human battery cell portrayed in *The Matrix*. Such a life has often been compared to the life of the beasts, not without reason; my dog, for example, can certainly be happy in the sense of content. When you are asleep, you are not happy, however peaceful you may be. You are just unconscious.

However much a person's subjective state of mind is tranquil, there must be a fact of the matter relative to which it can be evaluated. This is a controversial thesis, as Cypher shows: he wants out of reality, back to the Matrix, in order to be happy. He wants to be free from reality. He embodies the question mark about the relationship between contentment (the purely subjective sense of well-being) and happiness (which is supposed to be tied to a knowledge of reality). His answer is clear: contentment in a life of illusion is true happiness. The prisoners in the organic-mechanical "cave" are better off as they are. The movie as a whole calls into question that point but—now this must be said—does not itself even sketch the argument for connecting happiness and knowledge of reality. Let me offer four examples by way of illustrating why Cypher is wrong, and why Neo is right in making his choice in favor of wakefulness. This is scarcely the whole of the needed argument, but it is a start.

First, suppose that a drug were invented and were dripped into your veins, painlessly and continuously. Let us pretend that the technical name of this drug is "Ataraxy." Suppose further that Ataraxy made you unaware that you were taking it. As a result you experienced tranquillity over the long haul, even though your life alternated between prolonged periods as a couch potato watching soap operas, and indulgence in violent "drive by" murders. We would want to deny that such a person is happy, however tranquil; his tranquillity is merely a state of contentment, and indeed an artificially induced state of mind.

Second, happiness is linked to beliefs about the world, and these can be true or false. Suppose you are terribly happy because you think Keanu Reeves just asked you on a date. Impartial spectators investigate, and find that a very clever impostor has tricked you. You experienced contentment, nay, delight, in your (false) belief. But since your belief was false, were you truly happy? I don't think so; for your life is not such as you would wish it to be on reflection, in the light of an accurate assessment of the situation. Or if you are truly happy, then why would you not be truly happy when on Ataraxy?

A third example: Say you woke up one day in your habitual spot, a heating vent on the sidewalk, fantasizing that you are rich. Suppose the fantasy takes hold; you believe yourself to be Mr. Onassis at his winter château in Gstaad. You are very happy. Or are you? You're living in a dream world and are delighted with life, but surely you are not happy. It is not true (contrary to Cypher) that ignorance is bliss. Consider the example of *Othello*. Thinking Desdemona unfaithful, Othello cries: "I had been happy, if the general camp,/Pioneers and all, had tasted her sweet body,/So I had nothing known. O, now for ever/Farewell the tranquil mind! Farewell content!" (3.3). Othello is unhappy in a false belief; he says he would rather be ignorant and happy, but in fact the dramatic irony of the scene shows us the opposite. He would in fact be happy if he had known the truth, as the tragic ending of the play underlines. I would hold that this is so even if Desdemona had been unfaithful.

Consider a fourth example. Suppose you habitually drank too much moonshine and then regretted it the next morning. Suppose you went on like that for years. While high, you were content; in the cold light of sobriety, as you contemplate your bloodshot eyes and pudgy face in the morning's mirror, you realize that you are terribly unhappy, and that the contentment you found in the bottle was a flight from the underlying deficiency of your life. It was a flight into ignorance and forgetfulness. It seems to me that in one form or another this sort of experience is common, and reveals several important truths, one of which is that one cannot be happy if one harbors a well-grounded standing dissatisfaction with oneself, with how one really is. And that suggests that to be happy one must have the sort of desires one would want; in reflecting on myself, I must affirm that I am basically ordered in such a way as I would want to be, if I am to count myself happy.

Examples such as these suggest that while happiness is inseparable from a state of mind, it is distinguished from contentment because it is also inseparable from an arrangement of one's life, and more deeply because any such arrangement of one's life must be evaluatively linked to a notion of what sort of life is worth living

The various kinds of self-delusion on which an erroneous sense of happiness may be built all suffer from three defects.

First, they are unstable; self-delusion tends to be evanescent and destroyed by daily reality—as when after a fine day of fantasizing, your stomach is empty rather than full of Onassis's caviar. If we are willing to count a person happy whose state of mind depends on false beliefs, then happiness is completely subjectivized. As such, it is vulnerable. What you don't know *can* hurt you, like an Agent from behind.

Second, happiness by self-deluded fantasy seems truncated. As you lie on the heating vent, you picture the adoration bestowed on the wealthy and powerful, you imagine yourself its object; but you do not know their lives, their conversations, their failures, their triumphs. The image you conjure up of your dream life is a cartoon, a truncated partaking and does not measure up to its own object. Your happiness is bogus.

Hence the third point: Since your experience is that of a fantasy rather than of the real thing, whatever "happiness" you derive is not a product of your being, or doing, the real thing. If, when high on booze, you imagine yourself happy because beloved by a family to which you are devoted, whereas in fact your family is in tatters precisely because of your drinking, is your "happiness" of the same quality or depth as that which stems from really being loved by a family to which one really is devoted? Is the imagined happiness of partaking of Mr. Onassis's luxurious life as deep, as intense, as complex, as that which you would experience if you were actually partaking?

The confusion of happiness with contentment is widespread. Many people would choose as Cypher does. The recognition, often belated, that happiness and contentment are distinct, is perhaps not as widespread, but it is the sort of stuff of which the wisdom of the elders is made. The end-of-a-life feelings of regret and shame supply some evidence, I think, that we naturally connect happiness with some objective state of affairs.

Happiness is a feeling; but I add that it is not this or that feeling. It is more like that feeling or felt quality that attends many other feelings one has in the course of a life one has assessed as being rightly oriented. I am suggesting (the full argument cannot be presented on this occasion) that happiness is linked to a reflective affirmation of the sort of person one is. Happiness is linked to second-order desire (the desire to have the desires one has and in the way one has them). Contentment may be thought of as the subjective sense of satisfaction of desire(s), the kind

Cypher enjoys at dinner. Happiness is the satisfaction that one is desiring the right things in the right way, as when Neo knows he must choose the difficult path of saving Morpheus's life. There is therefore a connection between happiness and our conception of happiness. In order to have happiness, one needs a right understanding of reality—the reality about oneself and about what is truly the case in the world.

Three Theses on Happiness

By way of fleshing out this view just a bit further, I propose three theses on happiness. The first is that tranquillity is connected with the long-range sense of happiness discussed above, and so with the notion of a proper ordering of soul. Happiness is best understood, at the start, in terms of tranquillity. One general feature of happiness so understood is that it captures the connection between happiness and being at rest. It is at rest in the sense of lacking significant discord; it is peaceful, at a deep level. Further, it is at rest in the sense of being something like coming to a stop rather than like a process of moving towards a goal. It is more like an end state, a completion or fulfillment, than a condition of lacking and overcoming of lack. "Tranquillity" is the term usually used to translate the Greek term "ataraxia," a term that is the natural competitor to "eudaimonia," which is the one that Plato and Aristotle use. The latter is normally translated as "happiness," and less often as "blessedness"; ataraxia is also difficult to translate, and "tranquillity" is something of an approximation. Understanding happiness as tranquillity helps us to see that the enemy of happiness is anxiety. I have in mind not so much anxiety about this or that event—the sort of anxiety you have about getting back to the *Nebuchadnezzar* before the Agents catch you—but rather a general anxiety about things being out of kilter, not stable, not holding, potentially dissolving—the kind of "splinter in your mind" that keeps you awake at night.

This brings me to my second thesis about happiness, which is that one fundamental view associates happiness with ataraxia (tranquillity), and the other follows Aristotle in associating happiness with activity (*energeia*). The debate between Stoics and Aristotelians, in other words, articulates basic alternatives. Aristotelians define happiness as activity of the soul in accordance with excellence (*arete*). Happiness is the *summum bonum*, and the highest good for a person consists in excellence in his proper function (*ergon*), that is, in the proper activity or work of the psyche. There is a place, if a problematic one, for "external goods" (like decent food and a safe environment) in this picture; happiness is not just the exercise of virtue. This is what one might call an objectivist definition of happiness, and it has several obvious advantages. It provides us with a means of assessing claims to happiness and of explaining how people can be mistaken in thinking they are happy when in fact they are (as *The Matrix* portrays) nothing more than human batteries. As already noted, this is useful with respect to the "happy slave" or "happy tyrant" problem. It links up happiness with ethics and with how one leads one's life as a whole. It provides a basis for distinguishing between happiness and contentment.

Putting aside problems of making sense of the notions of soul, natural function, and excellence, and the famous difficulty of reconciling practical and theoretical virtue, however, this definition does not link up clearly with the experience of happiness. Aristotle says that excellence (*arete*) is not a *pathos* (*Nicomachean Ethics* II.v.3), and never says that happiness is a feeling (a *pathos*). Since happiness is *energeia*, its activity would seem at odds with the passivity connoted by the term "pathos." And as an activity in accordance with virtues that by definition are not feelings, it would be strange if happiness were understood by him as a feeling or emotion. Happiness is rather more like Neo's active decision making and discovery of truth about self and world, than like a lazy virtual tryst with the woman in red.

Finally, a third thesis about happiness: that neither of the two basic alternative views of happiness is alone adequate. I have mentioned some reasons why I think this true of happiness as Aristotelian activity. In spite of my endorsement of the association of happiness with tranquillity, however, one cannot accept that association without emendation. The tranquillity view of happiness tends to be associated with *apatheia*, with passionlessness, with a leveling out of the emotions, with detachment or indifference. This is precisely because of the close association of tranquillity with rest, peacefulness, and the other qualities already spoken of; and the contrary association of the passions, emotions, and attachment with perturbance, discord, motion. Yet to live a life of tranquillity so understood rightly strikes us as barren, dry, uninspired, as forsaking precisely much that is of value in human life.

Happiness as tranquillity in this long lasting, structural sense is compatible with anxiety and lack of contentment in the everyday sense. It is not so much equanimity as it is equipoise, balance, coherence and settledness in one's basic stance. At the level of lived experience, on this account, one can and indeed must have all sorts of passions, attachments, commitments. These may well be turbulent at times; they certainly put one's happiness, in the sense of mood, at risk, and in that sense they put one's happiness in the hands of others.

The Matrix as Mirror

Happiness as tranquillity requires evaluative assessment of my life; otherwise it would be difficult to distinguish between contentment and tranquillity. This assessment is, in the broadest, a philosophical one. From Socrates on down through the tradition, the questions "Who am I?" and "What sort of person ought I to be?" are fundamental to the philosophical enterprise. Philosophical recognition may often (to recall a point offered at the start of this essay) require personal experience, not just abstract argumentation. And art—including movies such as *The Matrix*—can both portray a problem, and, by holding up a mirror to the spectator, instigate reflection about its relevance and solution. This chapter is but a sketch of that reflection.[3]

---

[3] I am grateful to Eduardo Velasquez (Washington and Lee University) for the invitation to discuss *The Matrix* with his seminar "Film, Fiction, and the Politics of Popular Culture" on May 28th, 2001, and to the students for their illuminating thoughts. One of them—David Newheiser—kindly provided me with secondary sources relating to the movie. I am also grateful to William Irwin for his helpful suggestions. My discussion of happiness is drawn from the unedited manuscript of my *Adam Smith and the Virtues of Enlightenment* (Cambridge, 1999), Chapter 5. I am grateful to Cambridge University Press for permission to draw upon the book.

12

We Are (the) One! Kant Explains How to Manipulate the Matrix

JAMES LAWLER

Two Theories of Illusion

In what is arguably the most powerful scene in *The Matrix* we see endless transparent towers containing artificially cocooned, naked and wired human bodies. This, we discover with a shock, is Reality. Everything else that seemed to transpire to this point in the story, as people come and go, living their humdrum and frantic lives in our modern urban beehives, is Appearance, Dream, Illusion.

Since ancient times, philosophers from Plato to Buddha have been telling us that our supposed real world is hardly more than a shadow of the true reality. Perhaps the most sophisticated set of arguments to the effect that the world we see around us is a "mere appearance" is found in the work of Immanuel Kant. Kant argues that even the so-called objective properties of physics rest on subjective human projections. Although there is a Reality that somehow plays a part in the constitution of the appearances and the phenomena of experience, this Reality is not to be found in the realm of sensible appearances. The world we see and feel around us involves the projections of human consciousness. It is not the independently existing reality it appears to be.

Who is responsible for this hoax perpetrated on the human audience? For Kant, it is not some external being, like Descartes's malicious demon, that creates the illusory appearances of ordinary experience. We human beings deceive ourselves. In projecting the world of our own experience, we attribute to it an independent reality and thereby alienate our own freedom. This abdication of creative human freedom is the fundamental generating pattern or "matrix" of the socio-economic and political world in which most people find themselves enslaved to others.

Two Matrices

In *The Matrix* powerful machines with artificial intelligence control most, though not all, of humanity. It might therefore seem that *The Matrix* is more Platonic or Cartesian than Kantian in its portrayal of the source of the illusion as external rather than internal. And yet the intelligences that imprison human beings in the Matrix must control their captives according to the captives' own wishes. We learn in the film that the beings that have almost succeeded in governing mankind have had to alter their original program—the Matrix governing the nature of the seeming world—to comply with implicit human wishes.

Agent Smith reveals to Morpheus, whose mind he is trying to break, that there have been two Matrices, two different fundamental patterns and programs for governing the experiences of captive humanity: "Did you know that the first Matrix was designed to be a perfect human world? Where none suffered, where everyone would be happy. It was a disaster. No one would accept the program. Entire crops were lost." Agent Smith speculates on the reason for this anomaly: "Some believed we lacked the programming language to describe your perfect world. But I believe that, as a species, human beings define their reality through suffering and misery."

Just as contented cows create the best milk, contented humanity produces the best bio-energy, the necessary lifeblood for the intelligent machine masters. The Matrix was designed to occupy the mind while the sleeping organism performs its function as a battery for the soul-snatching machine intelligences. Paradoxically, what turns out to fit humanity's instinctive needs for a contented sleep is not an ideal world of happiness, but the familiar rat-race world of suffering and misery in which we, the audience, are actually living. By its veto power to choose among possible Matrices, sleeping humanity is unconsciously, instinctively, in charge of the program.

Agent Smith describes the cognitive dissonance produced by the first Matrix: "The perfect world was a dream that your primitive cerebrum kept trying to wake up from. Which is why the Matrix was redesigned to this: the peak of your civilization." The implication is that we choose our own illusions, instinctively rejecting a certain idea of the perfect world. Even when subject to the malicious demons and their dream towers, humanity gets what it wants. But why would people want *this* world of suffering and misery, rather than the world of happiness of the first Matrix?

Two Theories of Liberation

If *The Matrix* suggests two theories of imprisonment, external and internal, it also proposes two corresponding theories of liberation. Throughout the film the audience is asked to question not only whether indeed Neo is "the One," but what it means to be the One. At the beginning of the film, Choi recognizes Neo's powers even within the Matrix as a computer hacker who helps individuals manipulate the computer systems that control their lives. As he hands Neo two thousand dollars for a computer disk, Choi says: "You're my savior, man. My own personal Jesus Christ." But this kind of "liberation" is only a foreshadowing, perhaps a caricature, of true liberation.

The history of philosophy gives us two opposing interpretations of the idea of salvation. In the Platonic version, where the source of the illusion is external to the deluded human beings, the agent for overcoming the illusion is also externalized. An exceptional human being, a "philosopher king," is needed to guide humanity away from the shoals of misery and self-destruction and towards . . . what? The harmony and the contentment of a well-ordered existence. But something like this idyllic world has already been proposed by the controllers and rejected by the dreamers within the dream world itself.

In traditional Christianity, the Savior is an exceptional individual unlike others, a God-man capable of raising the dead, and, after his own death, bringing himself back to life. It is this traditional understanding of "the One" that predominates in the minds of the characters of the film until all such traditional expectations are fully overturned in the final scene of the film.

The other alternative, defended by Kant, is that of the modern philosophical Enlightenment philosophy, the principles of which are embedded in the United States Constitution. The only society worth having is one in which free people rule themselves. The slaves can only be truly free if they free themselves. If freedom from shackles is handed to them without their own efforts, they will quickly fall back into servitude. Kant argues that no one can save us but we ourselves. This self-liberation of humanity is the destiny that each of us must discover for himself or herself. In Kant's conception, Jesus is not an exceptional being who saves a helpless humanity, but the model of our own inner God-like potential to save ourselves.

Kant's conception that the perceived world is a self-imposed illusion, rather than one completely determined by an outside deceiver, is intimately connected with his view that every human being has a destiny to participate in the self-liberation of humanity. Kant's argumentation in defending these inter-related conceptions can convince the reader of their validity, and in this way strengthen the ideas that are visually and dramatically presented in *The Matrix*.

Philosophical Implication of Copernicus's Revolution in Astronomy

In his *Critique of Pure Reason* (1781), Kant called for a revolution in philosophy "according to the hypothesis of Copernicus." This Copernican revolution in philosophy means that our philosophical ideas—the way we think generally about the world we live in—ought to catch up with the implications of modern science. These implications are nowhere so obvious as in the discovery of Copernicus that the sun does not revolve around the earth, *as it appears to do*, but rather the earth goes around the sun, *contrary to appearances*.

Today we smugly laugh at the naivety and perhaps the arrogance of the older visions of the universe that placed our little blue planet (as it is seen from space) in the center of a vast universe. But let us give due credit to the ancient philosophers, such as Aristotle, who defended the geocentric world picture. After all, they merely formulated in general terms what we still today perceive with our own eyes to be the case. We directly *see* the sun going around the earth through the "vault" of the sky. We see the sky as a huge dome enclosing the flat plane of the earth that extends out from our physical bodies to the surrounding circular horizon. If we reject the ancient cosmology of Aristotle, we must accept the idea that the "world" as we actually perceive it is an illusion.

The geocentric view of the world is an extension of a more fundamental feature of perception, which we might call its egocentric nature. We directly see the physical world as if it were centered on our individual physical bodies. That is the way things seem or appear to us. The world I actually perceive centers on me, on my physical self. It is the same for each of us. But a little reflection tells us that the world in itself cannot be like this. When children take body-centered perception to be reality, we call that egocentrism. When adults persist in seeing themselves as the center of the universe, we call that egotism.

I Am the One

Egotism is a central category of the moral dimension of life. Egotism consists in taking one's own individual physical existence as the primary basis of one's choices. Ultimately, the egotist believes that he is "the One," the center of the universe, the being for which everything has been made. Each individual spontaneously, naturally believes in her or his mysterious election as a special being, as *the* special being. Experience, however, soon teaches most of us that other beings have the power to limit us, to prevent us from realizing our desires. Other beings too act as if they are "the One." To solve this contradiction, it is necessary to recognize that we—humanity in general, all intelligent beings in the universe—are in our oneness the true center of existence.

The basic choice of morality is a choice between two contradictory conceptions or Matrices of reality: there is the world of separate independent and competing egos, and the world of shared humanity. The egotistical world is connected to the appearances of physical bodies separated from each other in space and time, and colliding with one another according to laws of deterministic causality. On the other hand, there is the world as it comes to be seen from the standpoint of moral consciousness: a world of human unity and freedom. If the first is reality, the second must be an illusion. If we believe that the matrix of morality is real, then the matrix of separation must be an illusion.

In *The Matrix,* the moral choice for truth, freedom, and humanity is symbolized by the choice of the red pill. The red pill awakens the individual to Reality; the blue pill puts one back into the sleep of self-centered illusion. This choice however must be tested. There is a crisis in the unfolding of the commitment of the person who first chooses to awaken and live according to truth, only to discover that the realization of this choice in practical terms is doubtful.

What Is Reality?

The ultimate meaning of moral choice is, in Kant's terms, the duty to create "the Highest Good." The Highest Good is the creation of a world that combines freedom and happiness.[1] If such a lofty vision turns out to be illusory, then the initial choice is also unreal. In that case, only one possibility remains: to live one's own separate egotistical life by adapting as well as possible to the external circumstances of one's existence.

Because of the seemingly overwhelming power of the controllers, Cypher comes to the conclusion that the lofty goals of the *Nebuchadnezzar*'s crew are illusory. Cypher's initial choice of the red pill is tested by hard experience. He realizes that the initial freedom and reality outside the Matrix are, for the crew of the *Nebuchadnezzar,* only transitional moments in the realization of an ultimate freedom and an ultimate reality, which only exist in the minds of their believers. He recognizes that they are seeking a mythical Promised Land, symbolized by the name of the last free human city, Zion. Morpheus's vision of freedom and reality is the ultimate illusion, he concludes, using rational empirical estimates to draw practical conclusions.

In his justification of his betrayal of Morpheus, Cypher exposes his own superficial interpretation of freedom and reality. "If you would have told us the truth," he says to the body of Morpheus, "we would-a told you to shove that red pill right

---

[1] See James Lawler, "The Moral World of the Simpson Family: A Kantian Perspective," in William Irwin, Mark T. Conard, and Aeon J. Skoble, eds., *The Simpsons and Philosophy* (Chicago: Open Court, 2001), 147–159.

up your ass!" "That's not true, Cypher," Trinity argues with him, "he set us free." Cypher replies: "Free, you call this free? All I do is what he tells me to do. If I have to choose between that and the Matrix, I choose the Matrix."

The freedom that Morpheus has in mind is not mere separation from the Matrix, not mere individual freedom to strive for one's separate individual happiness, but participation in a destiny or Fate that has as its ultimate goal the higher liberation of humanity. This goal cannot be merely the replication "in reality" of our modern so-called world—the "peak of civilization"—but a different, better world, a world of human perfection that combines freedom and happiness.

Trinity's reply here is therefore inadequate, since she merely distinguishes between the illusion of existence within the virtual reality program of the Matrix, and mere physical existence with its illusions of egocentric perception: "The Matrix isn't real!" she says. Cypher's answer touches on a deeper truth. "I disagree, Trinity. I think the Matrix could be more real than this world. All I do is pull the plug here. But there, you have to watch Apoc die."

The contrast between the illusory world of the Matrix and the world of ordinary physical perceptions on board the *Nebuchadnezzar* is only the starting point for the film's exploration of the themes of illusion and reality, slavery and freedom. The initial contrast between illusion and reality, so startlingly depicted in the towers of sleeping humanity, is not complete. What is truly exciting, what captivates the audience along with Neo himself, is not life outside of the Matrix, but life within it— once its true nature is understood.

The Postulates of Morality

We seek to create a perfect world of universal happiness—Kant agrees so far with the first Matrix of the controllers. But this perfect world has certain conditions or requirements that make it incompatible with any possible world designed by alien captors. The Highest Good is a world in which people are not only happy, but also worthy of being happy. Their happiness must be earned through their own free, responsible actions.

We can now understand why sleeping humanity persists in demanding the rat-race world of the end of the millennium.

When the AI controllers offered them an idyllic world in which their needs were satisfied and all miseries alleviated, they recognized that such an illusion of happiness must *be* an illusion. It must be an illusion because the belief in separation persists even in dreams as the basic matrix of experience. And that belief in separation results inevitably, even dreamers recognize, in competition, struggle, and in the division between winners and losers. Happiness is possible only on the basis of a radically different principle, one in which free human beings act on the basis of their true unity, not their apparent separation.

The moral quest to create the Highest Good is tested against the seemingly hard reality of a world that appears to contradict its existence. The moral individual tends to feel powerless against the forces of a world built on completely different principles. The ideal Matrix of morality seems powerless to overcome the physically based Matrix of egotism. In order to avoid despair, the individual has to have faith in the possibility of *realizing* the moral ideal as the Matrix of a fully developed world. Kant distinguishes three aspects of this faith, which he calls the Postulates of morality. The Postulates of moral consciousness are: Freedom, God, and Immortality.

Against our feelings of powerlessness to realize the goals of morality, the Postulates describe what we must believe if we are to remain faithful to our basic moral choice. These beliefs are essentially those of liberators, of the saviors of humanity. Through the Postulates, we learn to follow through on our mission in life, which is to be the Ones who can create the world of the Highest Good, who can reach the promised land of Zion, the kingdom of heaven on earth.

Kant stresses that it is necessary to *believe* in the reality of moral experience. It is not possible to have scientific *knowledge* of this reality, he thought, because scientific knowledge consists in explaining experience according to deterministic physical, psychological, and socio-economic laws. But the essence of moral experience is its anti-deterministic nature, the freedom of the will. Since we cannot *know* (scientifically) this freedom without reducing it to its opposite, we must have a kind of faith in our own freedom to choose. This faith in human freedom—despite all the deterministic laws of our sciences—is the first "postulate" of moral experience.

The Postulate of God

One for all and all for one. That is the slogan of truly free individuals. That is the new principle, the alternative Matrix of the *Nebuchadnezzar* and Zion. It is the third Matrix, which is still incomplete and mysterious, still to be fully realized. In order to see the new Matrix of the united, sharing mind of humanity through to its ultimate implications, the destruction of the old Matrix, it is necessary to believe or postulate not only that freedom exists, but that free people have the power to create the Highest Good. A second postulate is therefore necessary: the postulate that free individuals, tuning in to the reality of our moral Oneness, have the power to realize our highest goals. If separation can create a world of external power, unity should have the power to create a radically different world. In this alternate world of Zion, the power of united humanity runs through each individual who opens up to it.

Kant calls this second postulate the postulate of God. In the traditional religious beliefs connected to the old civilization, God is regarded as the external distributor of justice. God metes out happiness to the good, and punishments to the evil, if not in this life and on this earth, then in the world of the afterlife. This conception implies that the ordinary human individual is powerless to achieve these goals of justice.

The world of the Matrix, modeled on the year 1999—the peak of modern civilization at the end of the millennium—is based on the sense of powerlessness that each individual feels before the seemingly external forces of nature and civilization. The root or Matrix of this sense of powerlessness is the belief in separation. Thus Morpheus tells Neo what Neo already knows: "You've felt it your entire life, that there's something wrong with the world. You don't know what it is, but it's there, like a splinter in your mind, driving you mad. . . . The Matrix is everywhere. It is all around us."

In the post-millennial religion of the New World of Zion, however, the potential of natural and human forces is not alienated and externalized in economic or political powers, whose theological counterpart is an external, all-powerful God. These external powers of contemporary life are epitomized in *The Matrix* by all-powerful intelligent machines. In the counter-world of Zion, however, the underlying, unifying Life Force can run through each individual who opens up to it by recognizing the illusion of separate existence.

In the Oracle's waiting room, a neo-Buddhist "Potential" tells Neo: "Do not try and bend the spoon. That's impossible. Instead . . . only try to realize the truth." "What truth?" asks Neo. "There is no spoon . . . Then you'll see, that it is not the spoon that bends; it is only yourself." We cannot bend the spoon—we cannot change so-called external reality—if, following deterministic science, we believe that it is an independent material substance that is separate from us. If however we recognize the truth that it is one with us, that it is part of us, then we need only bend ourselves, and the spoon will bend.

The "self" in this case is not the separate, isolated ego, but the higher Self, in unity with the All. God-like power will be ours if only we give up the illusion of separation. Neo must learn, not that he is *the* One—a special being apart from everyone else—but that he is One with all existence. He is, of course, "the One" who first fully understands this truth.

Fear and Trembling

The world of the Matrix is a world of fear. Interpreting oneself to be a separate physical being, vulnerable to the powerful forces of the physical and social universe, each individual must be afraid. The fundamental fear is fear of death, the extinction of that fragile physical existence. Fear of death presupposes that the individual fixes on his separate physical existence as the ultimate reality.

According to the belief-structure of the Matrix, we can never escape from fear. In the opening sequence of the film, Neo's first step toward freedom places him perilously on the ledge of his corporate tower. Then, he lets his fear govern his action. The second time he confronts the fear of falling occurs in the virtual reality Construct. He is being initiated into the power of manipulating the illusion. He is discovering the exhilaration that comes from *consciously* living in the illusion. The key to uncovering one's power is to release all fear. "You have to let it all go, Neo," Morpheus tells him. "Fear, doubt, and disbelief. Free your mind." Neo falls into the abyss only to discover the illusory nature of his fear.

And yet, Neo in physical form still bleeds. Why is this? Neo: "I thought it wasn't real." Morpheus: "Your mind makes it real." Neo: "If you're killed in the Matrix, you die here?" Morpheus: "The body cannot live without the mind."

The meaning of this enigmatic pronouncement becomes clear only with the unfolding of the logic of these ideas. Neo's initial distinction between the "reality" of life outside the Matrix, and the illusion within it, is simplistic. Those who are conscious of a reality outside the Matrix can become freer and more powerful within it. But existence within the Matrix, conversely, affects existence outside of it. Even outside the Matrix, the body is dependent on the beliefs of the mind.

The key to the realization of Neo's destiny consists in his rejection of the fear of death. Neo realizes his destiny when he chooses to give up his life for Morpheus, in accord with the prophecy of the Oracle.

Rather than expound a deterministic Fate, the Oracle gives him a choice: either his own life or that of Morpheus. "You're going to have to make a choice. In the one hand, you'll have Morpheus's life. And in the other hand, you'll have your own. One of you is going to die. Which one will be up to you."

The central elements in the prophecy of the Oracle are the Postulates of morality. First there is the postulate of freedom. Neo originally rejects the idea of Fate because he wants to be in control of his life. He doesn't want an external power to govern his actions. He wants always to be free to choose. The fulfillment of Neo's Fate is here presented as a matter of choice. As has been the case all along, Neo can choose differently. He could have chosen the blue pill and lived within the relative certainties of the dream-life in the Matrix. The choice of the red pill, and truth, brings with it the risk of unforeseeable fears, and the enmity of the controlling powers of existence. Now the Oracle tells him that he must choose between saving himself and saving Morpheus.

Secondly, in the prophecy of the Oracle, there is the belief in our Potential, our Power. In Kantian thought, we need to bolster our moral choice with the belief in the power of its realizability—against all the appearances to the contrary. The postulate of God is the postulate that links our moral choice for the Highest Good to belief in the power to realize this goal.

At first it would seem that belief in a divine power of realization or a Savior is an admission that we ourselves are powerless. But for Kant, morality requires that *we ourselves* be capable of realizing our moral duty. It follows that the God or God-man ("the One") that we postulate should not be regarded as a separate being who performs the miracle for us. God should be seen as an extension of ourselves as we transcend the limitations of physical separateness. In the dynamic of the film, there is a development from belief in an external savior to belief in our own God-like power, as united humanity, to save ourselves. This is our true inner "potential." This understanding is evident in the final speech of "the One" at the conclusion of the film.

Turning Point: The End of Fear

The third element of the prophecy clearly relates to death and survival. Someone must die, and someone will survive. In the world of the Matrix, where the principle of separation rules, the win-lose logic of separation is an iron law. The Oracle gives Neo this unhappy news: he is not the One, and either he or Morpheus must die. Oracle: "Sorry, kid. You got the gift, but it looks like you're waiting for something." Neo: "What?" Oracle: "You're next life, maybe. Who knows? That's the way these things go."

The Oracle's prophecy is fulfilled to the letter. Neo saves Morpheus's life, loses his own, and then returns in his next life as the One. How and why this prophecy is fulfilled is the key to understanding the film.

In the process of saving Morpheus, Neo finds himself face to face with a seemingly invulnerable and all-powerful Agent. Despite their training in the Construct which gives them tremendous powers in the Matrix, the crew of the *Nebuchadnezzar* recognize one ultimate fear-based rule: If you see an Agent, the only thing you can do is to run. This is Cypher's "realistic" advice to Neo, coupled with Cypher's debunking of any idea that Neo is the prophesied Savior. Hence, the dramatic turning point occurs in the film when Neo deliberately faces Agent Smith. He has made his choice; he will take his stand and face his death. Neo realizes this Fate in complete freedom, choosing to save another person rather than preserve his own existence as a separate, vulnerable body.

Neo thereby overcomes the fundamental fear that governs the power of the Matrix both within the virtual reality world and outside of it in the so-called real world of physical bodies. The same basic rule applies to each world. If you believe that you can die, even in the world of illusion, you will really die in the physical world. The vitality of the physical body depends on the mind's belief in the ultimate power of death. This is the basic rule that regulates the Matrix. Your power, your reality, depends on your beliefs, and your beliefs are ultimately ruled by fear of death.

There remains only one step in the unfolding of Neo's Fate. It is necessary to give up the belief in death. When Neo's body flatlines, Morpheus says: "It can't be." Morpheus cannot believe in Neo's death, although Neo, by all the rules of physical so-called reality, is dead. Trinity, however, goes further. Speaking to Neo's dead body, she addresses his living spirit: "Neo, I'm not afraid anymore. The Oracle told me that I would fall in love, and that that man, the man that I loved, would be the One. So you see, you can't be dead. You can't be. Because I love you. You hear me? I love you." Thanks to Trinity's love and refusal to believe in death, Neo comes back to life. In accordance with the words of the Oracle, Neo returns in his next life as "the One."

Immortality and Reincarnation

The third postulate of moral life is the postulate of immortality. To fulfill one's destiny as a moral being it is necessary to give up belief in and fear of death. The postulate of immortality is necessary to the morally committed person, Kant argues, because within the limitations of one lifetime it is impossible for the individual to perform one's ultimate duty: to bring about the advent of the Highest Good.

The moral goal of bringing about the Highest Good is about our own world, not another one. Just as the postulate of freedom is about human ability in *this* world, so too must be the postulates of God and immortality. Thus, the immortality postulated by morality must be a "this-worldly" immortality. The traditional Christian doctrine of an otherworldly immortality does not suit the requirements of moral consciousness. The main alternative conception of immortality to the other-worldly immortality of traditional Christianity is the "this-worldly" immortality of Hinduism and Buddhism. The Oracle's seemingly off-hand reference to reincarnation and the monkish robe and shaved head of the boy "Potential" suggest the Buddhist perspective. The soul or spirit of the enlightened individual, according to Mahayana Buddhism, chooses to remain on the wheel of birth and rebirth in order to facilitate the universal enlightenment of all living beings. In Kant's early writing, *Universal Natural History*, the immortality that expresses his cosmological perspective is one in which the individual soul is reborn over and over again as it climbs the ladder of potential human perfection.[2]

The One who is to save humanity appears in three incarnations. In a first lifetime, which takes place prior to our segment of the story, he liberates a few individuals from the life pods of the Matrix. The Oracle prophesies that this liberator will return in a new lifetime to complete his destiny. *The Matrix* is mainly the story of the second lifetime of the One, in the persona of Neo, eminent hacker who takes the several leaps that bring him to the realization of his Fate. The final moments of the film give us a glimpse of the One in his third lifetime. The third lifetime fulfills the Oracle's prophecy that the One will destroy the Matrix. But this is a negative goal, which by itself would only lead to the reproduction in physical reality of the repressive world of 1999. What is the positive objective of the liberator's actions?

The Savior or the Teacher?

Liberation from the Matrix must be the creation of free human beings, not beings living contented lives of happiness without freedom. Sleeping humanity rejects the concept of the unearned happiness of slaves that is the projection of their AI controllers. But how is such liberation possible under the direction of a Philosopher King, or thanks to the beneficent acts of an all-powerful Savior?

Like the Christian Messiah Jesus, Neo dies and comes back to life. More crassly, and perhaps comically, Neo sweeps up into the sky, his open overcoat spreading out like Superman's cape.[3]

---

[2] Immanuel Kant, *Universal Natural History and Theory of the Heavens*, translated by Stanley L. Jaki (Edinburgh: Scottish Academic Press, 1981), 195–96.

[3] The text for the first script by Larry and Andy Wachowski clearly suggests this image. The screenplay includes the words: "There is a RUSH of AIR as the Boy stares up as Neo shoots overhead. His coat billowing like a black leather cape as he soars up, up, and away." See www.geocities.com/Area51/Capsule/8448/Matrix.txt

But Neo's final overvoice summation suggests a different interpretation: that the Savior is not an exceptional Superman, but a
universal Teacher. As a teacher who shows others how to be
like him, Jesus said of his follower: "The works that I do, shall
he do also; and greater works than these shall he do."[4]
Addressing the AI controllers, the One announces that his task
of universal liberation involves the teaching of unlimited potential: "I'm going to show these people what you don't want them
to see. I'm going to show them a world without you. A world
without rules and controls, without borders or boundaries, a
world where anything is possible."

The world without limits, where anything is possible, is a
world in which everyone has the power to shape reality, to
manipulate the Matrix. For this world to exist, it is necessary that
egotism be overcome, that we rise to an understanding of our
essential unity with one another. In this understanding we will
find our freedom, our intrinsic connection with the divine
power to realize our highest ideals, and our ability to transcend
the fear of death. "The One" may be the first superhuman being,
but he is not the last.

---

[4] John 14:12; *The Holy Bible*, Authorized (King James) Version (Chicago:
Gideons International, 1961).

Scene 4

Virtual Themes

13

Notes from Underground: Nihilism and *The Matrix*

THOMAS S. HIBBS

From *The Terminator* to *A.I.*, from philosophical debates about whether terms such as "soul" and "consciousness" should be relegated to "folk psychology," to political debates over the ethics of cloning, preoccupation with the nature and implications of technology shapes both low and high culture in contemporary America.

In the 1999 movie *The Matrix*, the concerns and interests of low and high culture merge. *The Matrix* has everything—an intriguing and intellectually ambitious plot, postmodern echoes of classic fairy tales, special effects that set a new standard for science-fiction films, and expertly choreographed and technically sophisticated martial-arts fight sequences. Yet, both in its plot and its philosophical musings, *The Matrix* draws upon themes and debates that predate the current fascination with technology and artificial intelligence. In a number of ways, *The Matrix* replays old debates about Enlightenment modernity.[1] The Enlightenment commitment to the mastery of nature through technological progress risks the degradation of humanity, just as an imprudent celebration of individual freedom paradoxically courts a homogenization of all mankind. In these and

---

[1] Admittedly, the "Enlightenment," as we now call a certain cluster of ideas which emerged in the eighteenth century, is a complex phenomenon. As will become clear in the body of this chapter, I will be concentrating on a certain strain of Enlightenment thought, one which is ably dissected by Dostoevsky.

155

other ways, liberal modernity is seen as a potential source of
nihilism, a human existence void of any ultimate purpose or
fundamental meaning, where the great questions and animating
quests that inspired humanity in previous ages would cease to
register in the human soul.

Dostoevsky, Enlightenment Utopia, and Nihilism

Among the most important thinkers (for example, Nietzsche,
Tocqueville, and Arendt) who have detected a subtle link
between Enlightenment modernity and nihilism, one of the most
neglected is Dostoevsky.[2] Yet, there are striking resemblances
between many of the issues addressed in *The Matrix* and
Dostoevsky's *Notes from Underground* (1864), a work in which
Nietzsche claimed he could hear "the voice of blood." *Notes
from Underground* is a satirical diatribe against a certain strain
of western Enlightenment thought that had begun to infiltrate
Russia. An amalgam of humanitarian socialism, romanticism,
utilitarianism, and rational egoism, N.G. Chernyshevsky's *What
Is to Be Done?* is the target of Dostoevsky's polemics.
Chernyshevsky's text, which Lenin credited with reinforcing his
own revolutionary propensities, develops the utopian ideas of
the French socialist, Charles Fourier.[3] Dostoevsky's underground
man rails against the utopianism of the Enlightenment designers
of the modern city, who claim that their applied social science
will enable them to tabulate, regulate, and satisfy every human
longing. In a protest against the "rational" reconstruction of
society, the underground man opts to live in his sordid underground cell.

The underground man suffers from a paralyzing hyper-
onsciousness. Whereas the "healthy man of action" sees no difficulty with the laws of nature as applied to human life (indeed
he finds them consoling), the overly conscious individual real-

---

[2] For a discussion of nihilism in philosophy and as it relates to contemporary
popular culture in America, see my book *Shows About Nothing: Nihilism in
Popular Culture from The Exorcist to Seinfeld* (Dallas: Spence, 1999).

[3] For a discussion of the historical and polemical context of *Notes from
Underground*, see Joseph Frank's *Dostoevsky: The Stir of Liberation,
1860–1865* (Princeton: Princeton University Press, 1986), pp. 310–347.

izes the incompatibility between the mechanical determinism of natural science, on the one hand, and human deliberation and choice, on the other. The hyperconscious individual confronts the "stone wall" of the laws of natural science and the result is psychic "inertia" (p. 13).[4] He expounds:

> Science itself will teach man . . . that in fact he has neither will nor caprice . . . and that he himself is nothing but a sort of piano key . . . and that, furthermore, there also exist in the world the laws of nature; so that whatever he does is done not at all according to his own wanting, but . . . according to the laws of nature. (p. 24)

The goal of social science is to establish a logarithm for human desire and choice and to predict the future course of human life. Thus, there will "no longer be any actions or adventures in the world" (p. 24). Given this conception of science and of what is considered rational, the underground man's protests can be nothing but negative, a repudiation of reason, health, and science in the name of an irrational freedom. So he opts for passivity over action, isolation over community, and spite over the rational pursuit of happiness. But even this is self-defeating; as he notes, the "spite in me (according to the laws of nature) undergoes a chemical breakdown."

To the attentive reader, however, the underground man offers more than a dark negation of Enlightenment social science. He points out contradictions inherent in the Enlightenment project. The chief contradiction, the one that preoccupies the underground man and is the source of his unrelenting and paralyzing dialectic, concerns freedom. Enlightenment theorists promise liberation from various types of external authority: familial, religious, and political. But an unintended consequence of the implementation of Enlightenment theories is the elimination of freedom. The problem here is stated succinctly by Shigalyov, the theorist from Dostoevsky's *Demons*: "I got entangled in my own data, and my conclusion directly contradicts the original idea I start from. Starting from unlimited freedom, I conclude with unlimited despotism." How does this happen? One source of the

---

[4] All references to *Notes from Underground* are from the superb recent translation by Pevear and Volokhonsky (New York: Knopf, 1993).

elimination of freedom is the method of the nascent social sciences, which admit as real only what is verifiable according to the criteria of mathematical-mechanical, natural sciences. Another source is Enlightenment naivety about the ease with which theory can be translated into practice. The implementation of the theory requires both the correction of human nature and the radical restructuring of society; thus is the compulsory and violent nature of the project made clear.

The gap between theory and practice evinces a deeper difficulty with the Enlightenment project. In attempting to detect and regulate human desires, in treating man as a rational egoist, Enlightenment theorists have miscalculated. They suppose that what profits a human being is transparent to rational scrutiny and that all evil will diminish with education and political reorganization. But they overlook not only the fact that increased violence and desire for blood often accompany so-called progress in civilization but also that human beings have a deeper sort of desire, a desire for "truly independent willing." To exhibit their own freedom, the underground man insists, they will deliberately choose that which is harmful and self-destructive. Here the underground man anticipates Nietzsche's claim that human beings would "rather will nothing than not will." As is often the case in Nietzsche, so too in *Notes from Underground*, nihilism is not an end in itself but a protest or preparatory moment. Negation, it is hoped, will give way to affirmation. Thus the underground man confesses that he does not want to remain an "anti-hero" who merely inverts and rejects the theories of his contemporaries. It is "not at all the underground that is better, but something different, completely different, which I thirst for but cannot ever find. Devil take the underground" (p. 37).

The paralysis, spite, and nihilism that the underground man embodies are not alternatives to Enlightenment theory; on the contrary, they are its logical consequence. As he taunts his opponents at the very end: "I have merely carried to an extreme in my life what you have dared to carry even halfway" (129–130). Dostoevsky's book is a polemical *reductio ad absurdum* or better *reductio ad nihilum* of the theories espoused by his opponents.

Neither Utopia nor Nihilism: *The Matrix* on Human Life as a Quest

The enlightenment, rationalist project raises the question of what is real, what is human, and to what extent freedom and self-knowledge are still possible. As the underground man describes it, the Enlightenment project for society is an extension of modern mathematical physics, based on the reductionistic assumption that whatever is real is susceptible to quantitative analysis. Given such assumptions, the problem of human freedom and self-knowledge becomes acute. A related problematic informs the opening scenes of *The Matrix*. As Morpheus comments in one of his first conversations with Neo, "we're inside a computer program" where you have only a "residual self-image." He then asks, "How do you define the real? . . . electronic signals interpreted by the brain." The world of the Matrix is a world of "neural interactive simulation." The "anatomizing of man," as Dostoevsky's underground man calls it, dissolves the very possibility of human self-knowledge.

Whether or not it is actually underground, the cramped *Nebuchadnezzar* has the same feel as the underground man's cell. With its technological gadgets and their capacity artificially to affect human consciousness, the ship, operating on a "pirate signal" that "hacks into the Matrix," is a lesser version of the Matrix itself. But it has neither the naive, unreflective self-confidence enjoyed by the human constructs of the Matrix, nor the sense of omnipotence and autonomous control of the agents of the Matrix. Rooted in the "desert of the real," the rebel band struggles to ascertain clues about humanity's past, to gain a clearer understanding of what their task is in the present, and to recover a positive orientation toward the future.

Opting for the "desert of the real" over a constructed but more comfortable and orderly "reality" has its costs. There is, first, the unsettling fact that what one has taken to be real is in fact merely a fiction, that, as Morpheus explains, the "world has been pulled over your eyes to blind you from the truth," that you have been enslaved in the prison of "your own mind." Just as in Dostoevsky, so too here the false sense of freedom is accompanied by an illusory sense of our own unity, self-control and dominion over the future. A more adequate conception of freedom grows from a sense of uncertainty and internal division and leads to a more complex appreciation of humanity. Morpheus asks Neo whether he has not had the sense that "something is wrong in the world," a sense that you "cannot explain but feel." We must begin with a sense that something is awry, which, if investigated further, will initiate a quest. As Morpheus puts it, "it's the question that drives us—what is the Matrix? The answer is out there and it will find you if you want it to."

"The answer is out there" calls to mind "the truth is out there," the slogan of the popular and long-running television series, *The X-Files*. Although the central plot-line of *The X-Files* concerns the control of the earth by alien rather than articial intelligence, it shares much in common with *The Matrix*. Both stories play upon fears that some inscrutable and malevolent power—be it aliens, complex machines, the government, bureaucracy, or technology itself—has surreptitiously substituted a fictional world for the real world. But the situation is even worse than this; for, the enslaving tyrant is not a clearly identifiable, external force, which we have only to identify and then find the means of eliminating. Instead, the power is exercised in and through us, constituting in large measure who and what we are. The great danger—the one that can naturally generate nihilism—is that, having lost our grip on the real, we shall forever wallow in a world of illusion. If there are not sufficient clues to find our way out of the constructed universe, we risk a debilitating psychic vertigo, a loss of any sense of who and what we are and where we're headed. In such a situation, an investigation of the roots of our dilemma could be but a parody of the quest for truth. (It is significant that *The X-Files* couples "the truth is out there" with other slogans such as "trust no one" and "believe the lie.") As Adrienne MacLean, a perceptive commentator on *The X-Files,* puts it,

> Scully and Mulder are literally and figuratively alienated, penetrated, and probed to the molecular level by omniscient and omnipotent forces who have infiltrated like television and, now, computers, virtually everything in our lives . . . Scully and Mulder trust each other . . . Yet everything they think they know is wrong. Television has taught them the arts of insight but not how to formulate a point of view. It has sent them on a quest for identity, but taught them also never to trust what they find . . . The media-

driven milieu of *The X-Files* suggests that the whole world is now the same place, all of it's accessible, all of it at once sage, dangerous, restricting, liberating.[5]

Although MacLean's claim that the quest motif on *The X-Files* is utterly fruitless is open to debate, her description nonetheless captures a very real possibility for the show's characters. Given the similarities in plot-line between *The X-Files* and *The Matrix*, the characters in the film would seem vulnerable to the same fate as the characters on the television show. Indeed, narratives that begin with such radical claims about human alienation, about our inability to distinguish truth from fiction, reality from the construction of a wily artifice, run two diametrically opposed risks: that of never finding a way out of the entrapment and that of offering superficial solutions, what the literary and cultural critic Mark Edmundson calls modes of "facile transcendence." In his book *Nightmare on Main Street*, Edmundson argues that contemporary American culture is shot through with a dialectical battle between two sorts of narratives: the debased Gothic and "facile strategies of transcendence."[6] Neither strategy overcomes nihilism: the former immerses us in it while the latter provides only the illusion of escape. How does *The Matrix* fare on this score?

There is much evidence that the film wants to avoid these two poles; its alternative path is especially evident in its treatment of the issue of human freedom. The notion that our lives have been constructed for us is particularly irksome to our sense of freedom and personal control. As Neo says in his response to Morpheus's question about whether he believes in fate: "No . . . because then I wouldn't be in control." That Neo is operating with an impoverished conception of freedom is clear not only from this conversation with Morpheus but also from the Oracle's gentle mocking of him on this issue. As he prepares to leave her, she tells him he can forget the hard truths that she has revealed to him: "You'll remember you don't believe in fate. You're in control of your own life." But what Morpheus calls fate

---

[5] Adrienne MacLean, "Media Effects: Marshall McLuhan, Television Culture, and 'The X-Files'," *Film Quarterly* 51 (Summer 1998), pp. 2–9.
[6] *Nightmare on Main Street: Angels, Sadomasochism, and the Culture of the Gothic* (Cambridge: Harvard University Press, 1997), p. 77.

is not the same as the elimination of freedom perpetrated by the Matrix. Morpheus's notion of fate eclipses the divide between a shallow conception of freedom as complete control over one's life and a thoroughgoing determinism. In the references to Neo as the One for whom Morpheus has been searching all his life, there are suggestions that fate is actually a sort of providence. A prophecy of the Oracle, Morpheus explains, predicts the "return of a man who will be free of the Matrix." The relationship, however, between whatever powers of fate or providence may be operative and the power of human choice is left prudently understated. The best example of the film's ambiguity on this issue occurs in the scene where Cypher is about to "unplug" and thus kill Neo. He mockingly asserts that if Neo is the One, a miracle will disrupt his plans and keep Neo alive. Immediately, Cypher is killed by another member of the resistance.

Of course, very few ever entertain the paradoxes of freedom. Dostoevsky's underground man dwells on the contradictions of freedom in the utopian world, contradictions that the character Cypher embodies in *The Matrix*. In a pivotal sequence in the film, Cypher turns traitor and begins unplugging his colleagues in the resistance. When he is discovered, he admits that he is returning to the Matrix, that he's tired of doing what Morpheus tells him and that the Matrix is "more real." Morpheus himself has predicted that many are so "hopelessly dependent on the system that they'll fight to protect it." Cypher consciously chooses to relinquish willing, to abandon freedom for comfort, security, and an absence of struggle.

Morpheus explains that the Matrix is a "computer-generated dream world" whose goal is to keep human beings "under control." Their project is to "change the human being into a battery." Here we find a striking parallel to the theorists satirized by Dostoevsky, who liken the human being to a "piano key," a reference Dostoevsky may well have derived from Denis Diderot, the French materialist Enlightenment philosopher. In 1769, Diderot wrote, "We are instruments endowed with sense and memory. Our senses are piano keys upon which surrounding nature plays, and which often play upon themselves."[7]

---

[7] From *Conversation Between D'Alembert and Diderot*, quoted in *Notes from Underground*, p. 133.

Later Agent Smith confirms and amplifies Morpheus's description of the Matrix's project. He speaks of the "billions of people just living . . . oblivious." When he admits that the first design plan, which attempted to construct a human world void of suffering, was rejected by the humans, Agent Smith concedes one of the underground man's points, namely, the necessity of suffering for free beings. "Humans," Agent Smith observes, "define reality through misery and suffering." But Agent Smith and his cohorts share the utopian designers' view of natural, human life as an affliction, even an illness. As Agent Smith puts it, "human beings spread like a virus . . . and we're the cure." This echoes the belief, which the underground man imputes to his enemies, that in order to realize the dictates of reason human nature itself must be corrected. Like all utopian theorists, Agent Smith has a naive faith in progress. He states, "It's evolution, Morpheus, evolution; the future is our world."

Another parallel emerges concerning the absence of self-consciousness and self-knowledge. According to the underground man, the theorists deprive not only others but also themselves of self-knowledge. If they had any self-awareness, they too would be afflicted with inertia. Morpheus tells Neo, "the Matrix can't tell you who you are." Is there also the implication that a deficit of self-knowledge played some role in humanity's original act of hubris, which gave birth to AI in the first place? In his description of the source of the Matrix, Morpheus strikes a note of utopianism: He relates that in the early twenty-first century "all humanity is united" and in unison creates AI.

In this, *The Matrix's* depiction of humanity and its creation mimics the classic structure of the horror genre, with *Frankenstein* as prototype, where the creative ambitions of science generate a creature whom it cannot control and who turns against its maker. But in *The Matrix*, the creature, AI, having gained the upper hand, seems doomed to repeat the unknowing errors of humanity. The Matrix itself is now engaged in a utopian scheme of social reconstruction. What is the way out of this cycle?

Escaping the Matrix: A Victory for Humanity or Technology?

The answer seems to have much to do with a complex conception of freedom that the character Neo moves toward in the

course of the film. Yet it is on precisely this score that the conclusion of the film is highly ambiguous. Part of the problem here
is that in many ways *The Matrix* opts for the typical Hollywood
action-film ending, with the super-hero taking on a slew of evil-
doers. Of course, the sophisticated technology of *The Matrix*
renders its denouement more creative and more subtle than the
endings of films in the *Die Hard* or *Terminator* genre. Still, the
film has been rightly celebrated more for its special effects than
its crafting of plot and character. As Neo comes to transcend the
constraints of the ordinary human body and begins to exercise
powers possessed by comic-book super-heroes, improved technique overshadows the quintessentially human traits that Neo
has had to develop to prepare to wage war against the Matrix.

Until the final battle Neo seems quite vulnerable, resisting
and then only gradually accepting his role in the fate of humanity. Even when he elects to risk everything to battle against the
Matrix, the outcome remains in suspense. In the pivotal fight
with the Agent in the subway, he is shot and apparently dead.
Trinity, revealing the Oracle's prophecy that she would fall in
love with the One, insists, "you can't be dead because I love
you." She kisses Neo, and when he revives, she chides him,
"Now get up." Although we have had hints all along of a growing attachment between Neo and Trinity, the relationship is
insufficiently developed to carry this sort of dramatic weight.
And this is a serious flaw in the film. Why? The way to overcome
the threat of nihilism in *The Matrix* is through the recovery of
distinctively human traits and ways of living. Central among
these traits is the sense of human beings as distinct individuals
capable of loyalty, love, and sacrifice. Whereas the characters of
Neo, Trinity, and Morpheus are complex, different, and com-
plementary, the Agents of the Matrix are impersonal, generic,
and interchangeable. Is not this the significance of the name
"Smith" for the Agent who spends the most time on screen?

Whatever might be the flaws in the film's downplaying of the
human elements, it is Trinity's love for Neo that not only revives
him but also immediately precedes his manifestation of superhuman powers. He stops bullets and transcends the rules of
gravity; defying the solidity of bodies, he dives inside an Agent
who then explodes.

Having won a crucial battle with the Agents of the Matrix,
Neo warns them that he will reveal all things to all people and

then they will enter an uncertain and unpredictable world. As he puts it, "I know you're out there. I can feel you now. I know that you're afraid. You're afraid of us. You're afraid of change. I don't know the future. I didn't come to tell you how this is going to end. I came to tell you how it's going to begin . . . I'm going to show these people what you don't want them to see . . . a world without you, a world without rules and controls, without borders or boundaries . . . where anything is possible. Where we go from there is a choice I leave to you." Here Neo ignores all sorts of complications: he underestimates not so much the continued opposition of the Matrix as the likely resistance of complacent, still enslaved humans. The lesson of Cypher seems to have been forgotten. One also wonders whether the more complicated account of freedom that the film spends a good deal of time developing has here been sacrificed to a shallow conception of human freedom as autonomous self-creation, whether the film falls prey to the facile transcendence criticized by Edmundson. In fact, Neo's prophecy echoes the situation of humanity, described by Morpheus, at the end of the twentieth century, when a united humanity realized its peak moment of creativity and gave birth to artificial intelligence. Is Neo unknowingly promising yet another utopia?

Of course this may be asking too much in the way of consistency and clarity of a Hollywood movie. But this film, perhaps more than any other in recent memory, aspires to a kind of philosophical gravity. It wants us to take its philosophical musings seriously. And this makes the concluding words especially disappointing. Rife with platitudes, the statement seems less apt for *The Matrix* than for some other film, perhaps called *Neo's Excellent Adventure*. Alas, the ending does reflect a concern to which Hollywood gives much consideration in its crafting of endings: paving the way for a sequel.

14
Popping a Bitter Pill: Existential Authenticity in *The Matrix* and *Nausea*

JENNIFER L. MCMAHON

Early in *The Matrix* the main character, Neo, is faced with an existential choice. This choice is encapsulated quite literally in a choice between a red and a blue pill. Neo is given the pills by the character, Morpheus, immediately after Morpheus tells Neo that what he believes to be the world is instead a fabrication "that has been pulled over [his] eyes to blind [him] from the truth." Morpheus informs Neo that if he takes the red pill the true nature of things will be revealed, whereas if he takes the blue pill his perception of things will remain unchanged. Given their opposite effects, the pills represent the means through which Neo can either elect to wake from his slumber or sustain his dream. Thus, Neo's choice between the red and blue pills symbolizes the existential choice between living honestly and living in ignorance. Neo swallows the red pill and the plot unfolds.

Virtually all existential philosophers speak at length of the sort of choice Neo makes between honesty and ignorance, or truth and illusion. Though some use different terminology, they tend to describe it as a choice between authenticity and inauthenticity. Existentialists define authenticity as a state in which the individual is aware of the true nature of the human condition. In contrast, inauthenticity is defined as a state in which the individual is either ignorant of the true nature of reality or in denial with respect to it. The existentialist view is that existence is without any inherent purpose or underlying design. Existentialists assert that humans invest the world with order and meaning. They stress the freedom implied by, and the responsibility that accompanies this investiture, as well as the anxiety it can elicit. Common themes that existential philosophers discuss include absurdity, alienation, anguish, and authenticity. While Neo's choice involves a number of these items, it is most clearly a choice between authenticity and inauthenticity.

When describing authenticity and inauthenticity, existentialist philosophers tend to privilege authenticity over inauthenticity. For example, prominent existentialists such as Albert Camus, Martin Heidegger,[1] and Jean-Paul Sartre clearly elevate authenticity and scorn inauthenticity. In their philosophic works, these individuals describe inauthenticity in uniformly negative terms. Sartre refers to inauthenticity as bad faith.[2] Camus describes it as intellectual suicide.[3] Heidegger asserts that living inauthentically not only leads to "the levelling down of all possibilities,"(*Being and Time*, p. 119) but also to "the phasing out of the possible as such" (p. 181). In contrast, these existentialist philosophers describe an authentic lifestyle positively as one that is courageous, full of "majesty" ("Absurd Reasoning," p. 40) and "free of illusions"(*Being and Time*, p. 245). Oddly, despite the positive terms that existentialists use to describe authenticity, their literary portraits of characters who approximate or achieve it are discouraging, if not downright depressing. Whereas inauthentic characters are described as existing in tranquil ignorance, characters approaching authenticity are

---

[1] Admittedly, Heidegger's assertion in *Being and Time* (Albany: SUNY Press, 1996) that "the inauthenticity of *Dasein* does not signify a *lesser* or *lower* degree of being" (p. 40) has led some to question whether Heidegger actually privileges authenticity over inauthenticity. However, it seems evident that this assertion is made to clarify that authenticity and inauthenticity are modes of the same being rather than two categorically different types of being. Importantly, asserting that authenticity and inauthenticity are modes of the same being does not preclude Heidegger from considering one as a superior mode. Heidegger's negative descriptions of inauthenticity make it clear that he sees it as inferior.

[2] Jean-Paul Sartre, *Being and Nothingness* (New York: Washington Square Press, 1956).

[3] Albert Camus, "An Absurd Reasoning," in *The Myth of Sisyphus and Other Essays* (New York: Vintage, 1955).

depicted as anxious, alienated, and bordering on insanity. Because of the preponderance of such depictions, existential literature seems to suggest that the movement toward authenticity entails anguish, social dislocation, and sometimes madness. These consequences compel one to ask whether authenticity is indeed preferable to inauthenticity. Though authenticity may represent an honest awareness of the human condition, perhaps ignorance is bliss. Perhaps it is better to choose the blue pill. In what follows, I shall examine authenticity and inauthenticity and the benefits and burdens of each. I shall use *The Matrix* and Sartre's existential novel *Nausea* to support my claims, as characters in these works illustrate the pros and cons of both states. Though this essay will question the appeal of authenticity, it will conclude with an argument for it. Despite the challenge it represents, I shall argue that the benefits of authenticity outweigh its burdens and that a unique sort of serenity can be achieved in this state. I shall argue for the red pill.

Red or Blue? Neo and Cypher concerning Authenticity and Ignorance

Like the classics of existential literature, the popular film *The Matrix* illustrates both the unpleasant consequences of authenticity and the appeal of inauthenticity. This film depicts a future state when, after a long and world-ravaging conflict, computers conquer the human race and enslave it as their energy source. The Matrix is the virtual reality created by the computers that both placates, and maximizes the energy output from, the human subjects who lie captive in a vast complex of energy pods. While the billions inside the Matrix exist in blissful ignorance of their true condition (as immobilized, expendable energy cells for the artificial intelligence that dominates earth), a small number of individuals are free of its digital illusion. Unlike their captive counterparts, these individuals are painfully aware of humanity's authentic state. They constitute a resistance force that seeks to undermine the oppression by the Matrix. As a result, they live on the run from the computers that attempt to annihilate them. While the philosophic implications of *The Matrix* are numerous, the liberation of the character, Neo, and the choice made by the character, Cypher, illustrate the point addressed here concerning authenticity.

The character Neo illustrates the agony that accompanies the move to, and the achievement of, authenticity. Ensconced in the Matrix since birth, Neo exists unaware that the world in which he finds himself is an illusion. However, with the aid of Morpheus and his band of rebels, Neo is brought out of captivity. Rescued from his pod, Neo is like the prisoner brought from Plato's cave.[4] He too is brought from ignorance to enlightenment. Like the prisoner's emancipation, Neo's liberation from ignorance is painful. He experiences both physical and mental anguish. Neo's eyes hurt because he has "never used them before." His lifetime of captivity has left his body atrophied. Indeed, his limbs are so emaciated they require extensive electronic stimulation to give them sufficient strength to afford mobility. Though the physical pain that Neo experiences is acute, arguably the mental anguish is more severe. Indeed, he experiences a sort of cognitive shock. Morpheus apologizes to Neo for the mental anguish he endures, admitting that rescues of adults from the Matrix are rare because the psychological trauma is too great for most to endure. Ultimately, Neo's liberation from the virtual world of the Matrix compels him to admit that everything he believed to be real was an illusion. Worse yet, as Morpheus welcomes him "to the desert of the real," Neo realizes that reality is more terrible than he had ever imagined. Neo's experience turns his understanding upside down. It disorients him, pains him, and hands him more responsibility—and more "truth"—than he ever had or wanted.

Where Neo was freed late from the Matrix, Cypher was liberated when he was relatively young. Thus, he lives most of his life aware of the true nature of the human condition. In the film, Cypher illustrates the attraction of inauthenticity by opting for ignorance. After enduring years underground in harsh conditions, in perpetual fear of annihilation, and with little hope of improvement in his state, Cypher finds himself unable to bear his existence any longer. Consequently, he sells out Morpheus and the rest of his rebel companions for the opportunity to have his memory erased and his body returned to the Matrix. Over a virtual dinner with Agent Smith who arranges for his return,

---

[4] See Chapter 1 of this volume for a thorough comparison of Neo and Plato's prisoner.

Cypher explains his choice, stating, "I know this steak doesn't exist. I know that when I put it in my mouth the Matrix tells my brain it is juicy and delicious. After nine years, you know what I've realized?—ignorance is bliss."

Though we scorn Cypher for his choice, we can also sympathize with him. The apocalyptic reality with which he is faced is distressing to imagine, let alone admit. After all, who among us would choose a life spent in subterranean passages, under perpetual threat, where every meal represents the eternal recurrence of viscous gag-eliciting goop? While Cypher forfeits autonomy, honesty, and the opportunity for genuine experiences and human connections to return to virtual world of the Matrix, his choice will alleviate the extreme anxiety and discomfort that accompany authenticity. In his shoes, we too might opt for the illusion.

Sartre on Stomaching Existence

In his novel *Nausea*, existentialist Jean-Paul Sartre illustrates that the circumstances need not be those of science fiction for authenticity to seem unbearable or inauthenticity to present itself as a refuge. Where the characters and circumstances in *The Matrix* are extraordinary, Sartre's novel chronicles an ordinary man's discovery that existence is not as he assumed. In *Nausea,* the main character, Roquentin, comes reluctantly to an awareness of the true nature of reality. Where Neo possesses fantastic abilities and is characterized essentially as a savior, Sartre goes to great lengths to emphasize Roquentin's averageness. Roquentin is a historian of no acclaim. He writes books and frequents cafés. He lives in a rather mundane city in 1930s France. He is of modest means. He has a small and nondescript apartment. Indeed, the only thing unusual about Roquentin is his shocking red hair. Similarly, this common man's enlightenment begins not with a thrilling hovercraft rescue from gelatinous incarceration, but after a disquieting experience at the beach where the presence of a pebble in his hand engenders disgust and intractable fear. Unable to shake the disturbing feelings that this experience generates, Roquentin states, "something has happened to me."[5] Though he tries to dismiss his response to

---

[5] Jean-Paul Sartre, *Nausea* (New York: New Directions, 1964), p. 2.

the stone as "a passing moment of madness," (*Nausea*, p. 2) subsequent experiences lead Roquentin—and readers—to wonder whether he is going insane.

As we learn, Roquentin's experience with the pebble is just the beginning. Rather than improve, Roquentin's situation gets worse. Indeed, for Roquentin it appears that the bizarre has become commonplace as his mundane existence takes on a hallucinogenic quality. Similar to the experience Neo has upon ingesting the red pill, Roquentin's perceptions become increasingly distorted. For example, upon taking a friend's hand in greeting, Roquentin drops it in horror because it feels like "a fat white worm" (p. 4). Similarly, he is paralyzed by fear when he grabs a door-knob and it seems to grab him back and hold his attention "with a sort of personality" (p. 4). These experiences prompt Roquentin's confidence in reality to slip and he begins to think that, "nothing can ever be proved" (p. 13). When Roquentin looks in the mirror to get his bearings, he finds no solace. He finds no comfort because when he looks he, "understand[s] nothing of [his] face" (p. 16). Instead, he sees only something "on the fringe of the vegetable-world, at the level of jellyfish . . . the insipid flesh blossoming and palpitating with abandon" (p. 17). Likewise, when Roquentin looks at his hand and sees instead a crustacean, the impression is so intolerable that he stabs himself in the hand (p. 100).

As a result of his experiences, Roquentin's life becomes strangely disconcerting. It loses its order and continuity. Roquentin describes his life as becoming "jerky, [and] incoherent" (p. 5). He states anxiously, "nothing seemed true; I felt surrounded by cardboard scenery which could quickly be removed" (p. 77). As his perceptions repeatedly defy his conventional understanding, Roquentin's world dissolves around him. For example, while riding the tramway Roquentin struggles to stay calm as a simple seat cushion takes on the appearance of the bloated belly of a dead animal. He agonizes, "things are divorced from their names. They are there, grotesque, headstrong, gigantic and it seems ridiculous to . . . say anything about them. I am in the midst of things, nameless things . . . defenceless" (p. 125). Not surprisingly, Roquentin's experiences cause him to feel increasingly isolated, disoriented, and "full of anguish" (p. 55).

Though it appears that Roquentin is losing touch with reality, at the end of *Nausea* it becomes evident that he is, in fact, becoming aware of its true nature. As Sartre makes clear, what Roquentin's experiences reveal is that "the diversity of things, their individuality, [are] only an appearance, a veneer" (p. 127). Roquentin's experiences inform him that "the world of explanations and reason is not the world of existence" (p. 129). They show him that the orders and values we believe are intrinsic to the world and the things in it are instead "the feeble points of reference which [we] have traced on their surface" (p. 127). In *Nausea*, Roquentin confronts the unwanted and overwhelming truth that humans exist in—and are confined to—a world that lacks essential order and meaning. As Sartre explains in *Being and Nothingness*, though it does not create it, human consciousness gives order and purpose to the world. Without the structuring activity of consciousness the world exists as an indeterminate totality, an awesome undifferentiated whole. At the root of the chestnut tree, "[this] World, the naked World suddenly [reveals] itself" (p. 134) to Roquentin. With his previous experiences pushing him toward it, Roquentin finally becomes formally aware of the true nature of existence. He recognizes that the order and purpose he took to *be* reality is instead a construct consciousness *places upon it*. Rather than relish the truth that is revealed, Roquentin states, "I hated this ignoble mess. [Existence] mounting up, mounting up as high as the sky, filling everything with its gelatinous slither . . . I choked with rage at this gross, absurd being" (p. 134). Nauseated at the sight of existence's true nature, Roquentin describes existence as a "messy suffering" (p. 174) that both disgusts him and makes him "afraid" (p. 160).

Authenticity: Our Aversion to It and an Argument for It

In both *The Matrix* and *Nausea*, the main characters come to an awareness of the true nature of the human condition. As they illustrate, this awareness is unpleasant and met with resistance largely because the truth it reveals is terrifying. Morpheus acknowledges the burden of authenticity when he tells Neo, "I didn't say it would be easy, I just said it would be the truth." We see the desire to escape this burden evidenced not only in

Cypher's choice to return to the Matrix, but also in Mouse's fascination with his virtual woman in red and Neo's nostalgia for the noodle shop when he first re-enters the Matrix.

Importantly, both *The Matrix* and *Nausea* illustrate that authenticity is difficult not only because the truth it reveals is hard to stomach, but also because inauthenticity is the norm. Existentialists agree that most people are inauthentic. They attribute the prevalence of inauthenticity both to psychological resistance and social indoctrination. As Roquentin's and Neo's experiences make evident, the true nature of reality is not necessarily something humans *want* to see. Rather, existence contains numerous phenomena that we would prefer to deny. Death, suffering, and meaninglessness are three obvious examples. Most people have difficulty accepting these aspects of existence. However, authenticity entails accepting all aspects of reality, not just those with which we are comfortable. Existentialists assert that inauthenticity is pervasive because most people *do not want to know* the hard truths of existence. Instead, people prefer to comfort themselves with a vast array of lies about life. These lies range in size from major metaphysical fibs to the tiny tales we tell ourselves, but they are all lies we *want* to hear. As *The Matrix* illustrates, instead of aspiring to the Oracle's injunction, "Know thyself," most people prefer to flee the facts and remain in a "dreamworld" of their own—or someone else's—design.

Like psychological resistance, social indoctrination is a powerful deterrent to authenticity. As existentialists explain, most people are so thoroughly conditioned to believe that the world *is* the way they have been taught to see it that they resist any alternative. This indoctrination, and the resistance to change it encourages, makes becoming authentic more unlikely by making it alienating and making it appear as a movement into madness.

The prevalence of inauthenticity makes moving toward authenticity alienating primarily because it requires the individual who is becoming authentic to accept an understanding of things that is at odds with that of the majority. As Morpheus indicates, "most people are not ready to be unplugged." Most people are not ready for authenticity because they have been conditioned to accept, and are not psychologically ready to relinquish, the comfortable illusions they have about life and that they share with others. Consequently, most people will resist authenticity themselves and will renounce anyone who seems to be moving toward it. This resistance is evident in the antagonistic treatment of Roquentin in *Nausea* as well as in the characterization of unfreed individuals in *The Matrix* as "hardware" that will actively subvert efforts at revolution. As Roquentin states, "it is so important [for most people] to think the same things all together" (p. 8). Because of the pervasiveness of inauthenticity, the person who moves toward an honest awareness of the human condition loses the support of others precisely when she needs it most. Indeed, the seemingly ubiquitous desire to be like others and the social prohibitions against "deviant" behavior are sufficient to keep most people from ever achieving authenticity.

In addition to disclosing a burdensome truth and compelling social estrangement, the transition to authenticity also tends to appear as a movement toward, and elicit feelings of, madness. Certainly Neo suffers feelings of madness. Arguably, Sartre's character Roquentin illustrates this effect even more clearly. Repeatedly, Roquentin questions his sanity. After his experience with the pebble, he speculates that he might be "insane" (p. 2). Similarly, after a dizzying array of dissociative experiences, Roquentin concludes that others are likely to place him in "the crazy loon category" (p. 64). As Roquentin demonstrates, the movement toward authenticity both represents, and is experienced as, a movement toward insanity because the understanding achieved in authenticity transcends what has been established as "normal." Consequently, the individual who approaches or achieves authenticity not only appears mad to others, it is likely that she feels crazy herself.

Given what has been said about authenticity, it's hard to see why anyone would want to achieve it. As the existentialists admit, achieving authenticity entails not only accepting that the world has no intrinsic order or purpose, but also that we are fragile and finite creatures who bear complete responsibility for ourselves and the meanings we create. Given the burden of this awareness and the feelings of estrangement and insanity it can cause, it is easy to see why individuals prefer to remain ignorant of the nature of the human condition and insulated from the truth.

Though inauthenticity does seem to have some notable advantages over authenticity, the latter is still preferable. There are several reasons for this. First, while living inauthentically does alleviate anxiety, it does not eradicate it. For existentialists such as Sartre, Camus, and Heidegger, anxiety issues from the nature of our being. Thus, the only possible way to eradicate anxiety is to annihilate ourselves. This hardly seems a desirable option. After all, if death marks our end, then we will not be around to appreciate the eradication of anxiety that it brings. According to Sartre, Camus, and Heidegger, anxiety is an inescapable aspect of our being. It is part of our being because humans all have a sense of their constitution, a visceral concern for being that is rooted in an intuitive awareness of their true nature. Like the "splinter in the mind" that Morpheus describes, Sartre, Camus, and Heidegger believe that we all have a sense of the fragility and dependency of our nature that fosters feelings of anxiety. Existentialists recognize that we can disguise— or deny—this awareness, but they assert that we cannot eradicate it. Inauthenticity is precisely this attempt to disguise or repress what we know in our gut but do not want to admit to our mind. When one lives inauthentically one covers over the true cause of one's ontological insecurity and attributes this feeling instead to some mundane cause. For example, instead of attributing the generalized anxiety we experience to existence itself, we instead tend to attribute it to some localized source, like work, another person, or the lack of a particular object or status. We do this largely because attributing ontological insecurity to a mundane source gives us the impression that this insecurity can be controlled or even eradicated. We figure if we get the job, or get the right car, our insecurities and dissatisfactions will be eliminated. However, since inauthenticity represents a "flight . . . from [oneself]" (*Being and Time*, p. 172) and we cannot escape what we are, an inauthentic life is characterized by a certain desperate fervency and perpetual effort. Whether we want to admit it or not, most of us are familiar with this insidious cycle. Sadly, because of its internal dynamic, inauthentic individuals exist on the run from their being while at the same refusing to acknowledge the actual cause of their flight.

In addition to failing to eradicate anxiety and necessitating a sort of "life on the run," living inauthentically also has the negative consequence of limiting an individual's freedom. As existentialists explain, when one lives inauthentically one covers over not only the true nature of the world, but also the true nature of the individual. For existentialists, though humans find themselves in a situation they did not choose, they are free to determine themselves within that situation. Because this freedom is frightening, individuals often seek to deny it. Individuals who live inauthentically live in denial of their freedom. Consequently, they live without a genuine awareness of their own possibility. Individuals who are inauthentic do not admit the true extent of their choice. For example, instead of embracing the opportunity they have to create themselves, they instead adopt predetermined identities. They slip into roles that were dictated to them rather than crafted by them. Ultimately, inauthentic individuals cannot make genuinely informed or autonomous choices because they refuse to be honest about the actual state of affairs and because they make choices that are in keeping with their determined roles, rather than choosing for themselves. By removing responsibility, living inauthentically gives individuals some comfort. However, it does so at the expense of individual autonomy.

Though authenticity entails that one accept some disturbing facts, unlike inauthenticity, it lets one live honestly. Given the impossibility of actualizing one's potential and making informed choices in a state of inauthenticity, authenticity seems eminently preferable to living a lie. While the move to authenticity disrupts one's conventional understanding and forces one to dispense with certain illusions about the world, it need not induce madness. Instead, by allowing one to admit the nature of existence and the true cause of one's concern, becoming authentic not only creates a situation where genuine choices can be made, it also can compel a unique sort of serenity and existential appreciation. Sartre illustrates this when, despite the initial horror of his experiences, Roquentin comes to the awareness that existence is "a perfect free gift" (*Nausea*, p. 131) and a "fullness which man can never abandon" (p. 133). Indeed, by the end of the novel, existence has been transformed from something that arouses disgust to something bordering on the delicious when Roquentin describes it as "dense, heavy, and sweet" (p. 13). As Sartre illustrates, when Roquentin finally admits the true nature of existence, his nausea lessens. It transforms from a stifling, "insipid idea" (p. 5) which makes him sick into a poignant—and bearable—appreciation of the human condition and the burdens it brings (p. 157). When he accepts the true nature of existence,

Roquentin stops running and starts living. The nightmarish experience that constitutes the bulk of the novel ends and Roquentin commits himself to the arduous and unglamorous task of existing day by day "without justification and without excuse" (*Being and Nothingness*, p. 78). Despite the disturbing picture it paints, *The Matrix* also ends on a positive note. Though seeing the true nature of reality initially affects Neo in much the same way it does Roquentin, he too overcomes his nausea and seizes the grand opportunity that existence represents. Indeed, at the end of the film, it appears that Neo is poised not only to forge his own future, but also to lead humanity out of its oppression.

As Roquentin and Neo illustrate, the insights that authenticity brings are only unbearable as long as we resist them. Though existence may not be everything we want, it is only overwhelming if we insist that it be something other than it is. If one lets go of these expectations, one can see things as they are. Only at this point can one fully appreciate and make use of the remarkable gift of existence. While authenticity may not conform to our conventional definition of bliss, living authentically affords individuals a unique serenity because it ends the maddening run from our being that characterizes inauthenticity. It represents an opening up to ourselves and an acceptance of what is. Though the truth of existence may be sobering, it is all we have and all we are. Regardless of its attraction, if Heidegger is right and our being is time and our time is finite, then it would be madness to waste one's time—and thus one's being—living inauthentically. Either way, as Neo reminds us, the future is up to us. Take the red pill.[6]

---

[6] Special thanks to those who attended my presentation at the International Conference on "Madness and Bliss in Literature and the Visual Arts" (2000) and to Dr. Peter Fosl and the students at Transylvania University. I am grateful to these individuals for the commentary they provided on the two lectures upon which this chapter is based. Their comments and criticisms were of great assistance in the preparation of this chapter.

15

The Paradox of Real Response to Neo-Fiction

SARAH E. WORTH

The Matrix is one of a burgeoning genre of films, philosophical in nature, that specifically question the way we understand and function in reality. This is clearly a theme Hollywood is beginning to take more seriously. *The Matrix*, *Fight Club*, *eXistenZ*, and *The Thirteenth Floor* (all released in 1999) deal with the unreliable distinction between appearance and reality and the possibility that there are different "levels" or "versions" of reality. These movies come out of a tradition of films such as *Brazil* (1985), *Total Recall* (1990), *Lawnmower Man* (1992), *Lawnmower Man 2: Beyond Cyberspace* (1996), and even the more recent *Truman Show* (1998).

    The Matrix suggests that the "real" reality is much worse than the illusion we live in (though we are too unenlightened to know it), and *Fight Club* suggests that underdeveloped and undernourished aspects of our personalities can take on a life of their own—and do quite a bit of damage. *The Thirteenth Floor* and *eXistenZ* delve into different kinds of questions about different levels of virtual reality and whether we can ever know that the reality we are in at any given time is the real one. All of these films, except for *eXistenZ*,[1] assume that there is some sort

---

[1] It could be argued, in the case of *eXistenZ*, that by the end of the film Cronenburg throws into question the very idea that there is a firm way of distinguishing between reality, virtual realities, and fiction.

of differentiated, "real" reality; that if we ever came across this reality we would be able to identify it; and that this reality should function as something we strive for.

Earlier than all of these films was *Star Trek*'s Holodeck where the fortunate members of the Starship *Enterprise* were able to cross the barrier from being an observer of fiction to being an active participant, experiencing in a very real way what it is like to enter into a fictional space and to interact within the fiction in a meaningful way. One of the most compelling features of the Holodeck (for the viewers, not the participants) was that the program, on occasion, would get stuck or freeze and the "real" player would get caught in the "fictional" story. Thus the question of what was truly real came into question in an important way, since if the player couldn't get the program to work then he or she was going to be stuck permanently in another world—a false world—from which they had come. In a significant way, this is the problem all of these movies present to their viewers. That is, we watch as Neo struggles with understanding two different worlds (represented by his choice of the red and blue pills) but at the same time we, as viewers, are choosing for ourselves the world represented by the red pill ("Choose the red pill and you will stay in Wonderland") as we engage ourselves in the fictional space the film creates for us. The more we "lose ourselves" in the fiction, the further we choose to enter this altered reality in a way psychologically similar to the way Neo entered his new reality, the inhabitants of the Starship *Enterprise* enter the Holodeck, Douglas Hall and Jane Fuller enter simulated worlds in *The Thirteenth Floor*, or the way Allegra Gellar and Ted Pikul enter the simulated game world of *eXistenZ*.

Questioning Reality

Questions about the difference between appearance and reality, with their venerable Platonic and Cartesian sanction, will always be compelling. Let us, however, focus on a different, though related set of questions. How do we, as spectators, interact with the film itself and how does this parallel the kinds of questions the characters face in the film? How is it that we can get caught up in a fiction in a way similar to that in which the characters in these films get caught up in the different versions of reality that they experience? What this ultimately comes down to is the question: Why is it that we have emotional responses to fiction when we know what is happening isn't real?

Narrative is the important aspect of communicating the gist of a story. I can say in a conversation that I had a dream of a very different reality, but an extended narrative will communicate a more detailed meaning of the event and is likely to produce a more emotional response in the listener. A listener will get the gist of the story and the setting in a detailed *narrative* but will get only the facts from my *report* that the event took place. Thus, we can take into account all kinds of stories—documentaries (fact), docudramas (based on fact), historical fictions (fiction based on historical fact), and loosely defined fiction (any kind of "made up" story). The important thing to remember is that we respond emotionally to all of these—whether we know them to be true or not. We respond to fiction, knowing it to be a fiction, and we respond even more strongly to vivid and expressive narrative descriptions. We are attracted to fictions because we enjoy the ways that we respond to them. We generally respond more fully when the story is superior, that is, when the narrative is better developed. To better understand our responses we need some further explanation of the relationship between fictions, our beliefs about them, and our responses to them.

Why Respond to Fiction?

Our responses to fiction produce a complicated set of problems. First of all, what is included under the heading of representation or fiction would incorporate everything from literature to TV to big-screen film to virtual-reality games. The problem is not entirely that the story is fictional or that it is false, but that it is a re-presentation of a story—true or otherwise. Why do we purposely experience things—and enjoy these experiences—which we know are not real? This is generally known as the "paradox of fiction." The paradox can be constructed as follows:

(1) We only respond emotively to things that we believe to be real,

(2) We do not believe fiction is real, and

(3) We respond emotionally to fiction.[2]

To explain the first part of this, logically, it wouldn't seem that I would have an emotional response to a story you told me, if I knew beforehand that it wasn't true—for example, if you were to say, "What I am about to tell you isn't true" and then continue by saying, "I have a good friend who was so distraught over a romantic relationship that she threw herself in front of a train." Logically and practically there would be no reason for me to be concerned at all about your friend or for me to have any sort of emotional response to your story. But we do have emotional responses to fictional and false stories all the time.

All sorts of answers are often given as explanations as to why we do have these responses. Answers range from suggestions that there is a "willing suspension of disbelief" (first proposed by Samuel Taylor Coleridge) to claims that any sort of empathy for the characters can produce an emotional response in the viewer or reader.[3] Since I do not find any of these convincing, what I would like to suggest is that the way we empathize with fictional characters has more to do with the way the story is told than any real distinction between a true reality and some other manufactured or simulated reality or that it has anything to do with a willing suspension of disbelief. Whether it is the set of *The Truman Show*, a virtual reality world, or the reality provided Neo in *The Matrix*, when the observer becomes emotionally involved, it is because of the story.

Part of the problem is that we don't *believe* that what we are watching is true. This is the key component that makes this a paradox. At first, Neo did not believe that what he found after he took the red pill could be what was truly real until the parts

---

[2] The paradox of fiction is a general category, two subcategories of which would be the paradox of tragedy (How can we derive aesthetic pleasure from tragedy?) and the paradox of horror (Why do we enjoy horror when it is presented through representation?).

[3] Jerrold Levinson does an excellent job of explaining the competing theories. See his "Emotion in Response to Art: A Survey of the Terrain," in Mette Hjort and Sue Laver, eds., *Emotion and the Arts* (Oxford: Oxford University Press, 1997), pp. 20–34.

of the story he was told began to make sense to him. Even then,
for a long time, he continued to question different aspects of
what this new reality had to provide. So what we believe about
what is real and what isn't determines how psychologically and
emotionally connected we become to a particular story. A belief
of one kind or another is not going to provide a sufficient paradigm for us to talk of justified or genuine emotions when the
technology has changed the nature of the fictions that we experience to the degree that it has. *The Blair Witch Project* aside, we
"believe" when we are watching a movie that what is happening isn't "real," isn't really happening. But the technology, especially with the technology provided by IMAX films, which have
more of an effect on our senses than a traditional film, and even
the award-winning special effects in *The Matrix*, seems to get us
caught up in the film in ways that go well beyond our simple
belief that what we are seeing isn't really happening. The point
doesn't seem to be that *we don't believe* what is happening is
real, but rather that the way the story is told (and now the special effects which influence the realness of the way the story is
told) seems to be more influential over how we respond to the
story.

Some of the new fictional media even threaten to blur the
line between the real and fictional worlds that we experience—
some of it may have even made that line irrelevant. That is, we
have not come to any conclusions as to whether or not we are
able, imaginatively, to enter into fictional spaces in the same
way that Neo enters the Matrix. And as Neo is told repeatedly,
"you can't be told what the Matrix is, you have to see it yourself." Neo has to choose the red pill in order to experience this
very different reality for himself. This is similar to the fact that I
will never have the same experience or emotional response
when someone tells me about a movie or a novel as when I see
it or experience it for myself. Is it even possible that we, as
viewers, could have the same sort of access to our fictional
spaces that Neo had while he was in the desert of the real?
Kendall Walton suggests that we experience fictions psychologically, in similar ways as children do physically when they play
their games of make-believe.[4] That would imply, however, that

---

[4] See Kendall Walton, *Mimesis as Make-Believe* (Oxford: Oxford University
Press, 1990).

we really are able to enter into a fictional space in a way that is relevantly similar to the way Neo enters the reality that is the Matrix. Although we do not physically enter into another space, being able to explain the resulting emotional effects by saying that it is a cognitively similar experience would relieve us of the burden of explaining why we respond to things we believe not to be "real." That is, if the experiences are cognitively similar, a "belief in the reality of" or the clear distinction between "real" and "unreal" becomes not just blurred but irrelevant.

Don't misunderstand however. It is clear that we do not have to *believe* what is going on in the film in order to be affected by it. In fact, we *cannot* believe what is happening if we are to have an emotionally appropriate (aesthetic) response. This is especially true when it comes to tragedy or horror.[5] Generally, we are not amused by others' tragic lives nor do we derive pleasure out of watching people chased, stalked, or murdered. But in the context of a fiction, we often enjoy these things. We can enjoy them, however, only if we do not believe they are happening. We can enjoy watching Neo fighting Morpheus, after Neo has learned through a programmed computer simulation of a combination of martial arts, only if we know that neither of them is really being hurt. This goes even further with the kinds of special effects that *The Matrix* employs, since what the viewer sees is what it would be like if time slowed down or even stopped. Since we know that this can't happen, or it at least isn't part of our experience, we can still allow it to influence our response to the movie. (The bounds of these situations are also being stretched by the media with a new genre of voyeuristic television shows like *Survivor*, *Real World*, and *Big Brother*. We may even get to the point where we *do* want to know the presentation is "real" in order to derive aesthetic pleasure out of it.)

We Enter with Alice

The Matrix makes a number of clever and important references to *Alice in Wonderland*. Alice had many of the same problems in facing her strange new reality as did Neo. From the very

---

[5] See Noël Carroll, *The Philosophy of Horror or Paradoxes of the Heart* (New York: Routledge, 1990), and Peter Lamarque, "How Can We Pity and Fear Fictions?" *British Journal of Aesthetics* 21 (1981), pp. 291–304.

beginning, Neo (still Thomas Anderson at that point, outside the rabbit hole) was told to follow the White Rabbit (tattoo), which ultimately led him to the true reality. Once Neo arrived, Morpheus said to him, "I imagine right now you are feeling a bit like Alice—tumbling down the rabbit hole." These explicit references make it clear that the kind of experiences the creators of the film were allowing Neo to have are parallel to the experiences that the viewers have of the film. As viewers, we watch and become increasingly more involved in the new reality that Neo experiences and we acclimate to the different reality at the same time Neo does. Since *Alice in Wonderland* is a fiction we are nearly all familiar with, we are taken (the viewers of the film and Neo at the same time) into a new wonderland of our own.

When we enter into a fictional world, or let the fictional world enter into our imaginations, we do not "willingly suspend our disbelief." Coleridge aside, we cannot willingly decide to believe or disbelieve anything, any more than we can willingly believe it is snowing outside if all visual or sensory cues tell us otherwise. When engaging with fiction we do not *suspend a critical faculty*, but rather *exercise a creative faculty*. We do not actively suspend disbelief—we *actively create belief*. As we learn to enter into fictional spaces (and I do believe this is something that we have to learn and that requires skills we must practice and develop[6]) we desire more and more to experience the new space more fully. We want to immerse ourselves in the new world, just as Neo begins to immerse himself in the real world outside the Matrix. To do this we can focus our attention on the enveloping world and use our creative faculties to reinforce the reality of the experience, rather than to question it.

How does technologically sophisticated fiction, more and more like "real" events, produce emotive responses? Some argue that we have to understand the way emotions work in response

---

[6] This claim might seemingly be questioned because of the fact that *children* seem to do this with relative ease. Children do not have to train to play games of make-believe and they seem to become fully and easily absorbed in fictional and imaginary worlds of their own making. It would seem, however, that as Walton argues, adults are psychologically engaged in fictional experiences in similar ways as children are physically in their games of make-believe. Although children do this quite naturally, training to do this as adults seems to be something that we have to re-learn.

to real events in order to understand how we respond emotively to fiction. This may not be the way to go, however, as it seems that the belief requirement that is missing from our interactions with fictional situations does not prohibit us from profoundly similar experiences physically and phenomenologically. If we *feel* the same and have relevantly similar emotional responses, why cannot the experience be said to be real? In many ways it can, but we are now getting into an area where fictional spaces and real spaces overlap and even unite. In the same way, the two worlds in *The Matrix* begin to overlap and unite. At one point, after Neo has been shaved and placed in his new digs, Morpheus takes him into an all white room. Neo is surprised to find that he is dressed the way that he would have been earlier. Morpheus explains to him that this is his "residual self-image" and that it is the "physical image of your digital self." Neo's old self-image crosses over from one world to the next. Similarly, Cypher can't seem to give up the taste and texture of steak, even though he "knows" it isn't real. Our knowledge of what is real and what isn't real doesn't necessarily change the way we behave or respond to these things. We may have to face the possibility that the line that divides appearance and reality (in the Matrix and in our own lives) is not as clear as we once thought it to be. We may even need to actively make that line disappear in order to make sense of our interactions with fictions.

The Importance of Story-telling

In "reality," we make judgments about people and situations without having full information all the time—we must do this just to be practical, since the time it would take to gather all the information we assume would be prohibitive to living our lives. We fill in the gaps of knowledge with guesses and prejudices of our own. Thus, reality may not be as "real" as we tend to think of it, since we do a fair amount of the construction on our own. We do the same with fiction, as we assume those we read about have had relevantly similar human lives, that they function as flesh and blood humans unless otherwise noted, and we assume that they live in a world that works physically in the same way as does ours. In both cases, in reality and with fiction, we are given a skeleton structure of what is happening, and we use our imaginations to fill in the details. With fiction, the structure is carefully constructed so we are given nearly all the relevant information. In reality, on the other hand, the information we use as a basis to construct a coherent understanding of a situation is not given to us in a carefully constructed way. Rather, we pick up certain details and make a comprehensible story of our own, using our own prejudices and biases, working necessarily from our own perspective, which is determined largely by our culture. If this is the case and we do have to create and fill in significant parts of our own realities, we are in a sense, making up our own stories—and these stories are our lives. Roger Schank explains in his book on narrative and intelligence that

> We need to tell someone else a story that describes our experience because the process of creating the story also creates the memory structure that will contain the gist of the story for the rest of our lives. Talking is remembering . . . But telling a story isn't rehearsal, it is creation. The act of creating is a memorable experience in itself.[7]

We create meaning and memory through the hearing and telling of stories. Thus reality is more like fiction in terms of story creation than we originally thought, and the question of whether or not we must have a belief requirement in order to have a justified emotion seems now to be misguided.

Even if we do create our own stories to be reality (or our realities as stories) we still have a belief component missing from our assessment when we experience fictional simulations. If I believe that I am walking across the street, whether the cars are fictional or not, I am able to assess that I am in some mortal danger if I stay too long. If I make this assessment while playing a virtual reality game, I am not physically in any danger. Understanding how narrative undermines the distinction between reality and fiction does, however, make the paradox disappear in a certain sense. That is, the problem that we respond differently to fiction and reality no longer holds because the distinction between them has changed. If we put the fiction-reality distinction aside and look to what it is that

---

[7]Roger Schank, *Tell Me a Story: Narrative and Intelligence* (Evanston: Northwestern University Press, 1998), p. 115.

connects our understanding of both, namely how we comprehend narrative, we can begin to work with a more unified problem, one that will not always, ultimately, lead us to a paradox.

Experiencing Neo's Narrative

I am not suggesting that fiction and reality are the same or even that they are at times indistinguishable. There is a clear distinction between the epistemological (knowing what is real) and the ontological (the existence of things as they are) that will forever differentiate those for us. But what I am suggesting is a much stronger emphasis on how we make sense of both—that is, through narrative and story-telling. The way the story is told, or how it is that we create the story and make sense of it is similar for both fiction and reality. If it is the narrative that we are ultimately responding to, then it does not matter how we construe the emotions to work in response to real experiences and fictional ones—this is a false dichotomy that will continue to leave us in a paradox.

Further, if it is the narrative that we respond to, and the narratives are getting better or at least more vivid through technological developments, then it would make sense that we have increasingly stronger affective responses, even though we "know" what we see or experience is not "real." With the current state of the technology, especially with the kinds of special effects *The Matrix* provides, we are able to more fully experience both worlds and respond emotively to both. By moving the focus of the debate away from the belief requirement needed for "justified" emotions and understanding the role of stories more fully we can connect the divergent spaces of the real and the representational. We can further see how it is that we function in similar ways to the characters in *The Matrix*. Neo experiences a new reality as we experience it along with him in parallel ways we never before imagined.

16

Real Genre and Virtual Philosophy

DEBORAH KNIGHT and GEORGE MCKNIGHT

In this essay, we look at *The Matrix* as an example of a "mixed-genre" film and consider how it engages a range of issues in philosophy. The Hollywood cinema has, historically, been deeply rooted in genre, and *The Matrix* repays examination as a genre film. But right away we must dispel a common misconception. While genre films inevitably rely on a range of familiar, recognizable, and recurring features and motifs, it would be a misconception to think that, just because a film is "genre," it is a no-frills, standardized narrative, lacking originality and unworthy of critical examination. Since most of the great films of the Hollywood cinema are genre films, such a conclusion would obviously be wrongheaded. We should also identify a common misunderstanding. Through much of the history of genre criticism—though certainly not in actual filmmaking—film genres have been treated as uniquely identifiable, reasonably homogeneous categories, and genre films have been treated as belonging wholly to one genre or another. Since at least the mid-1970s, what has always been true about genre films has become quite explicit—namely, that the very idea of a pure genre form is a theorist's fiction. Rather, the mixing of elements in genre films is the norm, not the exception.[1]

---

[1] Important recent work on genre films includes Rick Altman, *Film/Genre* (London: British Film Institute, 1999), and Steve Neale, *Genre and Hollywood* (London: Routledge, 2000).

The Matrix is unquestionably a mixed-genre film. Our argument is that, by considering the particular elements that make up the mix, we can find the narrative roots of *The Matrix*'s more obviously philosophical themes. And *The Matrix* certainly has its fair share of philosophical thematics and allusions. It alludes to core issues from metaphysics and epistemology such as the nature of truth and belief, the distinction between appearance and reality, as well as the possibilities and limits of knowledge. What, for instance, counts as a justifiable true belief in a virtual world? *The Matrix* alludes to central themes from ethics and moral philosophy, such as the question whether our will is free or whether in fact we are deterministically controlled by forces outside ourselves. Philosophers will immediately note parallels between *The Matrix* and such canonical texts as Plato's *Republic*, especially the Allegory of the Cave, and Descartes's *Meditations on First Philosophy*, notably the Dream Hypothesis. And we should not forget the spiritual and religious allusions which run from Nietzsche's *Übermensch* through Zen Buddhism to apocalyptic Christianity, nor what *The Matrix* has to tell us about technology and science. Arguably, any properly philosophical consideration of *The Matrix* needs to recognize what is going on at the level of genre in the film. When the film's genre inheritance is acknowledged, it becomes easier to see the literary roots of its dominant philosophical motifs, and also to understand why, whatever philosophical questions the film alludes to, it does not propose *philosophical* answers, only genre ones.

The Matrix and Genre Films

To think in genre terms about films and other narratives is to think about overlapping inscriptions, conventions, and story paradigms. These overlaps cross-classify familiar textual categories, potentially drawing on sources as diverse as those used in *The Matrix*, for instance: medieval Romance literature, a range of recognizable film genres, popular "shoot 'em up" video games, and even such contemporary cultural "texts" as Goth and grunge fashion. Thinking in genre terms involves recognizing how a particular genre film fits into a complex set of industrial, historical, and communicative exchanges between producers and consumers of genre fictions. To "read" a film in genre terms is also to consider how audiences come to genre films with expectations based on their previous engagement with similar sorts of films. In the case of *The Matrix*, that might involve such things as fan recognition of Keanu Reeves from *Speed* (Jan de Bont, 1994) and *Johnny Mnemonic* (Robert Longo, 1995), fondness for films with futuristic settings—for instance *Blade Runner* (Ridley Scott, 1982/1991)—where humanity is in crisis, and familiarity with such contemporary cultural manifestations as comic-book narratives and computer games. To assess a film in genre terms is to see how the thematic meanings of various genres impact our understanding of the film in front of us. Perhaps the most important element for *The Matrix* is the audience's familiarity with essentially inscrutable genre heroes—a tradition that ranges from the Western through to science fiction and which Keanu Reeves has virtually perfected in this film. If we approach the philosophical aspects of *The Matrix* by way of the question of genre, we find that most of what counts as "philosophical" is in fact already part of the film's genre inheritance.

The broadest useful set of genre categories is wonderfully set out in Northrop Frye's classic *The Anatomy of Criticism: Four Essays*.[2] They are Tragedy, Romance, Comedy, and Irony/Satire. The characteristics of these master genres are abstractions from a wide range of narratives. As abstractions, they track dominant narrative trajectories, focusing simultaneously on the intended relationship between protagonists and audience, and the overall tone and teleology of the narrative. Tragedies concern protagonists who are superior in skills and knowledge to the members of their audience. For this reason, according to a tradition that dates back to Aristotle, we admire the tragic hero or heroine, and respond with fear and pity at his or her downfall. The Romance, as a master genre, is a quest story, an attempt to discover something as crucial as one's identity or to save one's society from a fallen existence if not certain doom. The protagonist of Romance undergoes a series of trials, through the course of which his or her true character is fully revealed. Perhaps the hardest genre to understand as a master genre is Comedy, given

---

[2] Northrop Frye, *The Anatomy of Criticism: Four Essays* (Princeton: Princeton University Press, 1957).

how easy it is to think that a comedy is just something funny, something that makes us laugh. The master genre of Comedy, by contrast, concerns the integration of an outsider figure into a community, and so involves the redemption of the qualities that initially marked the hero as "other." The master genre of Irony/Satire identifies narratives where the audience is clearly in a superior position to the protagonist, and where we should expect criticism of dominant social institutions.

Considered in terms of master genres, *The Matrix* is unproblematically a Romance. It is a quest narrative, and like so many quest narratives it combines three classic themes: the discovery, initiation, and full self-realization of the true hero, the threat to the rightful community, and the eventual romantic union of the hero and heroine, which also symbolizes or at least signals the triumph of their community over the evil forces that had threatened it.

What *The Matrix* deliberately does *not* do is position itself easily into any single consensus genre or subgenre. Consensus genres are the ones we talk about most easily when identifying movies. Familiar examples include: detective films, action films, horror films, thrillers, science fiction, musicals, romantic comedies, Westerns, swashbucklers, war films, biopics, teenpics, and many more. This is not to say that there is always a clear agreement in the critical literature about just how one demarcates genres. Some genre theorists emphasize shared conventions, iconographies, character types, and plotlines as the features that distinguish one genre from another. Others note that not all genres can actually be identified by, for instance, iconographies— iconography works for the gangster film but not for the biopic. Some genres get their names from the response they want to elicit from their audience—for instance, horror—while others get their names from the setting or location of their action, for example the Western, and still others get their names from their most striking devices as opposed to their iconography, for instance the musical. Other theorists, such as Linda Williams, have reconfigured consensus genres by linking melodrama, horror, and pornography within the term "body genres" which she identifies by such categories as bodily excess, ecstasy, perversion, originary fantasy, and temporality of fantasy. For instance, Williams explains the bodily excess in horror films in terms of violence, while ecstasy is shown by ecstatic violence or by blood.[3] Williams's notion of "body genres" cuts across consensus genre categories in ways that both draw upon our familiar knowledge of genres such as the horror film and, in the case of *The Matrix*, confront us with the innovative structuring of the threat posed to Neo, the stylized body movement in slow-motion action sequences, not to mention the final sequence where Neo's control over the threat of bodily violence is a final confirmation of his true role as Romance hero.

The Matrix as a Mixed-Genre Film

As any review of the film tells you, *The Matrix* draws upon the conventionalized features, structural elements, and thematics of a range of consensus genres and subgenres. Just how the mixed genre is described changes somewhat from critic to critic. For instance, *Splicedonline*'s Rob Blackwelder (http://www.splicedonline.com/99reviews/matrix.html) calls *The Matrix* a "virtual reality sci-fi thriller"—thus distinguishing it from, for example, a non-sci-fi virtual reality thriller such as *Disclosure* (Barry Levinson, 1994). Andrew O'Hehir from salon.com draws attention to *The Matrix*'s cinematic style which gives a European art-cinema inflection to the movie's many references, which include the films of John Woo, the *Alien* series, the *Terminator* series, and of course *Blade Runner*. O'Hehir adds that *The Matrix* "is all of those films, as well as a video game, a primer on Zen Buddhism, and a parable of the Second Coming." This means that *The Matrix* isn't just a mixed-genre film. In addition, it employs a broadly mixed set of core thematics drawn from its various narrative sources.

Every genre narrative needs to establish a dynamic between the familiar and the innovative. *The Matrix* solves this problem through pastiche, that is, by reassembling features from various consensus genres and subgenres into one coherent storyline. This reassembling begins, in fact, at the level of its master genre, and works down through *The Matrix* to include its constitutive consensus genres as well as the subgenres that inform its story-

---

[3] Linda Williams, "Film Bodies: Gender, Genre, and Excess," in Barry Keith Grant, ed., *Film Genre Reader II* (Austin: University of Texas Press, 1995), pp. 140–158.

line. Most obviously, this includes the thematics standardly invoked by consensus genres such as the action film, science fiction, and horror, along with a touch of the Western, not to mention thematics which characterize subgenres such as the innocent on the run thriller—since whatever else Thomas Anderson *aka* Neo is, he is an innocent on the run—and the Hong Kong martial-arts action film, which gives *The Matrix* its balletic fight sequences. The main features of these two key subgenres contribute to the film's suspense, not only ensuring that our hero is pursued by the Agents without fully understanding why they are after him, but at the same time providing the highly stylized mode of combat, mastery of which will eventually confirm that Neo is the One after all. Added to the master genre, consensus genres, and subgenres, the two main structuring elements of *The Matrix* are suspense (What is the fate of Neo, Morpheus, and Trinity?) and mystery (What is the Matrix?).

The master genre of Romance gives *The Matrix* its quest motif. It also establishes for us the idea of a fallen world in which the protagonist must struggle to save a threatened community that he did not initially realize he belongs to. Perhaps the most characteristically American film genre, the Western, also works from this basic Romance quest motif, in which an outsider figure has to discover his ability to act for the broader social good of a community in order to defend it against forces of evil. By referencing the Western, *The Matrix* continues a tradition linking science fiction to this most mythologically driven of American film genres, a connection already clearly established in *Star Wars* (George Lucas, 1977). Nevertheless, while *The Matrix* does reference the Western, these references are fleeting. The showdown in the subway between Neo and Agent Smith is iconographically a direct descendant of the Western shootout, but Thomas Anderson is certainly not a typical Western hero as embodied, for instance, by John Wayne. Rather, in the tradition of the Romance master genre, and not unlike Luke Skywalker, Neo is a neophyte, a beginner—someone who must be trained to develop the skills which most Western heroes have long since perfected. Nevertheless, like the great Western heroes before him and also like Luke, Neo becomes deputized to the cause of justice and thus must become the force of law and order in a radically disordered, dystopian society.

Doubtless the most dominant consensus genre at work in *The Matrix* is science fiction. The threat of a dystopian future world is a hallmark of the science-fiction genre, particularly when dealing with the effects of technology on human identity. Most genre films involve some sort of struggle between good and evil—a narrative paradigm that links the Western to science fiction. Where science fiction goes the Western one better is in its depiction of the forces of evil as uncanny and unimaginably powerful.[4] The contest between good and evil—which ultimately pits Neo, Trinity, Morpheus, and their crew against the Matrix and its Agents—depends upon still other familiar science-fiction thematics, for instance the idea that human civilization has developed its technology to the point of destroying the earth, thus bringing down a plague of global proportions and placing technological mastery in the hands of some non-human intelligence which in turn enslaves humanity both physically and mentally.

These features drawn from science fiction combine to let us imagine a future world that evokes the sort of terror usually associated with the horror film. Certainly the image of humans imprisoned in gelatinous pods restates the longstanding connections between *The Matrix* and films that work at the crossroads of science fiction and horror—pods being a motif that runs back through various science-fiction and horror films, for instance *Invasion of the Body Snatchers* (Don Siegel, 1955; Philip Kaufman, 1978). Further, this conjunction of science fiction and horror is exemplified by the confusion, at the core of *The Matrix*, between virtual reality and actuality. Many films have exploited the idea that the world of appearances is merely an elaborate illusion, but *The Matrix* develops this familiar theme through its portrayal of the virtual world which the pod people are programmed to experience. This virtual world is a human world not so very different from our own but one which emphasizes the coldest features of our contemporary existence, from soulless megacorporations through a leather culture nightclub life to the disparity of wealth between affluent urbanites and the social outcasts in the inner-city ghet-

---

[4] Thomas Schatz, *Old Hollywood/New Hollywood: Ritual, Art, and Industry* (Ann Arbor: UMI Research, 1983), p. 86.

toes. The deep genre connection between the master genre of Romance and the consensus genre of science fiction can be seen in the nature of the Matrix itself: the Matrix *is* the fallen world, the metaphoric desert behind the illusion of actual human society, the world where machine intelligence rules and God is dead. Indeed, in this virtual world, the Matrix is the "origin" of human life as we now understand it. Within the Matrix, human life itself is both a perverse parody of the myth of creation and an echo of the creation of life in horror films such as *Frankenstein* (James Whale, 1931). Thomas Anderson, portrayed from the beginning as both an innocent and yet as someone already engaged on a quest to discover the meaning of his existence, becomes our primary point of identification, and thus we—like Neo—are initiated by Morpheus into the truth of the Matrix.

The Matrix also exploits another favorite theme shared by both science-fiction films and horror films, namely the threat of the violation and possession of the human body. These ideas are worked out in the *Matrix* through a variety of scenes, including the bug that is implanted in Neo, the torture of Morpheus, the "squiddy" designed to search and destroy, the discovery that the apparent world is only a computer-generated virtual reality, and the revelation that the horrific future society holds humans captive as slaves within a virtual existence. Neo himself is already something other than wholly human. It is striking that there are two classes of humans in *The Matrix*: those who are "genuinely" human, and those such as Neo, Morpheus, Trinity, and the others who—thanks to being computer uploadable—represent a new stage in human existence.

The most distinctive aspects of *The Matrix* are the conjunction between its visual style and the steady escalation of viewer engagement orchestrated through progressively more elaborate and suspenseful action sequences. We can see this twinned focus on style and suspense running throughout the film—from how *The Matrix* is shot and edited, through its use of settings, to the Goth-grunge styles of the characters' clothing, eyewear, and weapons, to its central characters' "buff" and athletic bodies. There is reason to think that *The Matrix* presents us with a victory of style over narrative substance. Not everyone agrees; some critics, for example, celebrate the film's more cerebral sci-fi elements. But this should only remind us that a distinguishing feature of science fiction is its focus on Big Questions such as "What is the meaning of life?" and "What does it mean to be human?" Our familiarity with sci-fi means we shouldn't be surprised to find these sorts of questions raised by *The Matrix* as well. However, we should not assume that these Big Questions are raised in a philosophically significant way. Nor should we assume that they get any philosophically significant answers in the film.

Treating popular entertainment fictions from a philosophical perspective requires a certain delicacy. It is obviously just a matter of philosophical hubris to dismiss all so-called entertainment narratives as unworthy of philosophical consideration. On the other hand, it is not easy to justify the philosophical consideration of all entertainment narratives. How, then, should we approach *The Matrix*? Over a quarter century ago, Peter Jones, in *Philosophy and the Novel*, made it clear that literary texts and literary authors might raise points of philosophical interest without themselves being engaged in overtly philosophical discourse.[5] Jones's point was that philosophers can always interpret a novel so as to draw out its philosophical thematics. Jones's examples come from the canon of world literature: *Middlemarch*, *Anna Karenina*, *The Brothers Karamazov*, and *À la Recherche du Temps Perdu*. It may well seem as if *The Matrix* is crashing this canonical party. Still, in the first instance it's hard to say why Jones's idea shouldn't be applied to *The Matrix*. To treat *The Matrix* as Jones treats *Middlemarch* and the others would involve teasing out the important philosophical thematics from the film and offering them up for the sort of serious philosophical reflection that, for example, Jones uses to examine such topics as knowledge and illusion in Proust's great classic. So it seems possible and perhaps even plausible that *The Matrix*, in virtue of the philosophical themes it raises, should be treated seriously by philosophers. However, the very things that make *The Matrix* a splendid example of a mixed-genre film also raise the question whether it should merit serious philosophical examination. Let us look at those things now.

---

[5] Peter Jones, *Philosophy and the Novel* (Oxford: Clarendon, 1975).

The Matrix and the Fictional Genre Film

Given the plethora of consensus genres and their subgenres and the attendant difficulties in producing anything like a tidy categorization or definition of any particular film genre, Thomas Sobchack, with Northrop Frye as a model, opts for the bold step of "considering the fictional genre film as a single category that includes all that is commonly held to be genre film."[6] Sobchack is, in effect, arguing that the differences between the Western and the swashbuckler, or between the biopic and the teenpic—and even between the Western and the biopic—are smaller than the things that they share in common as genre films. Sobchack's move legitimates the idea that we should treat genres as inherently mixed, since to combine elements from any of the seeming "stand-alone" genres will in no way detract from the basic genre features that connect these consensus genres to one another. What distinguishes a genre film from a non-genre film? First, genre films focus on a story, and "not about something that matters outside the film" (pp. 102–03). Second, genre films always let us know who the hero is and who the villains are (p. 103). Third, Sobchack agrees that genre films are mimetic but like Northrop Frye he argues that what they imitate are *other films*, not "real life" (p. 104). Fourth, genre films are identifiable by their "compact sense of shape"—namely, their plot. In genre films, plot takes precedence over extended observational details about setting or psychology. In short, "what happens . . . is of most importance, not why" (p. 106). Fifth, characterization in genre films is always done by a kind of narrative "shorthand" (p. 107). As Sobchack says, "We know a character by what he wears as opposed to what he says or does" (p. 107). When Sobchack wrote these words about costumes in 1975, he might not have fully appreciated how apposite the remark would be with respect to the action heroes of the late twentieth century, decked out as they are in designer fashions. But there is more to this fifth point than just a remark about clothes. Sobchack

---

[6] Thomas Sobchack, "Genre Film: A Classical Experience," in *Film Genre Reader II*, p. 102. Further page references to the Sobchack article appear in parentheses in the text.

adds that, "once known, the character cannot change except in the most limited ways" (p. 107). This is superlatively true of such *Matrix* characters as Morpheus, Trinity, and the Agents, but is just as true of Neo, who cannot change because he is the Romance hero, trained by a master, embarking on a journey of self-realization that will eventually bring him into mortal combat with the forces of evil. This is how genre films operate.

But just how should we understand the idea that Neo is engaged in a journey of self-realization? Not in the sense of "self" typically understood within philosophy of mind and psychology. Protagonists like Neo do not have psychological depth or complexity. As Sobchack tellingly observes, genre characters are fundamentally their exteriors, their constant set of recognizable traits (p. 108). Which is only to say, they are *characters*, and what they imitate is not actual human individuals but other comparable characters. Genre heroes are "certainly far superior to us in what they can do; they may be limited as ordinary human beings, but they are unlimited as far as action. They can do what we would like to be able to do. They can pinpoint the evil in their lives as resident in a monster or villain, and they can go out and triumph over it" (p. 108). The narrative trajectory of *The Matrix* involves pinpointing where evil lies—namely, in the Matrix itself—and training Neo so that he can emerge victorious from a sequence of escalating encounters with the Agents. So even if Neo isn't persuaded until very late in *The Matrix* that he is the One, as competent consumers of genre fictions, we know full well that he must be. The matter is pre-established by genre convention. It has nothing to do with Neo as psychological personality, everything to do with narrative patterns. Neo is the Romance hero in a science-fiction world, the innocent whose discovery by Morpheus and confirmation by the Oracle propels him forward through a series of combats that define and reveal his true powers, and his true powers in turn reveal his identity as the One. Because he is a novice, an initiate, Neo does undergo *narrative* transformations—transformations that are programmatic in the Romance hero's recognition of his self and role—but these are not actual changes in terms of psychological reality. Neo's narrative trajectory takes him from a position on the sidelines to a centrally committed position in the fight against the Matrix. Neo is not so much an individual psychology as a narrative paradigm.

Criticisms that characters such as Neo lack psychological depth fail to recognize their role and function in relation to the plot of a genre narrative. If we recognize Neo as the Romance hero, we know that in due course he will triumph over the Agents and the Matrix which they represent—perhaps not in this film, but surely by the third sequel.

Philosophy and *The Matrix*

At the beginning of this chapter we mentioned that *The Matrix* alludes to many traditional themes from metaphysics and epistemology, moral theory, philosophy of religion, social and political philosophy, and the philosophy of science. Any good genre film is likely to offer comparable allusions. Romantic comedies, for instance, tend to ask the question, "What is the good life?" Westerns share with the hard-boiled detective film the question, "What sort of individual does it take to ensure justice within the community?" Science fiction is the most likely genre to raise the question "What does it mean to be human?" Philosophical allusions are not limited to any one genre. Nor should we imagine that every genre film asks such questions with the same degree of seriousness.

When *The Matrix* opened in 1999, philosophers could be found talking to one another, either in university corridors or at academic conferences, and they were telling each other the same story. In any introductory philosophy course you cared to name, after lecturing on, say, Plato's Cave or Descartes's First Meditation, students would either put up their hands in class or come up to you after the lecture and say: "It's just like in *The Matrix*." *The Matrix*'s philosophical allusions are many, and they are open enough to permit a range of philosophical interpretation and speculation. Students are quick to see parallels between the illusory world experienced by the prisoners in Plato's Cave and the humans trapped in pods by the Matrix. The prisoners, who have been raised from infancy in the Cave, and cannot distinguish mere images from reality, are indeed rather like the humans held captive in pods, who imagine that they are computer programmers or cyberhackers. Students are also quick to see that Neo's initial bewilderment over whether or not it is all just a dream is comparable to Descartes's Dream Hypothesis from his First Meditation. In both these cases, *The*

Matrix's allusions are primarily intended to promote suspense, anxiety, horror, and even terror, not philosophical reflection.

When someone like Peter Jones argues that philosophers can legitimately interpret the philosophical themes of novels such as *Anna Karenina*, it is important to recognize that Jones—like so many other critics before and since—is interested in thematically organic narratives. The general idea is that the sorts of stories that repay the serious attention given to them by someone like Jones—or for that matter by someone like Matthew Arnold or F.R. Leavis—depend upon a holistic, centralized set of core thematics. These are also novels which are thought to reward reflective reading. If they reward reflective reading, it is because they systematically direct readers into the fictional world of the story. *The Matrix*, by contrast, directs viewers to establish connections outside the film to comparable narratives. Genre texts depend for their recognizability on their viewers' familiarity with other texts, other sets of conventions, other storylines—even including philosophical themes and texts. So it is not hard to conclude that genre texts such as *The Matrix* are fundamentally centrifugal—their organizing principle depends upon our ability to make connections to things outside the text at hand. At the same time, the primary narrative devices of a film such as *The Matrix*—action, mystery, and suspense—do not allow viewers to linger over philosophically interesting themes or motifs. So we conclude that *The Matrix*, because it is an exemplary mixed-genre film, can only hope to use philosophical themes to trigger audience interest, but never intended to provide a forum for the solution of philosophical problems. In the meantime, *The Matrix* does resolve its genre problems: Our hero is discovered, he goes through a process of initiation, he at long last comes to trust his own powers, he survives the most serious confrontation against his enemies, and he returns to claim his lady love. These themes are as old as narrative.

What we have attempted to show is that the philosophical allusions found in *The Matrix* take their narrative significance from the film's genre inheritance, its position between its governing master genre of Romance and its particular mix of consensus genres and subgenres. "What does it mean to be human?" is a good question, but it is not one best answered through the close examination of a genre protagonist, since as we have argued genre protagonists are not psychological individuals or selves but rather figures whose characters are fixed and whose traits are unchanging. *The Matrix* raises questions of philosophical importance, but its objective isn't to provide any sort of philosophical argument or explication by way of an answer. For these reasons, we conclude that *The Matrix* is unquestionably an example of real genre, but only an instance of virtual philosophy.

De-Construct-Ing
The Matrix

17

Penetrating Keanu: New Holes, but the Same Old Shit

CYNTHIA FREELAND

The Matrix and *eXistenZ* were released in the same year (1999) and are often compared: both films take their characters through layers of computer-generated illusions and reality. Here I want to focus on a few key differences between the two movies. One difference which interests me as a feminist philosopher is that they adopt opposing pictures of the value of human flesh and bodies. This is linked to a second difference, namely, their attitudes toward their viewers. On both counts I find *eXistenZ* more satisfying. Let me preview my points here.

As its heroes become more able to bypass limitations of physical reality, *The Matrix* creates a naive fantasy of overcoming human flesh. The hero moves from being "penetrated" and connected to others, to being self-controlling and intact—even immune to bullets. *The Matrix* reveals an adolescent fear of the body as something that can veer out of control (something true of a real, changing, flesh-and-blood body). This fantasy suits geeky young males who yearn for autonomy and mental powers. By contrast, vulnerable and connected bodies are foregrounded in *eXistenZ*—especially for its hero. This film's vivid scenes of penetration and biomorphic connection show that bodies can be both delightful and disgusting. Bodies (and brains too) can leave one transported, or damaged and bleeding.

Because each film reflects on how virtual reality can be evil and mind-controlling, there are obvious ways they might address viewers' engagement with the "virtual reality" of movies.

eXistenZ develops this parallel, winding up with a prank that asks whether anything we have seen in the film is "real." In contrast, *The Matrix* ends with its savior hero freeing humans from our deceptive dreams. Although the film celebrates the liberation of human zombies from their spoon-fed visions, it ironically, and hypocritically, sucks viewers into its own virtual reality by offering an escapist fantasy fueled by knockout special effects. I prefer the playful intelligence of the layers of games in *eXistenZ*.

The two themes I want to explore are connected. By comparing virtual reality to the visions of a filmmaker, *eXistenZ* questions the place of our real human (or other) bodies in relation to the seductive visions of contemporary movies. Since *eXistenZ* confronts both its heroes and its viewers with the flesh in visceral, sometimes disgusting, forms, it does not feed fantasies of mental escape from the body. I see this film as offering a more intriguing vision of our potential as beings with both brains and bodies—one that feminists can find more potentially liberatory than that of *The Matrix*.

Bodies, Minds, Gender

The Matrix fetishizes a certain look in its stars. In the virtual world of the movie, the reality of their human flesh is covered up in well-co-ordinated ensembles of sleek black leather or latex. By contrast, *eXistenZ* revels in the goo of flesh, gore, and blood—of "wetware." These differences are evident in the films' parallel opening credit sequences. Both employ the metaphor of wholes built up from informational bits. The bits in *The Matrix* are fragments of computer code, green letters and numbers glowing against a black screen. The bits in *eXistenZ* are amorphous puddles of pink, cream, and gold which vaguely evoke cellular structures seen under a microscope. The metaphor here is biological not mechanical, analog not digital.

Many feminist philosophers have argued that western philosophy has been an affair of men seeking mental escapes from their bodies, from the reality of flesh and blood.[1] Such men

---

[1] See Genevieve Lloyd, *The Man of Reason: "Male" and "Female" in Western Philosophy* (Minneapolis: University of Minnesota Press, 1984) and Susan

include Plato, describing the world of transcendent Forms, Augustine and Aquinas, hoping for their souls' purity in heaven, and Descartes, establishing his identity as mind, not body. It is part of this tradition also to draw sharp distinctions between thinking and feeling. Men have traditionally been associated with rationality and "higher" mental faculties, women with the body, emotions, and "lower" faculties like child-bearing and nurturance. This mentalistic bias is evident again in the undoubtedly male perspective of *The Matrix*.

The differences in gender roles in the two films become clear when we focus on their male protagonists. The films star two of today's hottest male heart-throbs, Keanu Reeves and Jude Law. These are not men with the macho allure of a Clark Gable or John Wayne. With his delicate eyelids, Keanu/Neo looks as "pretty" as a girl when we first see him sleeping. He has very fair skin (another character in the film even comments on his whiteness), with no body hair. He moves gracefully, like a dancer. Jude/Ted has sculpted cheekbones and enviable eye-lashes; his Cupid's-bow lips make him seem pouty. Each hero is paired with a strong woman (or what seems like a strong woman) who occasionally takes the lead in directing his move-ments. At moments each is shown as vulnerable, unsure, and— most importantly—as penetrated. These scenes of male penetration, or of the insertion of new holes into the male body, are worth exploring.

Penetrating Keanu in *The Matrix*

The initial scene of penetration in *The Matrix* occurs when the evil Agents of the machine-run illusion, the Matrix, catch Neo and interrogate him. Restraining him, they insert a tracking device (a scorpion-type creature) through his navel, in a painful and creepy operation. Later, before the heroine, Trinity, and oth-ers in the radical group resisting the Matrix take Neo to meet their leader Morpheus, they remove the bug, in another scene of violent penetration. They apply a gun-like "scope" to Neo's navel to suck out the bug. He screams as they extract it.

Bordo, *Unbearable Weight: Feminism, Western Culture, and the Body* (Berkeley: University of California Press, 1993).

The next scene of penetration is probably the most disturbing of the movie. After Neo chooses the "truth" pill offered by Morpheus, he has a horrifying vision of humans as they really are. He sees countless naked bodies maintained artificially in fetal sacs by ugly bug-like machine "nurses." Each person is penetrated by a complex array of tubes that presumably feed it and remove bodily wastes. Their hairless pink bodies look disgusting and vulnerable, penetrated by black coils and plugs. As Neo gapes in horror, a keeper bug prepares to "flush" him, ripping out the plugs and cords interlacing his body. In a birth parody Neo is dumped down a slimy tube—presumably to be liquefied.

Rescued, Neo appears in a kinder, gentler scene of penetration. Again we see Keanu's nearly naked body displayed as he lies on a table. He is thoroughly penetrated now by gently waving acupuncture-style needles. The peacefulness and goodness of this penetration are emphasized by religious-sounding choral music on the soundtrack. Morpheus explains that Neo must be rebuilt because his muscles are atrophied from disuse. If only we could all lie back in gentle sleep with needles toning our muscles!

In this movie, Neo is so special that he can learn things instantly, with almost no effort. (Physical things, that is—it does take the dim and naive Neo/Keanu some time to catch onto the insight that he is "the One," the savior who will redeem all humanity by freeing them from the Matrix.) Knowledge and skills are quickly transmitted to the clever, deserving, and good-looking members of Morpheus's little cell of revolutionaries by instant programming or "uploading." This requires the insertion of a big "plug" into the back of a person's neck. So, in the next scene of penetration there is more violence, and Neo is obviously frightened when the connector device is slammed into the hole at the back of his neck. Through simulated physical training Neo learns skills, with effort transferred to his real body, leaving him tired or even sore. He learns quickly due to his "psychokinetics": we barely see him break a sweat. Although obviously freaky, the neck-plugs are never again emphasized and we see no other scenes of their insertion; rather, the group members simply lie back and we assume the plugs easily slide in with no pain or violence. These are good plugs with good penetration. They send people back into the Matrix with a new awareness that enables them to work against its presumed physical laws, leaping incredible distances and fighting off scores of flat-footed policemen.

This leads to the final scene of penetration I want to discuss, Neo's being pierced by bullets in his confrontations with the Agents. Despite being "the One" (or perhaps because of it), Neo must suffer and even die. But he is resurrected, apparently when Trinity (the Holy Spirit?) breathes life back into him by confessing to his inert real body aboard the ship that she loves him, and that the Oracle has prophesied she will love the man who is "the One"—so that he cannot really be dead. Neo magically returns to life with renewed confidence that even alarms his attacker Agents. Earlier he displayed a remarkable ability to dodge bullets; now he becomes impervious to them, and can even catch them in mid-air.

The allure of this new, savior Neo is that he is physically perfect and pristine—no penetration. He operates like this in the Matrix, which he can now see through. The Matrix is a neural-interactive simulation; obviously some simulations are beneficial, since training uses them. Within all the simulation scenes Keanu is more handsome, with longer hair, no neck-bolt, and outfitted in the now-notorious long black overcoat. Equipped with all the guns he could ever need, he dodges Agents' bullets. This perfect, exciting, memorable Keanu/Neo is intact, closed up, with no openings or flaws, no vulnerability—in short, with no relationship to his actual physical flesh-and-blood body. He has superceded the physical reality of the flesh.

It hardly needs mentioning, but must be mentioned, that the character of Trinity (Carrie-Anne Moss) occupies a typical subservient female role in this movie. The film opens promisingly with this "little girl" bravely confronting a gaggle of policemen and escaping. And when Neo meets her he is surprised (like all guys, she says) to learn that this brilliant hacker is a girl. But after these opening gambits, Trinity assumes the role of sidekick female. She has a few scenes of skill, but we never see this famous hacker do anything meaningful at a computer keyboard (she never examines the code of the Matrix, for example). She is there to be the love interest for Neo and to support his all-important enterprise of salvation. She provides stereotypical female nurturance and "connectedness" for the inexpressive, intact Neo. We see her bringing him food, watching, even sniffing him. Her love restores him to life toward the film's end. Besides deferring to Neo, she serves under Big Daddy Morpheus, the typical patriarchal leader, who looks not to her but to his son-figure, Neo, as humanity's savior.

Trinity is also a "babe" who is here to provide sex appeal.[2] She is celebrated by fans for "kicking butt," and she does accompany Neo in rescuing Morpheus, where she kills her share of men; but obviously her main job is decorative. Carrie-Anne looks damn sexy in skin-tight black latex and leather. Sure, she flies a helicopter, but even that gets messed up and she must be rescued by Neo. She is rewarded when they share a chaste kiss at the end, but the film has zero eroticism; the only man who shows any evidence of relishing sensual pleasures is Cypher, who is clearly evil.

The other important woman in the film is also stereotyped, "The Oracle" (Gloria Foster), a black woman with the insight and wisdom of a tribal sage. She appears as a kind of slum grandmother (dare I say "Mammy"?) dispensing fresh-baked cookies along with her prophecies. Anybody who resists my critique of the movie's stereotypes should answer this question: Why are there no female Agents in the Matrix? Even the machines are sexist here.

Penetrating Jude in *eXistenZ*

David Cronenberg, director of *eXistenZ*, has often depicted off-beat distortions of the male body, as with the decaying scientist in his best-known film *The Fly*. Cronenberg's movies have highlighted "deviant" sexuality and even "invaginations," as when the hero of *Videodrome* develops an abdominal aperture into which videocassettes are inserted. Some of his movies break down strict mind-body dualism, like *Scanners* with its telepathic hero. Cronenberg is interested in what he calls "the New Flesh," a vision of new bodies with new orifices, new sexual organs,

---

[2] The proliferation of fan websites is an indicator of this role. One site says, "Latex, firepower, and the ability to climb walls in slow motion. Man, does this gal have it all or what . . . ? I'm curious as to if they can get her outfit any tighter." Unidentified, website at http://members.tripod.com/twptracl0/id40.htm. (Carrie-Anne Moss plays a similar role opposite Val Kilmer in *Red Planet* [2000].)

and no clear gender distinctions.[3] I see him continuing this project in *eXistenZ*. By comparison, *The Matrix* seems boringly sexist with its same old set of characters: male hero aided by loving female partner, kind maternal advisor, and strong father figure.

In *eXistenZ*, Jude Law plays Ted Pikul, a neophyte in the virtual games industry who attends the test demo of a new game by brilliant designer, Allegra Geller (Jennifer Jason Leigh). After an audience member tries to assassinate Allegra and Ted escapes with her, she mistakes him for her security guard. She then wonders aloud why she has been stuck instead with a "PR nerd." This image of Jude as PR-nerd contrasts sharply with Keanu as hacker and black-clad warrior in *The Matrix*. *eXistenZ* undermines standard sex-role stereotyping by making the woman the computer whiz and decision-maker, while the man is often frightened and insecure. These gender realignments can be explored by examining some key scenes of penetration in this movie.

Unusually, Ted/Jude has never been fitted with a bioport, the opening in a human's lower spine that enables one to plug into virtual reality games run on "MetaFlesh game pods." These pods, constructed from synthesized amphibian parts with modified DNA, are connected to humans by plugging fleshy-looking "umbycords" into their bioports. The first scene of penetration involves Ted's being fitted with his bioport. His "feminine" role is evident as a kind of hysteria. Resisting surgery, Ted confesses, "I have this phobia about having my body penetrated [. . . pause . . .] surgically." He gets fitted with a black market bioport in a scene laden with homoerotic innuendo. "Gas" (Willem Dafoe) applies a huge gun-like structure to Ted's rear. As the latter bends over, Gas comments, "One thing you don't wanna do is miss with the stud finder." Ted's implied "feminization" is extended when Allegra immediately plugs a cord into Ted's new hole while he is still immobilized by anesthetic.

---

[3] Cronenberg explains that with "New Flesh," [Y]ou can actually change what it means to be a human being in a physical way . . . Human beings could swop [sic] sexual organs, or do without sexual organs . . . for procreation . . . The distinction between male and female would diminish, and perhaps we would become less polarized and more integrated creatures." Chris Rodley, ed., *Cronenberg on Cronenberg* (London: Faber and Faber, revised edition 1997), pp. 80–82.

The narrative arc of *eXistenZ* is different from that of *The Matrix*, where Neo/Keanu moves from a "bad, dirty" state of being full of plugs to a "clean, good" state of physical intactness. Instead, *eXistenZ* revels in scenes that show the penetration of game ports by game pods as a sensual, if messy and risky, physical business. Port penetration and pleasure are closely tied through the movie's imagery to other normal physical processes like eating and sex. The erotic dimensions of gaming and plugging in are highlighted in several scenes. Once when Ted inserts a mini-pod into Allegra's back, he begins licking her bioport. His reciprocal passivity is emphasized in a few minutes: After Allegra unzips his pants, Ted wails, "I'm very worried about my body . . . I feel really vulnerable."

These links between virtual game addiction and sexual urges are emphasized when Allegra experiences a compulsion to port into a diseased game pod. As the pod writhes and turns black, Allegra quickly becomes ill and infected. Desperate, Ted cuts her umbycord, but she starts to gush blood as he looks on helplessly. This scene drives home the point that like actual sex, the eroticism of games is risky. Connecting with and opening up both your mind and your body to others can be lethal.

eXistenZ evokes the fleshy physicality of virtual game architecture with many scenes that plunge us into the gooey inner workings of the pods. When Allegra's pod is fixed in a repair shop, the operation resembles open-heart surgery. Other scenes show the grim workings of a pod assembly plant for the firm Cortical Systematics. Ted finds himself skillfully slitting open frog bellies, which burst with gushing blood, to retrieve egg sacs, packaging and labeling them for distribution on the assembly line. The movie's near-obsession with goo culminates in a restaurant scene where Ted and Allegra get served a dish made of mutant amphibians. Here Ted's "penetration" extends to his compulsive eating of the disgusting dish, in order to retrieve a kind of gristle-gun that shoots human teeth as bullets. The contrast with Neo's clean, metallic guns and bullets could not be more stark.

Cronenberg says he had trouble casting the part of Ted because "to have a lead that is a woman means that when you talk to many male stars they are reluctant to play in the film . . . because they know they will be playing second fiddle to a woman who will be the focus . . . it's a very macho thing still."[4] The gender role reversal here is striking. Jude (indisputably a better actor than Keanu) plays his scenes with seeming relish, as wimpy, fussy, and hysterical. It is no wonder that a mainly male adolescent audience would find nothing to identify with here. And neither is Jennifer Jason Leigh's Allegra a "babe" female hacker like Trinity. Allegra is pretty, smart, and tough, but she is never subservient. Rather, she is wily and competitive to the point of "killing" Ted and thus winning at her own game.

Movies, Reality, and Illusion

Let's consider how the scenes of penetration I have reviewed are linked to the broader "messages" of their respective movies. Both *The Matrix* and *eXistenZ* raise questions about what it means to be seduced or deceived by artificial versions of reality. The illusions of the Matrix are created by a loathsome kind of penetration. So the story is about an escape from being plugged in. Neo uses his mental insights to become free of contaminating plugs and even bullet holes. At the end we see him flying, free of gravity, above other humans, as he dissolves the Matrix and offers them release.

But at the end of *eXistenZ*, we feel unable to tell the difference between reality and illusion, since we have learned, in a surprising coda, that the entire film we just watched was itself an illusion, the testing of a virtual game. Many aspects of this "outer" game mimic the inner game, and so viewers might well be perplexed about what was real and what an illusion. This confusion is epitomized when one frightened character asks, "Tell me, are we still in the game?"

These different endings show the two movies' strategies of reflecting on the power of film as a medium to create illusions. Ideally, to be consistent, *The Matrix* ought to enable viewers to recognize and reject the seductive illusions of movies in favor of

---

[4] See "Logic, Creativity, and (Critical) Misinterpretations: An Interview with David Cronenberg," conducted by Xavier Mendik, in Michael Grant, ed., *The Modern Fantastic: The Films of David Cronenberg* (Westport: Praeger, 2000), pp. 176–77.

their own more creative choices. But I suspect it works in the opposite way. The movie celebrates not freedom from the Matrix, but the indulgence in exciting filmic simulations. I realize this is not what it is supposed to be celebrating. But remember, things aren't attractive in non-Matrix conditions aboard the ship: Everything is gray and worn-looking, people are cold and eat goopy food. Unattractive, the crew have monk-like shaved heads, ragged clothes and (mostly) disfiguring neck-bolts. The image of Keanu that fans no doubt relish is rather as he appears in simulations: handsome, longer hair, no neck-bolt, black overcoat, flying through the air. It is only in the simulations that Keanu/Neo can display his awesome movement, speed, and power to kill.

My point concerns which cinematic world is more enticing, glamorous, and memorable: I contend it is the world of simulations. Fittingly, that's the world where we end, not on the ship where Neo's allegedly "real" body resides in potential new connection with Trinity. Instead, we see handsome overcoated Neo wandering among the masses in the Matrix, then zipping off through the sky, promising "a world without rules and controls, without borders and boundaries, a world where anything is possible." His flying, like his words, suggests that humans need not be bound by their physical bodies. The movie feeds escapist fantasies of a mental reality where the elect few are unencumbered by rules. (They certainly won't have to go to the office or work hard to learn new skills.) The vision the movie leaves us with is of Neo transcending physical reality, just like Superman. We viewers are urged to escape illusions, but hypocritically so, by a film that works hard to seduce us with its own remarkable visions.

In contrast, the plot of *eXistenZ*, a tissue of games-within-a-game, asks us to think about whether illusory reality is preferable to regular life. At the film's end we learn—or seem to—that Allegra's victory over Ted in the game of "eXistenZ" was an illusion that occurred in the demo run of yet another game, "transCendenZ." The characters of our movie emerge from "eXistenZ" to laugh and discuss their roles, commenting among other things on their ridiculous game accents. Suddenly we hear Jude talking in his normal British accent, not the flat Canadian accent he used earlier.

Whereas *The Matrix* dishonestly uses an arsenal of cinematic magic tricks to engage viewers in its illusory reality, *eXistenZ* constantly alludes to game-playing as a metaphor for film-making. This is brought out at the Country Gas Station when Gus says to Allegra, "I like your script, I want to be in it." Later, Allegra explains how different game authors weave cuts together in different ways—much like film directors and editors. *eXistenZ* does not offer simplistic judgment about whether plugging into games or movies is "bad for us." So it avoids the basic hypocrisy of *The Matrix*. Ted worries that game-playing involves an element of psychosis, but *eXistenZ* also shows the sheer fun of game-playing, as Ted learns when he pauses the game to find that ordinary reality is boring by comparison. The Matrix serves an ostensible aim of restoring human individuals to a reality of their own creation, all the while sucking audiences into a reality it never admits is just a movie. *eXistenZ* is the opposite: in its tongue-in-cheek way, as it pokes holes in the allure of games, it also gently reminds audiences that we enjoy fantasies because we are bored with real life.

Professional philosophers might say that both of these films offer amateur reflections on reality and illusion, with freshman-philosophy student conundrums along the lines of "What if I am a butterfly dreaming I am a man?" Both movies offer warnings about human dependence upon machines. But movies, with associated DVDs, sound tracks, sequels, and websites, are themselves simulations we viewers become "plugged into," even dependent upon, for our entertainment. Which movie encourages more reflection on this dependency, along with a more honest and intriguing vision of the pleasure of "connected" minds and bodies? I have argued it is the more overtly silly and grosser of the two, *eXistenZ*, rather than the allegedly deeper, slicker, more "liberatory" film, *The Matrix*.[5]

---

[5] Many thanks to Carolyn Korsmeyer and Steven Schneider for comments on an earlier draft.

18

The Matrix, Marx, and the Coppertop's Life

MARTIN A. DANAHAY and DAVID RIEDER

The Matrix does an especially good job of dramatizing the exploitation of the average American worker in late twentieth- and early twenty-first-century America from a Marxist perspective. The film is full of allusions to numerous social and economic themes that can be traced back to Karl Marx's work.

From UPS drivers with their handheld devices that indicate their position and times between deliveries, and data-entry clerks whose every keystroke-per-minute is counted, to customer service representatives whose per-call performance is monitored, American workers are increasingly under technological surveillance, century-old trends against which Marx wrote. If, in the nineteenth century, the old-time clock at the door to the workplace was a sign of capitalist oppression, today's management software that tracks employees' every move, in and outside of the office, differs only by degree. The increasing control of the worker by machines has long been a concern of Marxists, and *The Matrix* exemplifies the dystopic implications of these ongoing trends.

One of the most intense and horrifying moments for Neo is when he realizes that his entire life has been a half-truth. Neo is desperately holding himself up against the back of a chair, staring at a television set in the meaningless white space of the loading program. Morpheus, seated comfortably, channel-surfs a series of vibrant, tantalizing images of the city from which Neo has just escaped. Morpheus states, "You've been living in a dream world, Neo. This is the world as it exists today." On the television screen, snapshots of Neo's urban existence give way to a dark and dismal image of a burned-out city, the outcome of the war with the machines. The blinding white light in the loading program diminishes, and, a moment later, Morpheus and Neo find themselves surrounded by urban decay and misery. Morpheus announces, "Welcome to the desert of the real."

Neo is completely unprepared for Morpheus's presentation. He is overwhelmed, staggering backwards as he tries to keep his balance. Morpheus continues, answering the question that has kept Neo home alone, sitting at his computer night after night:

> What is the Matrix? Control. The Matrix is a computer-generated dream-world built to keep us under control in order to change a human being into this.

Morpheus holds up a Duracell battery, the coppertop battery. In the earlier scene where Neo had stepped into the back of the Cadillac with the "suicide doors," Switch had called Neo a "coppertop."

The "Coppertop" at Work

According to Marx, workers under capitalism do not recognize the relationship between their labor and the capital that they produce, because they have become "alienated" from the realities of work. They also do not recognize that they are forced to work, believing that they are operating in a "free" market in which they sell their labor voluntarily. In fact, Marx argues, they are exploited because they cannot choose how and when they work. They must accept the terms of their employment, which are dictated by the owners of capital.

The coppertop reference can be read as an expression of Marxist concerns over the plight of the worker, who, like slaves or conscripted soldiers, provides power for the machines. In his well-known *Manifesto of the Communist Party* (1848), Marx describes the exploitation of nineteenth-century factory workers in Europe, which is when and for whom he was writing:

> Modern industry has converted the little workshop of the patriarchal master into the great factory of the industrial capitalist. Masses

of laborers, crowded into the factory, are organized like soldiers. Not only are they slaves of the bourgeois class, and of the bourgeois State; they are daily and hourly enslaved by the machine, by the over-looker, and, above all, by the individual bourgeois manufacturer himself.[1]

For a growing number of people in the nineteenth century, work was increasingly meaningless. Workers were no longer asked to create personally meaningful products for their local constituencies, products in which they took pride. Rather, they were asked to work at tasks that were increasingly abstracted from the commodities that were ultimately sold back to them. Then as now, many jobs are still "coppertop," leading to alienation.

While people tend to talk of alienation as an individual and psychological experience, in Marx's work, alienation is a product of the way social relations are formed under capitalism. In other words, an individual's alienation is a product of the system. In the scene, "The gatekeeper," Morpheus seems to concur when he says the following to Neo:

> The Matrix is a system, Neo. That system is our enemy. When you are inside, and you look around, what do you see? Businessmen. Teachers. Lawyers. Carpenters. The very minds of the people we are trying to save. But until we do, those people are still a part of that system.

For Marx, social relationships under capitalism are expressed as relations between commodities (read: the system) rather than people, and workers themselves see their own labor as commodities to be sold in a market. Marx extensively analyzed the position of workers under capitalism, and while it may not be immediately obvious, work is an important aspect of the plot of *The Matrix*.

In his essay, "Wage-Labor and Capital," Marx explains the reason why work tends towards the status of "coppertop":

---

[1] Frederic L. Bender, ed., *The Communist Manifesto* (New York: Norton, 1988), pp. 61–62.

Labor power . . . is a commodity, neither more nor less than sugar. The former is measured by the clock, the latter by the scales.[2]

Under capitalism, the "commodity" that many workers sell to the companies and the factories for which they work is nothing more than their power. In *The Matrix*, this "reality" is overtly dramatized by the scenes of a naked and vulnerable humanity, floating quiescently in high-rises of coffin-like cubicles, plugged in to the power plant. Presumably, the power plant is reminiscent of a corporate building, all of its workers neatly stacked in cubicles, one floor on top of the next. This would make the human race in *The Matrix* a class of workers, the agents, the guardians of capital. The shots of the power plant help illustrate Morpheus's definition of a "coppertop" as someone who is "so hopelessly dependent on the system," as Morpheus puts it, that he is unable to break free of its exploitative dimensions.

Dialectical Reflections

The theoretical foundations of Marx's thought are derived, in part, from a novel reading of German philosopher G.W.F. Hegel's "dialectical" philosophies. In Marxist thought, dialectics is a theory of evolution or progress. It is based upon the Hegelian idea that the engine that drives motion and change in human history is the struggle of opposing forces. Someone who thinks dialectically thinks of the world as a constantly evolving place, a place in which life is never still. Moreover, a dialectician thinks of the world as a space in which oppositions between everything from individual molecules of matter to complex ideas are striving to reach new levels of consciousness and organization. Marxist Leon Trotsky likens "dialectical thinking" to the silver screen in the following passage:

Dialectical thinking is related to [everyday] thinking in the same way that a motion picture is related to a still photograph. The

---

[2] Robert C. Tucker, ed., *The Marx-Engels Reader*, second edition (New York: Norton, 1978), p. 204.

motion picture does not outlaw the still photograph but combines
a series of them according to the laws of motion.[3]

A dialectical thinker believes that a picture says a thousand
words, because every picture is a reflection of a network of pictures worldwide that are simultaneously competing for meaning.
A dialectical thinker never takes things at face value, because
life is always evolving in and around every single picture; nothing is ever "still."

In *The Matrix*, a "motion picture within the picture," portrays
Neo's dialectically evolving state of mind. This motion picture
en abyme is developed out of a series of reflections—in sunglasses, spoons, a mirror, and, at one point, the doorknob to the
Oracle's apartment. The individual reflections or "still pho-
tographs" combine to create a "motion picture" that runs on top
of the actual film. It portrays Neo's dialectical growth, as he
struggles to overcome his coppertop life.

In the first part of the film, the two scenes, "Down the rabbit hole" and "The real world," reflect Neo's transition from an
undialectical coppertop to a dialectically aware resistance
fighter. In "Down the rabbit hole," Neo is reflected back to us in
Morpheus's sunglasses. Neo has not made the choice yet. The
blue and the red pills are in Morpheus's outstretched hands.
They appear to correspond to the two lenses in Morpheus's
glasses. As if symbolizing the undialectical life that he leads as
a coppertop, the same image of Neo is reflected in both lenses.
Like a still photograph, Neo is the same person, from one
"frame," or lens, to the next. After Neo chooses the red pill, his
reflection begins to change. While he is waiting for Kansas to go
"bye-bye," the mirror to his right reflects a fragmented Neo; his
dialectical journey is beginning. Later, in "The real world," the
dialectical split between the dream world of the Matrix and the
real world is complete. Neo's "double-image" has changed.
When Morpheus holds up the coppertop battery, Neo's reflection is missing from the lens in which the blue pill in "Down the
rabbit hole" was reflected. Now, a coppertop battery takes its

[3] Trotsky, Leon. "The ABC of Materialist Dialectics," in *The Collected Writings of Leon Trotsky: Trotsky Internet Archive*, http://www.trotsky.net/works/1939-abc.htm.

place. In the other lens, the "real" Neo stands alone. Neo is dialectically aware. His journey is starting.

As the movie progresses, reflections of Neo illustrate his attempt to reconcile the two opposing sides of his identity. He struggles to overcome the opposing images of his life, the one in the Matrix, and the one in the "real world." Following this train of thought, Neo's Nirvana-like transformation into "the One" can be interpreted as follows: Neo has achieved a new level of dialectical consciousness, overcoming the oppositions between his alienated and unalienated lives. Neo is one, because Neo is no longer split between two worlds. A significant difference between *The Matrix* and Marxist thought is that "the One" is simply the first of two halves in a never-ending evolution. In other words, the "rabbit hole" is bottomless.

Cypher and Commodity Fetishism

In the second half of the scene, "Dealing for bliss," Cypher is sitting at a table in a restaurant across from Agent Smith. Cypher is busily slicing into a large, juicy cut of filet mignon. The sound from his knife and fork is heard as they scrape across the fine china plate, the red wine in his glass gently sloshing. Cypher is about to defect. He is tired of his life as a resistance fighter. After nearly a decade on the *Nebuchadnezzar,* he has given up, and he is willing to sell the lives of his entire crew for a second chance as a coppertop, plugged in to the Matrix. Agent Smith asks for his final answer, but, before Cypher answers him, Cypher states,

> I know this steak doesn't exist. I know that when I put it in my mouth the Matrix is telling my brain that it is juicy and delicious. After nine years, you know what I realize? Ignorance is bliss.

Cypher's last line is delivered as he bites down on a slice of the filet. As the scene ends, the vertical strings of a harp replace the vertical lines of impersonal green code that stream down the dreaded computer screens in the *Nebuchadnezzar.*

Cypher is well aware of the meaninglessness of the steak he is eating. He knows that it does not really exist. In Marxist terminology, the steak is a commodity, and the bliss that Cypher craves is "commodity fetishism." In the chapter, "The Fetishism of Commodities," in Volume I of *Capital*, Marx writes,

> A commodity . . . is a mysterious thing, simply because in it the social character of men's labor appears to them as an objective character stamped upon the product of that labor; because the relation of producers to the sum total of their own labor is presented to them as a social relation, existing not between themselves, but between the products of their labor.[4]

In this chapter, Marx describes the typical relationship that we, the workers of the world, have with the products that we produce. Some of Marx's terminology is hard to follow: "product of labor"; "relation of producers"; "social relations." It is easier to follow when we understand one basic concept. For Marx, every commodity in the world—cars; computers; software; shoes; furniture; books—exists because someone put their personal "labor power" into its production. Even the money that we use to buy commodities is a piece of someone's labor.

The problem is that we, the workers of the world, "fetishize" the commodities that we buy. In other words, we are oftentimes blind to the following fact: the commodities that we buy are produced by people just like us. The shoes that we buy, with the money that we earn, is made *for* workers *by* workers. We hear stories about fellow workers suffering in Asian sweatshops, but we buy our favorite brands of sneakers nonetheless. We drive cars on *our* way to work, which were created by workers, and we do not recognize the system of work in which we are enveloped. Whether we ignore these relations purposefully or not, many of us practice varying degrees of "commodity fetishism."

Thinking back to the question that has driven Neo's underground ambitions, Marx would have extended Morpheus's explanations. Sure, the Matrix is a dream world whose purpose is to control us. Moreover, the Matrix is the sum total of the human "labor power" that produces it, every day and every hour. Every sight and smell in the Matrix is a product of human

---

[4] See Marx's essay, "The Fetishism of Commodities and the Secret Thereof" in *Capital: A Critique of Political Economy* (New York: Modern Library, 1906), p. 83.

labor. But, for "mysterious" reasons, this reality is "fetishized," or, as Cypher puts it, blissfully ignored. As Marx says in the quote above, "the relation of producers to the sum total of their own labor is presented to them as a social relation, existing not between themselves, but between the products of their labor." In other words, the relationship that the global workforce shares as a class is clouded over by the "dream world" of commodities to which we relate more directly. Workers are unable to unite because their shared global experience as a class of laborers is covered over by the saccharine tastes, sounds, and views of commodities. There is nothing mysterious about the steak that Cypher is eating. He is well aware that the juiciness and the deliciousness of the steak are brought to him by the labor power in the power plant. But, he is tired of fighting against the saccharine world of the Matrix in order to eat "real" slop, and to live like a "real" pauper.

Wake up from What?

Is *The Matrix* part of a "real" capitalist Matrix? Twentieth-century Marxists Max Horkheimer and Theodor Adorno would say yes. In their essay, "The Culture Industry: Enlightenment as Mass Deception," they argue that the mass media, which includes radio, television, and film, contribute to a new level of "commodity fetishism" in capitalist societies.[5] The "extraterrestrial world" of Hollywood values and corporate brands is the *real* dream world—and it has enveloped us in its saccharine sweetness; which is why these Marxists want us to "wake up" from it. Paradoxically, *The Matrix* is part of the culture industry against which Horkheimer and Adorno rail. But, how is this possible? Clearly, it is a film about exploitation and grassroots resistance. Or is it?

One of Marx's most powerful insights concerning the extent to which capitalism exploits its labor forces is in his theory of surplus value. Marx wanted to find out how and where capitalists make profit. After careful analyses of all of the various aspects of the capitalist production cycle, he came to the

---

[5] The essay is in Max Horkheimer and Theodor W. Adorno, *Dialectic of Enlightenment*, translated by John Cumming (New York: Continuum, 1995), pp. 120–167.

following conclusion: capitalists make profit, or surplus value, by paying workers less than they have earned. It is oftentimes assumed that profit is a careful play of the rhythms of supply and demand: a capitalist sells a product when the price he can make exceeds the cost of its production. Marx realized that this happens too infrequently to be the basis of profit. He also realized that the cost of the raw materials that go in to production are essentially fixed. The only dimension that capitalists can systematically exploit is a laborer's pay. According to Marx, capitalists try to pay workers just enough to live, pocketing the rest. If a laborer works an eight-hour shift, he is basically paid the equivalent of five or six hours; the remaining two or three hours is from where the capitalist's profit is derived.

The Matrix is an unforgettable film, but it falls short of convincing its viewers to "wake up" in order to fight the exploitative powers that make the majority of us into coppertops in the real world. It falls short, in part, because it does not show us what the human race is missing while they are plugged in to the Matrix. Arguably, the two species—the humans and the machines—live a symbiotic relationship, and the dream world that Cypher wants to return is not really that bad. It looks relatively hip and urban, with "really good noodles," steady work, and a cool club scene. Humanity has to work to generate BTUs, but the Matrix has unlimited bandwidth and full color! In other words, humanity works, and they are paid exactly what they are worth.

If *The Matrix* really wanted to make a "Marxist" statement from which to wake up, the dream world of the Matrix would have been shot in black and white, symbolizing the extent to which the machines exploited the value of the coppertop's labor power. If the Matrix had been shot in black and white, and the "real" world in the *Nebuchadnezzar* had been in color, perhaps then the revolutionary future for which the humans were fighting would have looked as bright and colorful as did Oz when the real Dorothy said "bye-bye" to Kansas.

19

The Matrix Simulation and the Postmodern Age

DAVID WEBERMAN

Consider the following hypothesis: Some time during the years between 1966 and 1974, the world changed. Which is to say, *our* world changed. In a big way. Though not uncontroversial, many historians and scholars believe just this: that during these years we entered a new era, leaving behind the modern age, we now find ourselves in very different circumstances. We are now in what is referred to as the postmodern age or the condition of postmodernity.

What happened? Many things. Deindustrialization, suburbanization, and a dramatic increase in the flexibility of capital accumulation leading to what we now know as globalization.[1] In the arts and in architecture, ideals of purity and depth have given way to irony and the play of surfaces while the distinction between high and low or popular art has come to seem quaint and indefensible. Think of Andy Warhol or Madonna. In philosophy, many have been led to abandon their faith in an episte-

---

[1] The idea of "flexible accumulation" as well as the expression "the condition of postmodernity" come form one of the best books on the subject, David Harvey's *The Condition of Postmodernity* (Cambridge, MA: Blackwell, 1990). Harvey's book also supplies a more precise date for the beginning of postmodernity. On p. 39, Harvey quotes Paul Jencks as saying that modernism ended and the postmodern age began at 3:32 p.m. CST on July 15th, 1972 in St. Louis, Missouri with the dynamiting if the modernist Pruitt-Igoe housing development.

mological or ethical foundationalism—a rock-solid, axiomatic basis to support our knowledge and values. And, obviously, technology is a large part of the story. The first generation of children "nurtured" on a steady diet of television came of age during this time. And after television there followed the widespread proliferation of cable, video, fax machines, pharmaceutical mood enhancers, computers, cell phones, and the Internet.

Finally, all of this has had an effect on our thoughts, wishes, and feelings. How could it not? The nature of human experience has undergone and continues to undergo a transformation. The idea is that in a world without a real sense of place we have become spiritual nomads. In a world without seriousness, we are cynics and disbelievers. In a world with designer drugs, our personalities have plasticity, leaving authenticity behind as a nothing more than a hoax. And in a thoroughly mediatized world, we are . . . well, we are what? This brings us to *The Matrix* and to the Matrix, that is, to the film by the Wachowskis and to the network of refracted images itself in which, undeniably, we are all entangled to a degree never before known and for as far as we can see. Call it truth, call it the real, call it a rabbit hole. If the film is about all of this, then it's really about looking back at ourselves as we are now and soon to become even more so.

The film *The Matrix* was released in 1999, not 1969. Because of this it easily finds resonance among its viewers. We understand it; we recognize its power—not only as a futuristic science fiction, but as a commentary on who we are. It is not the first film or artwork to test these waters. But it is perhaps the most sustained (implicitly) philosophical film to address one of the central features of postmodern experience: the blurred or vanishing line between reality and simulation.

That *The Matrix* is about this vanishing line is clear. References to it are strewn throughout the dialogue. And the film makers give us a wink early on. In the scene in which Neo is visited at his apartment by hackers in need of digitized information, Neo reaches for the goods in a hollowed-out book which the camera reveals to be Jean Baudrillard's *Simulations and Simulacra*[2]—a postmodern work on the erosion of the real

---

[2] Originally, *Simulacres et simulation* (Paris: Éditions Galilée, 1981). Available in English as *Simulations* (New York: Semiotext(e), 1983). Morpheus's words later in the film, "This is the world as it exists today. Welcome to the desert of

and its displacement by simulated images. Yet while the film concerns this vanishing line, it is not immediately clear what it is saying, or rather showing, about it. Neither is it clear what exactly is postmodern or new about the film's story as an allegory for our age. This essay attempts to look at that line, to cast our gaze around the rabbit hole, to see what we've become.

My method is to consider four theses or propositions which are possible interpretations of what the film is saying, suggesting, or showing about the distinction between reality and simulation in our age of advanced technology. They are as follows:

I. It is ultimately impossible to tell the difference between the real and the unreal.

II. Reality can be simulated and improved on.

III. Simulated or virtual reality can (and probably will) be preferable to normal reality.

IV. Simulated reality is as metaphysically real as unsimulated reality, if not more so.

We should not simply assume from the start that each or any of these propositions is true. The point here is to reflect on the film's acceptance of or flirtation with these propositions and the ways in which they characterize our postmodern age in opposition to previous history. The hope is that, in the end, our rabbit hole might be better understood.

It Is Ultimately Impossible to Tell the Difference between the Real and the Unreal

After Neo first meets Morpheus, he learns that he's been right all along, that "there's something wrong with the world" and it has

---

the real," may also have been inspired by Baudrillard, for whom, postmodern America is one big desert where "you are delivered from all depth . . . a brilliant, mobile, superficial neutrality, a challenge to meaning and profundity, a challenge to nature and culture, an outer hyperspace, with no origin, no reference-points." See his *America* (London: Verso, 1988), p. 124 and pp. 1–13, 66–71, 123-126 as well as Baudrillard's *The Gulf War Did Not Take Place* (Bloomington: Indiana University Press, 1995).

something to do with the Matrix. He chooses the red pill to see "how deep the rabbit hole goes" and, as we know, soon learns that the only world he has ever known, seen, and tasted is an illusion, having no reality outside cyberspace. Just before his voyage into the real begins, Morpheus sensing Neo's puzzled disbelief asks him: "How would you know the difference between the dream world and the real world?" The message is clear. Neo has no way of knowing for sure what's real and what isn't.

Now, this, of course, is a *philosophical* problem, more specifically, an epistemological one. It is also an old one. Is it possible that we know nothing because all of our beliefs are false? Is there any way to show that we are not totally deluded about *everything*? Plato's *Republic,* 2,400 years old, tells of cave dwellers who take the mere shadows on the wall to be the real things themselves. They do not know what is real, having never encountered it, and are oblivious of their ignorance. For Plato this is an allegory for the condition of human beings who know only the material world and not the ideas or Forms which, Plato holds, stand behind them and make them possible. Much later, in the seventeenth century, Descartes entertains the possibility that all our beliefs might be false. In his *Meditations*, he aims to find a secure foundation for knowledge and, wanting to start from scratch, undertakes, in the first meditation, to show that all of our beliefs are susceptible to doubt. He begins with the unreliability of our senses but decides that this doesn't quite do the job. He then considers the possibility that we may be dreaming everything up. In fact, there is no surefire way to show that we are not dreaming. But Descartes reasons that we could not *always* have been dreaming since the contents of our dreams could not be generated from dreams alone and so must come from some other source. Descartes then considers the possibility that a malicious demon is systematically deceiving us such that every one of our beliefs is false. And with this possibility, and the attendant impossibility of proving this false, comes radical or global skepticism (which Descartes thought he could overcome by the means explained in his later meditations).

So we see that Morpheus's suggestion that we cannot really know for sure whether the world we experience is real or not *is* a respectable philosophical assertion (though there may be some good arguments against it). Is there anything new in what Morpheus says here? Only this. The thought of the malicious demon in the seventeenth century and until recently was an outlandish thought. Very few people were able to imagine how an all-powerful, mean-spirited entity could possibly implant beliefs into our minds. Nowadays, with the advent of computer simulation and the knowledge that the brain operates by means of electrical impulses, all of this seems possible, even if only remotely so. So *The Matrix* and other sci-fi films and books have made the job of philosophy teachers easier. Global skepticism is not so ridiculously far-fetched. With rapid advances in computer and brain science, maybe we'll one day arrive at the point where lifelike simulated images and experiences can be masterfully fed into our brains or central nervous systems. Maybe we're already there and maybe you're lying somewhere in a tub of goo thinking otherwise. *"How could you know the difference . . . ?"*

Still, the point here is that the claim that we cannot be sure that we can recognize the difference between reality and illusion is not philosophically new. But there's more to *The Matrix* than that.

Reality Can Be Simulated and Improved On

Start with the idea that there is only one real world and that it is exactly what it is and nothing else besides. Where then does the unreal, the illusory come from? And why are we sometimes fooled by it? The unreal may arise spontaneously in dreams and seems to fool us while we are dreaming. The unreal may also result from sensory or cognitive error, again spontaneously, and such as to lead to deception. In either case, the world co-exists with something else thanks to the powers and frailties of the mind. There is another way in which the real world comes to co-exist with something else. Human beings can *represent* the world in signs, language, and images. Consequently, we live in a world of things *and* of representations of things. Representations have been around since cave drawings and the beginnings of sign language. But theorists of postmodernity argue that we now live in a world thoroughly saturated with representations, both linguistic and pictorial. Words, signs, and especially images are ubiquitous and have usurped the immediacy of the material world, so much so that the world we experience is better described as a *spectacle* than as a space-time continuum filled with physical objects. Thus, Guy Debord, in his highly original *The Society of the Spectacle* (1967), writes:

> In societies where modern conditions of production prevail, all of life presents itself as an immense accumulation of spectacles. Everything that was directly lived has moved away into representation. The images detached from every aspect of life fuse in a common stream in which the unity of this life can no longer be re-established. Reality considered partially unfolds, in its own general unity as a pseudo-world apart, an object of mere contemplation . . . The spectacle is not a collection of images, but a social relation among people, mediated by images.[3]

According to Debord, there are now not only a lot more representations and images than before, but they form a network (matrix?) constituting a spectacle which is so much closer to us than the non-representational that the non-representational has become an unreconstructible abstraction. To illustrate this, look at your immediate surroundings and the extent to which their reality has been shaped by human fabrication and production with an eye to their eventual consumption. Or think of the place of the television or monitor screen in contemporary life or in an airport lounge.

The next step comes with computer simulation. Not only can we and do we produce and consume human-made representations of the world, we can now *simulate* the world. Simulation is a means of representing, in a life-like manner, objective processes and subjective experiences that may or may not have existed before, typically with the aid of computers. Thus we can simulate a car crash or the aroma of fried onions or the experience of weightlessness. And people are doing just this right now in labs in Texas and New Jersey and in IMAX theaters at your

---

[1] Guy Debord, *The Society of the Spectacle* (Detroit: Black and Red, 1983), p. 5. Originally *La société du spectacle* (Paris: Éditions Buchet-Chastel, 1967).

local museum. As a result we live in a simulated world, filled with the products of such simulation, called simulacra.

Now, at the beginning of our twenty-first century, computer simulation is clearly in its infancy. But it is rapidly progressing. The hardest part of it may not be replicating and modifying the ways things and people look, smell, sound, and behave but feeding all of this into the brain in a way that bypasses any awareness of the surrounding non-simulated world. But imagine that science and technology have come this far. Or rather let *The Matrix* imagine it for you. That's what the film does. Simulation begins with the staccato peck-peck-pecking at the keyboard (the certain sign in recent Hollywood films telling us that something interesting is about to happen) by means of which virtual reality is created. In *The Matrix*, cyberspace is beautifully depicted by white space without walls, floor, or ceiling as in the scene when Morpheus first shows Neo the "inside" of a computer program adorned with two red leather armchairs and a TV set (of prepostmodern 1950s vintage, appealing to our stubborn nostalgia for the days before the line had blurred) or in the scene when Neo and Trinity generously stock up on weapons to save Morpheus. Next, fill up the white space with whatever you'd like from guns and skyscrapers and swarms of business people to the woman in the red dress. Pipe all of this in through a steel rod inserted into the brain and wired into the appropriate receptors and, *voilà*, we get the fully simulated world of 1999 and it's the only world we know. *Formidable!*, as the French say.

Once all of this is granted, it seems rather easy, in principle, to see how a simulated world could be created and how our judgment of the real might yield to it. There is one aspect of it, however, that is confusing and maybe even poorly thought out by the film's writers: the self and its mental powers. Morpheus tells Neo that when a person is placed into a computer program such as the Matrix, he or she retains a "residual self image" and becomes "a mental projection of your digital self." What does this mean? It's not clear that it means anything, but we can give it a try. Neo, once unplugged and then loaded up into cyberspace, is very much a residuum of whatever he was in the real world, that is, on the *Nebuchadnezzar*. He has the same personality (that same Keanu Reeves *il-ne-sait-quoi*), the same memories (which incidentally were formed, strangely enough, not in the real world, but in the virtual one), the same will to be free, the same knowledge of ju jitsu (this, by contrast, was uploaded), and so forth. On the other hand, his person and powers in cyberspace are also a function of his capacity for mental projection. Thus, on the ju jitsu mats with Morpheus, he is told that if he is to win the fight, his mind will do it, not his body. His mind is strong enough (if not always his will or self-confidence) to defy gravity and bend spoons. It is not altogether clear where this power comes from. It could easily be punched in at a keyboard, of course, but that's not what happens. Neo himself lying inert in a chair is doing the work of manipulating his body and the physical world in cyberspace. What allows for this?

It would seem, at first, that simulation gives unlimited power to the keyboard operator and no power at all to the one (lying in the chair) to whom the world is being simulated. Or is this right? What if simulation could be more than this? A world is piped into your brain and, furthermore, your brain has the power not only to receive information from that world but to act on it (as in a video game) and because it is the cyberworld, not the real one, your powers are not limited by the familiar scientific laws. Maybe *The Matrix* is right about this, after all: very, very sophisticated simulation would in fact allow for a cyberself that both projects much of its real attributes and is able to surpass them as well by means of a strong and disciplined will. According to *The Matrix*, more powerful than the computer is the mind that engages with it. We'll have to wait to find out about this one, but it's hard not to be curious. Wake me up in a couple hundred years, or better yet, load me up there right now.[2]

So, not only can reality be simulated, it can be improved on. Why simulate it otherwise? This means that simulating reality is not only a matter of replicating its basic structure but making

---

[2] For experts on the film, this quiz-show question: According to *The Matrix*, what is most powerful of all? Incorrect answer: the mind or its will-power. Correct answer: Love. Recall that, toward the end of the film, in his struggle against the agents, Neo's mental powers are not sufficient for the task. As he lies dying or dead, what saves him and gives him the strength to prevail is Trinity's kiss.

whatever tweaks are necessary to bring it into line with our wishes. Virtual reality in *The Matrix* replicates not the bleak, gray wasteland of 2199 but the world as it was in 1999. Compared to the world of 2199, it is replete with bright colors, blue skies, and tasty food. Even compared to the "real" world of 1999, it's improved in certain ways, for example with the addition of the woman in the red dress or perhaps the elimination of poverty (for we see mainly business types and we mustn't forget that the machines want a docile human population and would be unwise to permit hunger and deprivation).

Yes, simulation is, for almost all intents and purposes, fundamentally an enhancement of reality. This brings us back to ourselves and our society. Haven't we reached a point where virtual reality is simply better than the real thing? Isn't it possible that the artificial flavor of banana is or could be made more pleasing than the banana itself? Or can't we imagine the day when the super-duper IMAX experience of the Grand Canyon far surpasses the experience of the big hole itself? Walker Percy, the philosophically-inspired novelist, once pointed out that it would be far better to encounter the Grand Canyon unexpectedly than to arrive there on a tourist bus. Imagine that the IMAX experience hooked you up to electrical impulses that temporarily eradicated any knowledge of the Grand Canyon's existence so that you could ride up to it on a horse and be completely taken by surprise. Given such a scenario, people might understandably say: "If you've only got three hours, take a pass on the Canyon and head straight for the IMAX. It's awesome. If you have more time, visit the real thing, it's not bad, though be prepared for a bit of a disappointment." And who can blame them? Which takes us to the next step.

Simulated or Virtual Reality Can (and Probably Will) Be Preferable to Normal Reality

Which is preferable, the real world or the enhanced virtual world? Which pill would you take—the blue one or the red? As we have just seen, given the appropriate technological advances as well as a competent and benevolent programmer, the virtual world will typically seem more attractive than the real one. Much more so. This is nicely illustrated in the scene in which

Cypher defects and goes to work for the inimitable Agent Smith. Cypher enjoying a succulent cut of beef and a fine glass of red wine says: "I know this steak doesn't exist. I know that when I put it in my mouth, the Matrix is telling my brain that it is juicy and delicious. After nine years, do you know what I realize? Ignorance is bliss."

The Matrix has juicy steaks; the real human world has bland gruel. The Matrix has great nightclubs; the real world has none. The Matrix has the woman in the red dress; the real world has . . . Trinity (oh well, there's always an exception). But the point is that the Matrix is a paradise of sensual pleasures compared to the real world. And Cypher is a hedonist through and through—a pleasure-seeker unwilling to put up with forever-deferred dreams and other idealist crap. He wants to return to cyber-reality and is willing to do what it takes to get out of another nine years of gruel. Not so the other *Nebuchadnezzar* team-mates. There's something more important to them than pleasure, namely, truth and freedom. Especially to Neo who reveals early on his distaste for and disbelief in fate because "I don't like the idea that I'm not in control of my life."

So, on the face of it, it looks as if the virtual world is only preferable to the shallow hedonist who's indifferent to the sin of self-deception, while the real world is preferable to anyone who cares about more important things such as truth, freedom, autonomy, and authenticity. In putting forth this message, we get an old-fashioned Hollywood morality tale. Very unpostmodern. And of course the whole plot of the film is driven by the noble battle for liberation from the tyranny of the machines and their evil Matrix. But the film, despite itself, presents us with two worlds in a way that shows us that Cypher is the one who is right. I believe that the only sensible path is to choose the simulated world over the real one.

Here's why. The Matrix does not just offer sensual pleasures. It really encompasses much more, in fact, it gives us just about everything we could want from the shallowest to the deepest of gratifications. Assuming the machines haven't made things unnecessarily impoverished, the virtual world gives us the opportunity to visit museums and concerts, read Shakespeare and Stephen King, fall in love, make love, raise children, form deep friendships, and so on. The whole world lies at our feet except that it's probably better than our world since the machines have every motivation to create and sustain a world without human misery, accidents, disease, and war so as to increase the available energy supply. The real world, on the other hand, is a wasteland. The libraries and theaters have been destroyed and the skies are always gray. In fact, you'd have to be out of your mind or at least seriously out to lunch to choose the real world (is that why Keanu Reeves seems so well cast in the role?). We're not talking base hedonism now, we're talking about, to use John Stuart Mill's words, "the higher faculties" and the deep and diverse types of gratification derived from them. Such gratification is to be found far more easily in The Matrix than in "the desert of the real."[3]

What about truth and freedom, autonomy, and authenticity? The machines probably don't mind what you do in the virtual world as long as it stays there. You can paint, you can make music, you can support the government or fight against it. You're free in every way that you're free now, you just can't do one thing: unplug or try to get others to unplug or kill Agents who are trying to stop people from unplugging. As for truth, there's really only one single important truth that eludes you: that none of this real. It's all only virtual. But it feels real as real can get. And there's no reason to suspect that it's unreal unless Morpheus or his team visits you. So should you care? Does it matter? Is it in the end really unreal? What makes it unreal? On to our last proposition.

---

[3] So while Neo chooses the red pill, I, along with Cypher, would choose the blue pill, albeit not simply for creaturely comforts and pleasures. There is, however, a third position. In "You Won't Know the Difference So You Can't Make the Choice," *Philosophy Now* (December 2000/January 2001), pp. 35–36, Robin Beck argues that "there are no rational grounds for making the decision" because "[e]pistemologically, the worlds are the same" given that either world seems "equally real" once either pill has been swallowed. Beck is right to say that either way we take our world to be the real one and so there's no difference on that score. But the world so taken is very different depending on which pill's been chosen, and the blue pill gives us by far the better world.

Simulated Reality Is as Metaphysically Real as Unsimulated Reality, if not More So

First, some lines from the theorist of postmodernity, Jean Baudrillard:

> The very definition of the real becomes: *that of which it is possible to give an equivalent reproduction* . . . At the limit of this process of reproducibility, the real is not only what can be reproduced, but *that which is always already reproduced*. The hyperreal . . . transcends representation . . .only because it is entirely in simulation . . .[A]rtifice is at the very heart of reality.[4]

When Morpheus takes Neo on his first tour of computer programmed cyberspace, Neo grasps at a leather armchair against the background of a bright white void and asks Morpheus: "Are you telling me this isn't real?" Morpheus responds: "What is real? How do you define 'real'?" This is not just a throw-away line or a mere rhetorical question. In the weird context of this film and our ever-weirder technological world, it is a legitimate question. Morpheus's next statement only confirms this. He says that the real is what we can "feel, smell, taste and see" and that this consists in "electrical signals interpreted by your brain." But if one's experience of a virtual reality is also a matter of electrical signals interpreted by the brain, then it would seem to follow that virtual reality is as real as reality.

In another scene Neo is being driven by car to the Oracle. Gazing out the window, he suddenly recognizes something and exclaims, "God, I used to eat there . . . really good noodles," only to fall back into his seat disappointed when it occurs to him that "I have these memories from life . . . none of them happened." But didn't they? He remembers them.[5] Unlike false memories (say, the kind that questionable psychotherapeutic practices are said to create), Neo's memories were experienced at one time as occurring in the present. His experience of the restaurant led to further visits to the restaurant. In other words,

---

[4] Baudrillard, *Simulations*, pp. 146, 147, 151.
[5] Which calls to mind the line from the 1960s song "Both Sides Now": "It's life's illusions I recall / I really don't know life at all."

his experience of the restaurant stands in a coherent relation to his other experiences and behavior. It even stands in a coherent relation to the experiences and behavior of other human beings, whom Neo brought to the restaurant in a virtual intersubjectively shared world.[6] In a way, then, those memories do in fact correspond to something that happened. One could, in principle, find traces of it in the brains of other human beings lying in pods plugged in to the Matrix.

The idea, mentioned a moment ago, that reality, and our knowledge of it, is rooted in the sensory impressions (seeing, touching, etc.) we have is a fundamental principle of philosophical empiricism—a philosophy that is no less influential today than when it was first developed in its modern form in the seventeenth and eighteenth centuries. According to David Hume, there can be no other justification for our knowledge, for our belief in what is real, than what we see, hear, smell, taste, and touch. Now one might object to this by saying that Neo and other human beings in the Matrix don't really see or hear anything at all. However, they have the same type of sensory impressions as we do. And since there is nothing that distinguishes their sensory impressions from ours, no external evidence accessible to them (as there is none for us) that would show them that their sensory impressions are mere imaginings, then it follows that for them the Matrix is as real as our world is for us since both are underwritten by the same type of sensory impressions.[7]

We also saw that Neo's earlier experiences were experiences of reality because they cohere with other experiences and other behavior, not only Neo's own but that of other human beings as well. This relies on something like a coherence notion of truth, according to which a belief such as "I used to eat in that restaurant with my buddies" is true if it coheres with most of our other

---

[6] Why intersubjective? In *The Matrix* it's not as if each individual has his or her own private Matrix, rather the entire human population is experiencing the same Matrix. What one person does there is witnessed and experienced by others.

[7] This point depends on accepting a certain principle of verification—according to which a claim is meaningful and true if and only if there is a possible method for verifying it. This principle is itself not without philosophical controversy

beliefs. That his experience coheres with and is a reliable basis for our behavior (also true of Neo's earlier experiences) is a central principle of pragmatism.

Still, a skeptic of all this, a cyberskeptic, will say that no matter how many sensory impressions one has of the virtual world and no matter how much they cohere within and between individuals, the cyberworld is not real because it does not exist in space. It is nowhere except in people's heads in the same way that other fictitious things (imaginary lovers or Santa Claus) might be in people's heads. But the cyberbeliever will respond: but the cyberworld does *exist* in space, in cyberspace. The skeptic will say that cyberspace is not *real* space. And the believer will then say *HELLO-O?*, of course it isn't "real" space, that's what makes it cyberspace. But the skeptic will respond that any space that isn't real space just doesn't count as space at all. According to this view, "cyberspace" is a mere metaphor; strictly speaking, "cyberspace" is an oxymoron.

Even granting that "cyberspace" is only a metaphor, we should note here that the cyberskeptic is assuming that spatiality is an essential feature of what can count as real. The assumption is that there is one and only one spatial-temporal continuum and that some of our beliefs and experiences correspond to what is in that continuum and some do not. If beliefs (or experiences) do not correspond, they are false (or non-veridical). Similarly, if something cannot be found in that continuum, it is not real. This assumption of the spatiality (and materiality insofar as materiality is defined in terms of spatiality) of the real is an assumption that some philosophers would reject. In fact, Plato rejected it. He held that numbers and, more generally, all Forms or ideas are real yet not spatial. (And Kant held that space is not a thing-in-itself, but belongs to the way subjects intuit the world.) So we see that the cyberbeliever shares some philosophical ground not only with empiricists, coherentists, and pragmatists but with Platonists (and perhaps Kantians) too. As does the postmodernist (at least, in many cases).

Plato held that the Forms or ideas were *more real* than material objects locatable in space. His reasons are complex but we might say, in a nutshell, that for Plato the Forms or ideas are more real because they are eternal and immutable and make possible the material world and our knowledge of it. Now, virtual reality is not eternal or immutable nor does it enable the unsimulated world we know (at least, not yet). Can any sense be given to the claim that simulated worlds are more real than nonsimulated worlds? Perhaps only this sense. If our future experience turns out to be such that simulated reality has a greater causal impact on our lived experience and actual behavior than nonsimulated reality, then, in one sense, a pragmatic sense, it will be more real. Whether this will turn out to be the case is not something that we can easily foresee at this point in time. Let's wait, oh, about two hundred years.

20

The Matrix: Or, The Two Sides of Perversion

SLAVOJ ŽIŽEK

When I saw *The Matrix* at a local theater in Slovenia, I had the unique opportunity of sitting close to the ideal spectator of the film—namely, to an idiot. A man in his late twenties at my right was so absorbed in the movie that he continually disturbed the other viewers with loud exclamations, like "My God, wow, so there is no reality!"

I definitely prefer such naive immersion to the pseudo-sophisticated intellectualist readings which project refined philosophical or psychoanalytic conceptual distinctions into the film.[1] It is nonetheless easy to understand this intellectual attraction of *The Matrix*: Isn't *The Matrix* one of those films which function as a kind of Rorschach test [http://rorschach.test.at/], setting in motion the universalized process of recognition, like the proverbial painting of God which seems always to stare directly at you,

---

[1] Comparing the original script (available on the Internet) with the movie itself, we can see that the Wachowski brothers were intelligent enough to throw out the clunky pseudo-intellectual references: "Look at 'em. Automatons. Don't think about what they're doing or why. Computer tells 'em what to do and they do it." "The banality of evil." This pretentious reference to Arendt misses the point: People immersed in the VR of the Matrix are in an entirely different, almost opposite, position compared with the executioners of the Holocaust. Another wise move was to drop the all too obvious references to Eastern techniques of emptying your mind as the way to escape the control of the Matrix: "You have to learn to let go of that anger. You must let go of everything. You must empty yourself to free your mind."

from wherever you look at it—practically every orientation seems to recognize itself in it?

My Lacanian friends tell me that the authors must have read Lacan; the Frankfurt School partisans see in *The Matrix* the extrapolated embodiment of *Kulturindustrie*, the alienated-reified social Substance (of Capital) directly taking over, colonizing our inner life itself, using us as the source of energy; New Agers see in it a source of speculations on how our world is just a mirage generated by a global Mind embodied in the World Wide Web.

This series goes back to Plato's *Republic*. Doesn't *The Matrix* exactly repeat Plato's device of the cave (ordinary humans as prisoners, tied firmly to their seats and compelled to watch the shadowy performance of (what they falsely consider to be) reality? The important difference, of course, is that when some individuals escape their cave predicament and step out onto the surface of the Earth, what they find there is no longer a bright surface illuminated by the rays of the Sun, the supreme Good, but the desolate "desert of the real."

The key opposition here is the one between the Frankfurt School and Lacan: Should we historicize *The Matrix* into the metaphor of Capital that has colonized culture and subjectivity, or is it the reification of the symbolic order as such? However, what if this very alternative is false? What if the virtual character of the symbolic order "as such" is the very condition of historicity?

Reaching the End of the World

The idea of the hero living in a totally manipulated and controlled artificial universe is hardly original: *The Matrix* just radicalizes it by bringing in virtual reality (VR). The point here is the radical ambiguity of VR with regard to the problematic of iconoclasm. On the one hand, VR marks the radical reduction of the wealth of our sensory experience to—not even letters, but—the minimal digital series of 0 and 1, of the transmission and nontransmission of an electrical signal. On the other hand, this very digital machine generates the "simulated" experience of reality which tends to become indistinguishable from the "real" reality, with the consequence of undermining the very notion of "real" reality. VR is thus at the same time the most radical assertion of the seductive power of images.

Is not the ultimate American paranoid fantasy that of an individual living in a small, idyllic Californian city, a consumerist paradise, who suddenly starts to suspect that the world he lives in is a fake, a spectacle staged to convince him that he lives in a real world, while all the people around him are effectively actors and extras in a gigantic show? The most recent example of this is Peter Weir's *The Truman Show* (1998), with Jim Carrey playing the small-town clerk who gradually discovers the truth that he is the hero of a 24-hour ongoing TV show: his hometown is constructed on a a gigantic studio set, with cameras following him continually.

Sloterdijk's "sphere" is here literally realized, as the gigantic metal sphere that envelops and isolates the entire city. The final shot of *The Truman Show* may seem to enact the liberating experience of breaking out from the ideological suture of the enclosed universe into its outside, invisible from the ideological inside. However, what if it is precisely this "happy" denouement of the film (let us not forget: applauded by millions around the world watching the last minutes of the show), with the hero breaking out and, as we are led to believe, soon to join his true love (so that we have again the formula of the production of the couple!), that is ideology at its purest? What if ideology resides in the very belief that, outside the closure of the finite universe, there is some "true reality" to be entered?[2]

Among the predecessors of this notion is Phillip K. Dick's novel *Time Out of Joint* (1959), in which a man living a modest daily life in an idyllic Californian small town of the late 1950s, gradually discovers that the whole town is a fake staged to keep him satisfied. The underlying experience of *Time Out of Joint* and of *The Truman Show* is that the late-capitalist consumerist Californian paradise is, in its very hyper-reality, in a way irreal, substanceless, deprived of material inertia. So it's not only that Hollywood stages a semblance of real life deprived of the weight and inertia of materiality: In late-capitalist consumerist

---

[2] It's also crucial that what enables the hero of *The Truman Show* to see through and exit his manipulated world is the unforeseen intervention of his father. There are two paternal figures in the film, the actual symbolic-biological father and the paranoiac "real" father, played by Ed Harris, the director of the TV show who totally manipulates his life and protects him in the closed environment.

society, "real social life" itself somehow acquires the features of a staged fake, with our neighbors behaving in "real" life as stage actors and extras. The ultimate truth of the capitalist utilitarian despiritualized universe is the dematerialization of "real life" itself, its reversal into a spectral show.

In the realm of science-fiction, one should mention also Brian Aldiss's *Starship*, in which members of a tribe live in the closed world of a tunnel in a giant starship, isolated from the rest of the ship by thick vegetation, unaware that there is a universe beyond. Finally some children penetrate the bushes and reach the world beyond, populated by other tribes.

Among the older, more "naive" forerunners, one should mention George Seaton's *36 Hours*, the early 1960s movie about an American officer (James Garner) who knows all the plans for the invasion of Normandy and is seized by the Germans just days before D-Day. Since he is taken prisoner unconscious following an explosion, the Germans quickly construct for him a replica of a small American military hospital, and try to convince him that he now lives in 1950, that America has already won the war and that he has no memory of the last six years—the intention being that he will reveal all he knows about the invasion plans. Cracks soon appear in this carefully constructed edifice . . . (Lenin, in the last two years of his life, lived in an almost similar controlled environment, in which, as we now know, Stalin had printed for him a specially-prepared one-copy edition of *Pravda*, censored of all news that would tell Lenin about the political struggles going on, with the justification that Comrade Lenin should take a rest and not be excited by unnecessary provocations.)

What lurks in the background is the pre-modern notion of "arriving at the end of the universe." In those well-known engravings, the surprised wanderers approach the screen or curtain of heaven, a flat surface with painted stars on it, pierce it and reach beyond—this is exactly what happens at the end of *The Truman Show*. No wonder that the last scene of this movie, when Truman steps up the stairs attached to the wall on which the "blue sky" horizon is painted and opens the door, has a distinctly Magrittean touch: Isn't this same sensitivity today returning with a vengeance? Do works like Syberberg's *Parsifal*, in which the infinite horizon is also blocked by the obviously "artificial" rear-projections, not signal that the time of the Cartesian infinite perspective is running out, and that we are returning to a kind of renewed medieval pre-perspective universe?

Fred Jameson perspicuously drew attention to the same phenomenon in some of Chandler's novels and Hitchcock's films. The shore of the Pacific Ocean in *Farewell, My Lovely* functions as a kind of "end or limit of the world," beyond which there is an unknown abyss; and it is similar with the vast open valley that stretches out in front of the Mount Rushmore heads when, on the run from their pursuers, Eva Marie Saint and Cary Grant reach the peak of the monument, and into which Eva Marie Saint almost falls, before being pulled up by Cary Grant.

One is tempted to add to this series the famous battle scene at a bridge on the Vietnamese-Cambodian frontier in *Apocalypse Now*, where the space beyond the bridge is experienced as the "beyond of our known universe." And the view that our Earth is not a planet floating in infinite space, but really a circular opening or hole, within the endless compact mass of eternal ice, with the sun in its center, was one of the favorite Nazi pseudo-scientific fantasies—according to some reports, they even considered putting some telescopes on the Sylt islands in order to observe America.

The "Really Existing" Big Other

What, then, is the Matrix? Simply the Lacanian "big Other," the virtual symbolic order, the network that structures reality for us. This dimension of the "big Other" is that of the constitutive alienation of the subject in the symbolic order: the big Other pulls the strings, the subject doesn't speak, he "is spoken" by the symbolic structure. In short, this "big Other" is the name for the social Substance, for all that on account of which the subject never fully dominates the effects of his acts, on account of which the final outcome of his activity is always something other than what he aimed at or anticipated.

However, in the key chapters of *Seminar XI*, Lacan struggles to delineate the operation that follows alienation and is in a sense its counterpoint, that of separation: Alienation *in* the big Other is followed by separation *from* the big Other. Separation takes place when the subject takes note of how the big Other is in itself inconsistent, purely virtual, "barred," deprived of the Thing—and fantasy is an attempt to fill out this lack of the

Other, not of the subject, to (re)constitute the consistency of the big Other.

For that reason, fantasy and paranoia are inherently linked: Paranoia is at its most elementary a belief in an "Other of the Other", into another Other who, hidden behind the Other of the explicit social texture, programs (what appears to us as) the unforeseen effects of social life and thus guarantees its consistency: Beneath the chaos of the market, the degradation of morals, and so forth, there is the purposeful strategy of the Jewish plot . . . This paranoid stance has acquired a further boost with today's digitalization of our daily lives. When our entire social existence is progressively externalized-materialized in the big Other of the computer network, it's easy to imagine an evil programmer erasing our digital identity and thus depriving us of our social existence, turning us into non-persons.

Following the same paranoid twist, the thesis of *The Matrix* is that this big Other is externalized in the really existing Mega-Computer. There is—there *has* to be—a Matrix because "things are not right, opportunities are missed, something goes wrong all the time." In other words, the movie's suggestion that this is so because there is the Matrix obfuscates the true reality that is behind it all. Consequently, the problem with the film is that it is not "crazy" enough, because it supposes another "real" reality behind our everyday reality sustained by the Matrix.

However, to avoid a fatal misunderstanding, the inverse notion that "all there is is generated by the Matrix," that there is *no* ultimate reality, just the infinite series of virtual realities mirroring themselves in each other, is no less ideological. In the sequels to *The Matrix*, we shall probably learn that the very "desert of the real" is generated by another matrix. Much more subversive than this multiplication of virtual universes would have been the multiplication of realities themselves—something that would reproduce the paradoxical danger that some physicists see in recent high-accelerator experiments.

Scientists are now trying to construct an accelerator capable of smashing together the nuclei of very heavy atoms at nearly the speed of light. The idea is that such a collision will not only shatter the atom's nuclei into their constituent protons and neutrons, but will pulverize the protons and neutrons themselves, leaving a "plasma," a kind of energy soup consisting of loose quark and gluon particles, the building blocks of matter that have never before been studied in such a state, since such a state only existed briefly after the Big Bang.

However, this prospect has given rise to a nightmarish scenario. What if the success of this experiment created a doomsday machine, a kind of world-devouring monster that would with inexorable necessity annihilate the ordinary matter around itself and thus abolish the world as we know it? The irony of it is that this end of the world, the disintegration of the universe, would be the ultimate irrefutable proof that the tested theory were true, since it would suck all matter into a black hole and then bring about a new universe, perfectly recreating the Big Bang scenario.

The paradox is thus that both versions—(1) a subject freely floating from one to another VR, a pure ghost aware that every reality is a fake; (2) the paranoiac supposition of the real reality beneath the Matrix—are false. They both miss the Real. The film is not wrong in insisting that there *is* a Real beneath the Virtual Reality simulation—as Morpheus puts it to Neo when he shows him the ruined Chicago landscape: "Welcome to the desert of the real."

However, the Real is not the "true reality" behind the virtual simulation, but the void which makes reality incomplete or inconsistent, and the function of every symbolic Matrix is to conceal this inconsistency. One of the ways to effectuate this concealment is precisely to claim that, behind the incomplete/inconsistent reality we know, there is another reality with no deadlock of impossibility structuring it.

"The Big Other Doesn't Exist"

"Big Other" also stands for the field of common sense at which one can arrive after free deliberation; philosophically, its last great version is Habermas's communicative community with its regulative ideal of agreement. And it is this "big Other" that progressively disintegrates today.

What we have today is a certain radical split. On the one hand, there is the objectivized language of experts and scientists which can no longer be translated into the common language accessible to everyone, but is present in common language in the mode of fetishized formulas that no one really understands, but which shape our artistic and popular imaginary universes

(Black Hole, Big Bang, Superstrings, Quantum Oscillation . . .). Not only in the natural sciences, but also in economics and other social sciences, the expert jargon is presented as an objective insight with which one cannot really argue, and which is simultaneously untranslatable into our common experience. In short, the gap between scientific insight and common sense is unbridgeable, and it is this very gap which elevates scientists into the popular cult figures of the "subjects supposed to know" (the Stephen Hawking phenomenon).

And on the other hand, the strict obverse of this objectivity is the way in which, in cultural matters, we are confronted with the multitude of lifestyles which we cannot translate into each other. All we can do is secure the conditions for their tolerant co-existence in a multicultural society. The icon of today's subject is perhaps the Indian computer programmer who, during the day, excels in his expertise, while in the evening, upon returning home, he lights the candle to the local Hindu divinity and respects the sanctity of the cow.

This split is perfectly rendered in the phenomenon of cyberspace. Cyberspace was supposed to bring us all together in a Global Village. Yet what effectively happens is that we are bombarded with the multitude of messages belonging to inconsistent and incompatible universes. Instead of the Global Village, the big Other, we get the multitude of "small others," of tribal particular identifications at our choice. To avoid a misunderstanding: Lacan is here far from relativizing science into just one of the arbitrary narratives, ultimately on an equal footing with Politically Correct myths, and so forth: Science *does* "touch the Real," its knowledge *is* "knowledge in the real." The deadlock resides simply in the fact that scientific knowledge cannot serve as the *symbolic* "big Other." The gap between modern science and Aristotelian common-sense philosophical ontology is here insurmountable. This gap emerges with Galileo, and is brought to an extreme in quantum physics, where we're dealing with laws which do work, though they cannot ever be retranslated into our experience of representable reality.

The theory of the risk society and its global reflexivization is right in its emphasis on how, today, we are at the opposite end of the classical Enlightenment universalist ideology which presupposed that, in the long run, the fundamental questions can be resolved by way of reference to the "objective knowledge" of the experts. When we're confronted with conflicting opinions about the environmental consequences of a certain new product (say, of genetically modified vegetables), we search in vain for the ultimate expert opinion. And the point is not simply that the real issues are blurred because science is corrupted through financial dependence on large corporations and state agencies. Even in themselves, the sciences cannot provide the answer.

Fifteen years ago ecologists predicted the death of the Earth's forests, but we now learn that the problem is too large an increase of forest growth. Where this theory of the risk society falls short is in emphasizing the irrational predicament into which this puts us, common subjects. We are again and again compelled to decide, although we are well aware that we are in no position to decide, that our decision will be arbitrary. Ulrich Beck and his followers refer to the democratic discussion of all options and consensus-building. However this does not resolve the immobilizing dilemma: Why should the democratic discussion in which the majority participates lead to better results, when, cognitively, the ignorance of the majority remains?

The political frustration of the majority is thus understandable. They are called upon to decide, while, at the same time, receiving the message that they are in no position effectively to decide, to objectively weigh the pros and cons. The recourse to "conspiracy theories" is a desperate way out of this deadlock, an attempt to regain a minimum of what Fred Jameson calls "cognitive mapping."

Jodi Dean[3] drew attention to a curious phenomenon clearly observable in the "dialogue of the mutes" between the official ("serious," academically institutionalized) science and the vast domain of so-called pseudo-sciences, from ufology to those who want to decipher the secrets of the pyramids. One cannot but be struck by how it is the official scientists who proceed in a dogmatic, dismissive way, while the pseudo-scientists refer to facts and argumentation, disregarding common prejudices. The answer, of course, will be that established scientists speak with the authority of the big Other, of science as an institution, but

---

[3] On whom I rely extensively here. See Dean's *Aliens in America: Conspiracy Cultures from Outerspace to Cyberspace* (Ithaca: Cornell University Press, 1998).

the problem is that, precisely, this scientific big Other is again and again revealed as a consensual symbolic fiction. So when we are confronted with conspiracy theories, we should proceed in a strict homology to the proper reading of Henry James's *The Turn of the Screw*. We should neither accept the existence of ghosts as part of the narrative reality nor reduce them, in a pseudo-Freudian way, to the "projection" of the heroine's hysterical sexual frustrations.

Conspiracy theories are of course not to be accepted as "fact." However one should also not reduce them to the phenomenon of modern mass hysteria. Such a notion still relies on the "big Other," on the model of "normal" perception of shared social reality, and thus does not take into account how it is precisely this notion of reality that is undermined today. The problem is not that ufologists and conspiracy theorists regress to a paranoid attitude unable to accept (social) reality; the problem is that this reality itself is becoming paranoiac.

Contemporary experience again and again confronts us with situations in which we are compelled to take note of how our sense of reality and normal attitude towards it is grounded in a symbolic fiction—how the "big Other" that determines what counts as normal and accepted truth, what is the horizon of meaning in a given society, is in no way directly grounded in "facts" as rendered by the scientific "knowledge in the real."

Let us take a traditional society in which modern science is not yet elevated into the "master discourse." If, in its symbolic space, an individual advocates propositions of modern science, he will be dismissed as a "madman." And the key point is that it is not enough to say that he is not "really mad," that it is merely the narrow, ignorant society which puts him in this position. In a certain way, being treated as a madman, being excluded from the social big Other, effectively *equals* being mad. "Madness" is not the designation which can be grounded in a direct reference to "facts" (in the sense that a madman is unable to perceive things the way they really are, since he is caught in his hallucinatory projections), but only with regard to the way an individual relates to the "big Other."

Lacan usually emphasizes the opposite aspect of this paradox: "The madman is not only a beggar who thinks he is a king, but also a king who thinks he is a king." In other words, madness designates the collapse of the distance between the

Symbolic and the Real, an immediate identification with the
symbolic mandate; or, to take his other exemplary statement,
when a husband is pathologically jealous, obsessed by the idea
that his wife sleeps with other men, his obsession remains a
pathological feature even if it is proved that he is right and that
his wife in fact sleeps with other men.

The lesson of such paradoxes is clear. Pathological jealously
is not a matter of getting the facts wrong, but of the way these
facts are integrated into the subject's libidinal economy.
However, what we should assert here is that the same paradox
should also be performed as it were in the opposite direction:
The society (its socio-symbolic field, the big Other) is "sane" and
"normal" even when it is proven factually wrong. Maybe it was
in this sense that the late Lacan designated himself as "psychotic." He effectively was psychotic insofar as it was not possible to integrate his discourse into the field of the big Other.

One is tempted to claim, in the Kantian mode, that the mistake of the conspiracy theory is somehow homologous to the
"paralogism of pure reason," to the confusion between the two
levels: the suspicion (of the received scientific, social, etc. common sense) as the formal methodological stance, and the posit-
ing of this suspicion in another all-explaining global
para-theory.

Screening the Real

From another standpoint, the Matrix also functions as the
"screen" that separates us from the Real, that makes the "desert
of the real" bearable. However, it is here that we should not forget the radical ambiguity of the Lacanian Real: it is not the ultimate referent to be covered-gentrified-domesticated by the
screen of fantasy. The Real is also and primarily the screen itself
as the obstacle that always distorts our perception of the referent, of the reality out there.

In philosophical terms, therein resides the difference
between Kant and Hegel: For Kant, the Real is the noumenal
domain that we perceive "schematized" through the screen of
transcendental categories; for Hegel, on the contrary, as he
asserts exemplarily in the *Introduction* to his *Phenomenology*,
this Kantian gap is false. Hegel introduces here *three* terms:
when a screen intervenes between ourselves and the Real, it

always generates a notion of what is In-itself, beyond the screen (of the appearance), so that the gap between appearance and the In-itself is always-already "for us." Consequently, if we subtract from the Thing the distortion of the Screen, we lose the Thing itself (in religious terms, the death of Christ is the death of the God in himself, not only of his human embodiment)—which is why, for Lacan, who here follows Hegel, the Thing in itself is ultimately the gaze, not the perceived object. So, back to the Matrix: the Matrix itself is the Real that distorts our perception of reality.

A reference to Lévi-Strauss's exemplary analysis, from his *Structural Anthropology*, of the spatial disposition of buildings in the Winnebago, one of the Great Lake tribes, might be of some help here. The tribe is divided into two sub-groups ("moieties"), "those who are from above" and "those who are from below"; when we ask an individual to draw on a piece of paper, or on sand, the ground-plan of his or her village (the spatial disposition of cottages), we obtain two quite different answers, depending on his or her belonging to one or the other sub-group. Both perceive the village as a circle; but for one sub-group, there is within this circle another circle of central houses, so that we have two concentric circles, while for the other sub-group, the circle is split into two by a clear dividing line. In other words, a member of the first sub-group (let us call it "conservative-corporatist") perceives the ground-plan of the village as a ring of houses more or less symmetrically disposed around the central temple, whereas a member of the second ("revolutionary-antagonistic") sub-group perceives his or her village as two distinct heaps of houses separated by an invisible frontier . . .[4]

Lévi-Strauss's main point is that this example should in no way entice us into cultural relativism, according to which the perception of social space depends on the observer's group-membership. The very splitting into the two "relative" perceptions implies a hidden reference to a constant—not the objective, "actual" disposition of buildings but a traumatic

---

[4] Claude Lévi-Strauss, "Do Dual Organizations Exist?", in *Structural Anthropology* (New York: Basic Books, 1963), pp. 131–163. The drawings are on pp. 133–34.

kernel, a fundamental antagonism the inhabitants of the village were unable to symbolize, to account for, to "internalize," to come to terms with, an imbalance in social relations that prevented the community from stabilizing itself into a harmonious whole.

The two perceptions of the ground-plan are simply two mutually exclusive endeavors to cope with this traumatic antagonism, to heal its wound via the imposition of a balanced symbolic structure. Is it necessary to add that things stand exactly the same with respect to sexual difference, that "masculine" and "feminine" are like the two configurations of houses in the Lévi-Straussian village? And in order to dispel the illusion that our "developed" universe is not dominated by the same logic, suffice it to recall the splitting of our political space into left and right: a leftist and a rightist behave exactly like members of the opposite sub-groups of the Lévi-Straussian village. They not only occupy different places within the political space; each of them perceives differently the very disposition of the political space—a leftist as the field that is inherently split by some fundamental antagonism, a rightist as the organic unity of a community disturbed only by foreign intruders.

However, Lévi-Strauss makes a further crucial point: since the two sub-groups nonetheless form one and the same tribe, living in the same village, this identity somehow has to be symbolically inscribed. But how is this possible, if the entire symbolic articulation, all social institutions, of the tribe are not neutral, but are overdetermined by the fundamental and constitutive antagonistic split? By what Lévi-Strauss ingeniously calls the "zero-institution," a kind of institutional counterpart to the famous *mana*, the empty signifier with no determinate meaning, since it signifies only the presence of meaning as such, in opposition to its absence: a specific institution which has no positive, determinate function—its only function is the purely negative one of signalling the presence and actuality of social institution as such, in opposition to its absence, to pre-social chaos.

It's the reference to such a zero-institution that enables all members of the tribe to experience themselves as such, as members of the same tribe. Is, then, this zero-institution not ideology at its purest—the direct embodiment of the ideological function of providing a neutral all-encompassing space in which social antagonism is obliterated, in which all members of society can recognize themselves? And is the struggle for hegemony not precisely the struggle for how this zero-institution will be overdetermined, colored by some particular signification?

To provide a concrete example: is not the modern notion of nation such a zero-institution that emerged with the dissolution of social links grounded in direct family or traditional symbolic matrixes, when, with the onslaught of modernization, social institutions were less and less grounded in naturalized tradition and more and more experienced as a matter of "contract."[5] Of special importance here is the fact that national identity is experienced as at least minimally "natural," as a belonging grounded in "blood and soil," and as such opposed to the "artificial" belonging to social institutions proper (state, profession . . .). Pre-modern institutions functioned as "naturalized" symbolic entities (as institutions grounded in unquestionable traditions), and the moment institutions were conceived as social artifacts, the need arose for a "naturalized" zero-institution that would serve as their neutral common ground.

And, back to sexual differences, I am tempted to risk the hypothesis that, perhaps, the same logic of zero-institution should be applied not only to the unity of a society, but also to its antagonistic split: what if sexual difference is ultimately a kind of zero-institution of the social split of humankind, the naturalized minimal zero-difference, a split that, prior to signalling any determinate social difference, signals this difference as such? The struggle for hegemony is then, again, the struggle for how this zero-difference will be overdetermined by other particular social differences. It is against this background that one should read an important, although usually overlooked, feature of Lacan's schema of the signifier: Lacan replaces the standard Saussurean scheme (above the bar the word "arbre," and beneath it the drawing of a tree) with, above the bar, two words one alongside the other, "homme" and "femme," and, beneath the bar, two identical drawings of a door.

In order to emphasize the differential character of the signifier, Lacan first replaces Saussure's single scheme with a signifier's couple, with the opposition man-woman, with the sexual

[5] See Rastko Mocnik, "Das 'Subjekt, dem unterstellt wird zu glauben' und die Nation als eine Null-Institution," in H. Boke, ed., *Denk-Prozesse nach Althusser* (Hamburg: Argument Verlag, 1994).

difference; but the true surprise resides in the fact that, at the level of the imaginary referent, *there is no difference* (we do not get some graphic index of the sexual difference, the simplified drawing of a man and a woman, as is usually the case in most of today's restrooms, but *the same* door reproduced twice). Is it possible to state in clearer terms that sexual difference does not designate any biological opposition grounded in "real" properties, but a purely symbolic opposition to which nothing corresponds in the designated objects—nothing but the Real of some undefined X which cannot ever be captured by the image of the signified?

Back to Lévi-Strauss's example of the two drawings of the village. Here one can see in what precise sense the Real intervenes through anamorphosis. We have first the "actual," "objective," arrangement of the houses, and then their two different symbolizations which both distort in an anamorphic way the actual arrangement. However, the "real" here is not the actual arrangement, but the traumatic core of the social antagonism which distorts the tribe members' view of the actual antagonism. The Real is thus the disavowed X on account of which our vision of reality is anamorphically distorted. (And, incidentally, this three-levels device is strictly homologous to Freud's three-level device of the interpretation of dreams: The real kernel of the dream is not the dream's latent thought, which is displaced or translated into the explicit texture of the dream, but the unconscious desire which inscribes itself through the very distortion of the latent thought into the explicit texture.)

The same goes for today's art scene, in which the Real does *not* return primarily in the guise of the shocking brutal intrusion of excremental objects, mutilated corpses, shit, and so forth. These objects are, to be sure, out of place—but in order for them to be out of place, the (empty) place must already be here, and this place is rendered by "minimalist" art, starting from Malevitch. Therein resides the complicity between the two opposed icons of high modernism, Kazimir Malevitch's "Black Square on White Surface" and Marcel Duchamp's display of ready-made objects as works of art.

The underlying notion of Malevitch's elevation of an everyday object into a work of art is that being a work of art is not an inherent property of the object: It is the artist himself who, by pre-empting the (or, rather, *any*) object and locating it at a certain place, makes it the work of art. Being a work of art is not a question of "why" but "where." And what Malevitch's minimalist disposition does is simply to render—to isolate—this place as such, the empty place (or frame) with the proto-magic property of transforming any object that finds itself within its scope into the work of art.

In short, there is no Duchamp without Malevitch. Only after the art practice isolates the frame/place as such, emptied of all its content, can one indulge in the ready-made procedure. Before Malevitch, a urinal would have remained just a urinal, even if it were to be displayed in the most distinguished gallery.

The emergence of excremental objects which are out of place is thus strictly correlative to the emergence of the place without any object in it, of the empty frame as such. Consequently, the Real in contemporary art has three dimensions, which somehow repeat within the Real the triad of Imaginary-Symbolic-Real. The Real is first here as the anamorphotic stain, the anamorphotic distortion of the direct image of reality—as a distorted image, as a pure semblance that "subjectivizes" objective reality. Then, the Real is here as the empty place, as a structure, a construction which is never here, experiences as such, but can only be retroactively constructed and has to be presupposed as such—the Real as symbolic construction.

Finally, the Real is the obscene excremental Object out of place, the Real "itself." This last Real, if isolated, is a mere fetish whose fascinating or captivating presence masks the structural Real, in the same way that, in Nazi anti-Semitism, the Jew as the excremental Object is the Real that masks the unbearable "structural" Real of the social antagonism.

These three dimensions of the Real result from the three modes of setting distance from "ordinary" reality: One submits this reality to anamorphic distortion; one introduces an object that has no place in it; or one subtracts or erases all content (objects) of reality, so that all that remains is the very empty place these objects were filling in.

The Freudian Touch

The falsity of *The Matrix* is perhaps most directly discernable in its designation of Neo as "the One." Who is the One? There effectively is such a place in the social link. There is, first, the One of the Master-Signifier, the symbolic authority. Even in social life in its most horrifying form, the memories of concentration camp survivors invariably mention the One, an individual who did not break down, who, in the midst of the unbearable conditions which reduced all others to the egoistic struggle for bare survival, miraculously maintained and radiated an "irrational" generosity and dignity. In Lacanian terms, we are dealing here with the function of *Y'a de l'Un*: even here, there was the One who served as the support of the minimum of solidarity that defines the social link proper as opposed to collaboration within the frame of the pure strategy of survival.

Two features are crucial here. First, this individual was always perceived as one (there was never a multitude of them, as if, following some obscure necessity, this excess of the inexplicable miracle of solidarity has to be embodied in a One); secondly, it was not so much what this One effectively did for the others which mattered, but rather his very presence among them (what enabled the others to survive was the awareness that, even if they are for most of the time reduced to survival-machines, there is the One who maintained human dignity). In a way homologous to canned laughter, we have here something like canned dignity, where the Other (the One) retains my dignity for me, in my place, or, more precisely, where I retain my dignity *through* the Other. I may be reduced to the cruel struggle for survival, but the very awareness that there is One who retains his dignity enables *me* to maintain a minimal link to humanity.

Often, when this One broke down or was unmasked as a fake, the other prisoners lost their will to survive and turned into indifferent living dead—paradoxically, their very readiness to struggle for bare survival was sustained by its exception, by the fact that there was the One *not* reduced to this level, so that, when this exception disappeared, the struggle for survival itself lost its force.

What this means is that this One was not defined exclusively by his "real" qualities (at this level, there may well have been more individuals like him, or it may even have been that he was not really unbroken, but a fake, just playing that role). His exceptional role was rather that of transference: He occupied a place constructed (presupposed) by the others.

In *The Matrix*, on the contrary, the One is he who is able to see that our everyday reality is not real, but just a codified virtual universe, and who therefore is able to unplug from it, to manipulate and suspend its rules (fly in the air, stop bullets, and so forth). Crucial for the function of this One is his virtualization of reality. Reality is an artificial construct whose rules can be suspended or at least rewritten—therein resides the properly paranoid notion that the One can suspend the resistance of the Real ("I can walk through a thick wall, if I really decide to . . ."—the impossibility for most of us to do this is reduced to the failure of the subject's will).

Here again, the film does not go far enough. In the memorable scene in the waiting room of the Oracle who will decide if Neo is the One, a child who is seen bending a spoon with his mere thoughts tells the surprised Neo that the way to do it is not to convince myself that I can bend the spoon, but to convince myself that *there is no spoon* . . . However, what about *myself?* Shouldn't the movie have taken the further step of accepting the Buddhist proposition that I, *myself*, the subject, do not exist?

In order to further specify what is false in *The Matrix*, one should distinguish simple technological impossibility from phantasmic falsity: Time-travel is (probably) impossible, but phantasmic scenarios about it are nonetheless "true" in the way they render libidinal deadlocks. Consequently, the problem with *The Matrix* is not the scientific naivety of its tricks. The idea of passing from reality to VR through the phone makes sense, since all we need is a gap or hole through which we can escape.

Perhaps, an even better solution would have been the toilet. Is not the domain where excrements vanish after we flush the toilet effectively one of the metaphors for the horrifyingly sublime Beyond of the primordial, pre-ontological Chaos into which things disappear? Although we rationally know what goes on with the excrements, the imaginary mystery nonetheless persists—shit remains an excess with does not fit our daily reality, and Lacan was right in claiming that we pass from animals to humans the moment an animal has problems with what to do with its excrements, the moment they turn into an excess that annoys it. The Real is thus not primarily the horrifyingly-disgusting stuff re-emerging from the toilet sink, but rather the hole itself, the gap which serves as the passage to a different ontological order—the topological hole or torsion which "curves" the space of our reality so that we perceive/imagine excrements as disappearing into an alternative dimension which is not part of our everyday reality.

The problem is a more radical phantasmic inconsistency, which erupts most explicitly when Morpheus (the African-American leader of the resistance group who believe that Neo is the One) tries to explain to the still perplexed Neo what the Matrix is. He quite consequently links it to a failure in the structure of the universe:

> MORPHEUS: It's that feeling you have had all your life. That feeling that something was wrong with the world. You don't know what it is but it's there, like a splinter in your mind, driving you mad. . . . The Matrix is everywhere, it's all around us, here even in this room. . . . It is the world that has been pulled over your eyes to blind you from the truth.
> NEO: What truth?
> MORPHEUS: That you are a slave, Neo. That you, like everyone else, was born into bondage . . . kept inside a prison that you cannot smell, taste, or touch. A prison of your mind.

Here the film encounters its ultimate inconsistency: the experience of the lack/inconsistency/obstacle is supposed to bear witness of the fact that what we experience as reality is a fake—however, towards the end of the film, Smith, the Agent of the Matrix, gives a different, much more Freudian explanation:

> Did you know that the first Matrix was designed to be a perfect human world? Where none suffered, where everyone would be happy? It was a disaster. *No* one would accept the program. Entire crops [of the humans serving as batteries] were lost. Some believed we lacked the programming language to describe your perfect world. But I believe that, as a species, human beings define their reality through suffering and misery. The perfect world was a dream that your primitive cerebrum kept trying to wake up from. Which is why the Matrix was re-designed to this: the peak of your civilization.

The imperfection of our world is thus at the same time the sign of its virtuality *and* the sign of its reality. One could effectively claim that Agent Smith (let us not forget: not a human being as others, but the direct virtual embodiment of the Matrix—the big Other—itself) is the stand-in for the figure of the analyst within the universe of the film: His lesson is that the experience of an insurmountable obstacle is the positive condition for us, humans, to perceive something as reality—reality is ultimately that which resists.

Malebranche in Hollywood

Another inconsistency concerns death: *Why* does one "really" die when one dies in the VR regulated by the Matrix? The film provides the obscurantist answer: "Neo: If you are killed in the Matrix, you die here [not only in the VR, but also in real life]? Morpheus: The body cannot live without the mind." The logic of this solution is that your "real" body can only function in conjunction with the mind, the mental universe into which you are immersed. So if you are in a VR and killed there, this death affects also your real body . . . The obvious opposite solution (you only really die when you are killed in reality) is also too short.

The catch is: Is the subject *wholly* immersed in the Matrix-dominated VR or does he know or at least *suspect* the actual state of things? If the answer to the former question is *yes*, then a simple withdrawal into a prelapsarian Adamic state of distance would render us immortal *in the VR* and, consequently, Neo who is already liberated from the full immersion in the VR should *survive* the struggle with Agent Smith which takes place *within* the VR controlled by the Matrix (in the same way he is able to stop bullets, he should also have been able to derealize blows that wound his body). This brings us back to Malebranche's occasionalism. Much more than Berkeley's God who sustains the world in his mind, the *ultimate* Matrix is Malebranche's occasionalist God.

Malebranche was undoubtedly the philosopher who provided the best conceptual apparatus to account for Virtual Reality. Malebranche, a disciple of Descartes, drops Descartes's ridiculous reference to the pineal gland in order to explain the co-ordination between the material and the spiritual substance, body and soul. How, then, are we to explain their co-ordination, if there is no contact between the two, no point at which a soul can act causally on a body or vice versa? Since the two causal networks (that of ideas in my mind and that of bodily inter-conections) are totally independent, the only solution is that a third, true Substance (God) continuously co-ordinates and medi-ates between the two, sustaining the semblance of continuity. When I think about raising my hand and my hand effectively raises, my thought causes the raising of my hand not directly but only "occasionally." Upon noticing my thought directed at rais-ing my hand, God sets in motion the other, material, causal chain which leads to my hand effectively being raised. If we replace "God" with the big Other, the symbolic order, we can see the closeness of occasionalism to Lacan's position: As Lacan put it in his polemics against Aristotle in "Television,"[6] the rela-tionship between soul and body is never direct, since the big Other always interposes itself between the two.

Occasionalism is thus essentially a name for the "arbitrary of the signifier," for the gap that separates the network of ideas from the network of bodily (real) causality, for the fact that it is the big Other which accounts for the co-ordination of the two networks, so that, when my body bites an apple, my soul expe-riences a pleasurable sensation. This same gap is targeted by the ancient Aztec priest who organizes human sacrifices to ensure that the sun will rise again: The human sacrifice is here an appeal to God to sustain the co-ordination between the two series, the bodily necessity and the concatenation of symbolic events. "Irrational" as the Aztec priest's sacrificing may appear, its underlying premise is far more insightful than our common-place intuition according to which the co-ordination between body and soul is direct—it's "natural" for me to have a pleasur-able sensation when I bite an apple since this sensation is caused directly by the apple: what gets lost is the intermediary role of the big Other in guaranteeing the co-ordination between reality and our mental experience of it.

And is it not the same with our immersion in Virtual Reality? When I raise my hand in order to push an object in virtual space, this object effectively moves—my illusion, of course, is that it was the movement of my hand which directly caused the dislocation of the object; in my immersion, I overlooked the intricate mechanism of computerized co-ordination, homolo-

---

[6] See Jacques Lacan, "Television," *October* 40 (1987).

gous to the role of God guaranteeing the co-ordination between the two series in occasionalism.[7]

It is a well-known fact that the "Close the door" button in most elevators is a totally redundant placebo, placed there just to give the individuals the impression that they are somehow participating, contributing to the speed of the elevator journey—when we push this button, the door closes in exactly the same time as when we just pressed the floor button without "speeding up" the process by pressing also the "Close the door" button. This extreme and clear case of fake participation is an appropriate metaphor of the participation of individuals in our "postmodern" political process. And this is occasionalism at its purest: according to Malebranche, we are all the time pressing such buttons, and it is God's incessant activity that co-ordinates between them and the event that follows (the door closing), while we think the event results from our pushing the button . . .

For that reason, it is crucial to keep open the radical ambiguity of how cyberspace will affect our lives: this does not depend on technology as such but on the mode of its social inscription. Immersion into cyberspace can intensify our bodily experience (new sensuality, new body with more organs, new sexes . . .), but it also opens up the possibility for the one who manipulates the machinery which runs the cyberspace literally to steal our own (virtual) body, depriving us of control over it, so that one no longer relates to one's body as to "one's own." What one encounters here is the constitutive ambiguity of the notion of mediatization.[8] Originally this notion designated the gesture by means of which a a subject was stripped of its direct, immediate right to make decisions; the great master of political mediatization was Napoleon who left to the conquered monarchs the appearance of power, while they were effectively no longer in a position to exercise it. At a more general level, one could say that such a "mediatization" of the monarch defines the constitutional monarchy: In it, the monarch is reduced to the point of a purely formal symbolic gesture of "dotting the i's," of signing and thus conferring the performative force on the edicts

---

[7] The main work of Nicolas Malebranche is *Recherches de la Vérité* (1674–75; the most available edition is Paris: Vrin, 1975).

[8] As to this ambiguity, see Paul Virilio, *The Art of the Motor*, Minneapolis: University of Minnesota Press, 1995).

whose content is determined by the elected governing body. And does not, mutatis mutandis, the same hold for today's progressive computerization of our everyday lives, in the course of which the subject is also more and more "mediatized", imperceptibly stripped of his power, under the false guise of its increase? When our body is mediatized (caught in the network of electronic media), it is simultaneously exposed to the threat of a radical "proletarization": the subject is potentially reduced to the pure dollar sign, since even my own personal experience can be stolen, manipulated, regulated by the mechanical Other. One can see, again, how the prospect of radical virtualization bestows on the computer the position which is strictly homologous to that of God in Malebrancheian occasionalism. Since the computer co-ordinates the relationship between my mind and (what I experience as) the movement of my limbs (in the virtual reality), one can easily imagine a computer which runs amok and starts to act liker an Evil God, disturbing the co-ordination between my mind and my bodily self-experience—when the signal of my mind to raise my hand is suspended or even counteracted in (the virtual) reality, the most fundamental experience of the body as "mine" is undermined. It seems thus that cyberspace effectively realizes the paranoiac fantasy elaborated by Schreber, the German judge whose memoirs were analyzed by Freud.[9] The "wired universe" is psychotic insofar as it seems to materialize Schreber's hallucination of the divine rays through which God directly controls the human mind.

In other words, does the externalization of the big Other in the computer not account for the inherent paranoiac dimension of the wired universe? Or, to put it in yet another way, the commonplace is that, in cyberspace, the ability to download consciousness into a computer finally frees people from their bodies—but it also frees the machines from "their" people . . .

Staging the Fundamental Fantasy

The final inconsistency concerns the ambiguous status of the liberation of humanity anounced by Neo in the last scene. As the result of Neo's intervention, there is a "SYSTEM FAILURE" in the

---

[9] The connection between cyberspace and Schreber's psychotic universe was suggested to me by Wendy Chun, Princeton.

Matrix; at the same time, Neo addresses people still caught in the Matrix as the Savior who will teach them how to liberate themselves from the constraints of the Matrix—they will be able to break the physical laws, bend metals, fly in the air . . . However, the problem is that all these "miracles" are possible only if we remain *within* the VR sustained by the Matrix and merely bend or change its rules: our "real" status is still that of the slaves of the Matrix, we as it were are merely gaining additional power to change our mental prison rules—so what about exiting from the Matrix altogether and entering the "real reality" in which we are miserable creatures living on the destroyed earth surface?

In an Adornian way, one should claim that these inconsistencies[10] are the film's moment of truth: they signal the antagonisms of our late-capitalist social experience, antagonisms concerning basic ontological couples like reality and pain (reality as that which disturbs the reign of the pleasure-principle), freedom and system (freedom is only possible within the system that hinders its full deployment). However, the ultimate strength of the film is nonetheless to be located at a different level. Years ago, a series of science-fiction films like *Zardoz* or *Logan's Run* forecast today's postmodern predicament: The isolated group living an aseptic life in a secluded area longs for the experience of the real world of material decay. Till postmodernism, utopia was an endeavor to break out of the real of historical time into a timeless Otherness. With postmodern overlapping of the "end of history" with full availability of the past in digitalized memory, in this time where we *live* the atemporal utopia as everyday ideological experience, utopia becomes the longing for the Reality of History itself, for memory, for the traces of the real past, the attempt to break out of the closed dome into smell and decay of the raw reality. *The Matrix* gives the final twist to this reversal, combining utopia with dystopia: the very reality we live in, the atemporal utopia staged by the Matrix, is in place so that we can be effectively reduced to a passive state of living batteries providing the Matrix with the energy.

---

[10] A further pertinent inconsistency also concerns the status of intersubjectivity in the universe run by the Matrix: do all individuals share *the same* virtual reality? Why? Why not to each its preferred own?

The unique impact of the film thus resides not so much in its central thesis (what we experience as reality is an artificial virtual reality generated by the "Matrix," the mega-computer directly attached to all our minds), but in its central image of millions of human beings leading a claustrophobic life in water-filled cradles, kept alive in order to generate energy for the Matrix. So when (some of) the people "awaken" from their immersion into the Matrix-controlled virtual reality, this awakening is not the opening into the wide space of the external reality, but first the horrible realization of this enclosure, where each of us is effectively just a fetus-like organism, immersed in the pre-natal fluid . . . This utter passivity is the foreclosed fantasy that sustains our conscious experience as active, self-positing subjects—it is the ultimate perverse fantasy, the notion that we are ultimately instruments of the Other's (Matrix's) *jouissance*, sucked out of our life-substance like batteries.

Therein resides the true libidinal enigma of this device. *Why does the Matrix need human energy?* The purely energetic solution is, of course, meaningless. The Matrix could have easily found another, more reliable, source of energy which would have not demanded the extremely complex arrangement of virtual reality co-ordinated for millions of human units. Another question is discernible here. Why does the Matrix not immerse each individual into his or her own solipsistic artificial universe? Why complicate matters by co-ordinating the programs so that all humanity inhabits one and the same virtual universe? The only consistent answer is that the Matrix feeds on the humans' *jouissance*—so we are back at the fundamental Lacanian thesis that the big Other itself, far from being an anonymous machine, needs the constant influx of *jouissance*. This is how we should turn around the state of things presented by the film. What this movie depicts as the scene of our awakening into our true situation, is effectively its exact opposition, the very fundamental fantasy that sustains our being.

The intimate connection between perversion and cyberspace is today a commonplace. According to the standard view, the perverse scenario stages the "disavowal of castration." Perversion can be seen as a defense against the motif of "death and sexuality," against the threat of mortality as well as the contingent imposition of sexual difference. What the pervert enacts is a universe in which, as in cartoons, a human being can survive any catastrophe; in which adult sexuality is reduced to a childish game; in which one is not forced to die or to choose one of the two sexes. As such, the pervert's universe is the universe of pure symbolic order, of the signifier's game running its course, unencumbered by the Real of human finitude.

As a first approach, it may seem that our experience of cyberspace fits perfectly this universe: Isn't cyberspace also a universe unencumbered by the inertia of the Real, constrained only by its self-imposed rules? And is not the same true of Virtual Reality in *The Matrix?* The "reality" in which we live loses its inexorable character; it becomes a domain of arbitrary rules (imposed by the Matrix) that one can violate if one's Will is strong enough . . . However, according to Lacan, what this standard notion leaves out of consideration is the unique relationship between the Other and the *jouissance* in perversion. What, exactly, does this mean?

In "Le prix du progrès," one of the fragments that conclude *The Dialectic of Enlightenment,* Adorno and Horkheimer quote the argument of the nineteenth-century French physiologist Pierre Flourens against medical anesthesia with chloroform. Flourens claims that it can be proven that the anesthetic works only on our memory's neuronal network. In short, while we are butchered alive on the operating table, we fully feel the terrible pain, but later, after awakening, we do not remember it . . . For Adorno and Horkheimer, this, of course, is the perfect metaphor of the fate of Reason based on the repression of nature in itself: his body, the part of nature in the subject, fully feels the pain, it is only that, due to repression, the subject does not remember it. Therein resides the perfect revenge of nature for our domination over it: Unknowingly, we are our own greatest victims, butchering ourselves alive . . . Isn't it also possible to read this as the perfect fantasy scenario of inter-passivity, of the Other Scene in which we pay the price for our active intervention into the world? There is no active free agent without this phantasmic support, without this Other Scene in which he is totally manipulated by the Other.[11] A sado-masochist willingly assumes this suffering as the access to Being.

---

[11] What Hegel does is to "traverse" this fantasy by demonstrating its function of filling in the pre-ontological abyss of freedom—reconstituting the positive

Perhaps, it is along these lines that one can also explain the obsession of Hitler's biographers with his relationship to his niece Geli Räubel, who was found dead in Hitler's Munich apartment in 1931, as if the alleged Hitler's sexual perversion will provide the "hidden variable," the intimate missing link, the phantasmic support that would account for his public personality. Here is this scenario as reported by Otto Strasser:

> Hitler made her undress [while] he would lie down on the floor. Then she would have to squat down over his face where he could examine her at close range, and this made him very excited. When the excitement reached its peak, he demanded that she urinate on him, and that gave him his pleasure. (Ron Rosenbaum, *Explaining Hitler* [New York: Harper, 1999], p. 134)

Crucial here is the utter passivity of Hitler's role in this scenario as the phantasmic support that pushed him into his frenetically destructive public political activity—no wonder Geli was desperate and disgusted at these rituals.

Therein resides the correct insight of *The Matrix*: in its juxtaposition of the two aspects of perversion: on the one hand, reduction of reality to a virtual domain regulated by arbitrary rules that can be suspended; on the other hand, the concealed truth of this freedom, the reduction of the subject to an utter instrumentalized passivity.[12]

Scene in which the subject is inserted into a positive noumenal order. In other words, for Hegel, Kant's vision is meaningless and inconsistent, since it secretly reintroduces the ontologically fully constituted divine totality, a world conceived *only* as Substance, *not* also as Subject.

[12] An earlier version of this chapter was delivered to the international symposium "Inside *The Matrix*," Center for Art and Media, Karlsruhe, Germany.

The Potentials

DANIEL BARWICK is Associate Professor of Philosophy at Alfred State College. He is the author of *Intentional Implications* and numerous articles. Barwick lectures widely on ethics, metaphysics, and assessment of general education. His students describe his teaching as follows: "You don't know what it is, but it's there, like a splinter in your mind, driving you mad."

GREGORY BASSHAM is Associate Professor of Philosophy at King's College, Pennsylvania. He is the author of *Original Intent and the Constitution* and the co-author of *Critical Thinking: A Student's Introduction*. Greg publishes widely in obscure journals on such topics as philosophy of law and Reformed epistemology. He thanks Bill Irwin for introducing him to Rob Zombie.

MICHAEL BRANNIGAN is Professor of Philosophy and Chair of the Philosophy Department at La Roche College in Pittsburgh, Pennsylvania. He is also Executive Director of the college's Center for the Study of Ethics. Besides numerous articles on Asian philosophy and ethics, he has authored *The Pulse of Wisdom: The Philosophies of India, China, and Japan* and *Striking a Balance: A Primer on Traditional Asian Values*. While recently "undergoing" a class on Eskimo rolling, he discovered that he is still oceans away from realizing the truth that there is no kayak.

MARTIN A. DANAHAY is Professor of English at the University of Texas at Arlington and has published widely in the areas of Victorian literature and culture, contemporary autobiography, and theories of oppression and resistance. He does not understand why the AI machines did not just make the human population into university professors; it would have taken eons of scholarly articles and books for them to figure out what Neo learned by taking one little pill.

GERALD J. ERION is Assistant Professor of Philosophy at Medaille College. His publications include papers on philosophy of mind and ethics. He has a problem with authority. He believes that he is special, that somehow the rules do not apply to him. Obviously, he is mistaken.

CYNTHIA FREELAND is Professor of Philosophy at the University of Houston. She is author of *The Naked and the Undead: Evil and the Appeal of Horror* (Westview, 1999) and *But Is It Art?* (Oxford, 2001), and editor of *Feminist Interpretations of Aristotle* (Penn State, 1998) and (with Thomas Wartenberg) *Philosophy and Film* (Routledge, 1995). She is willing to pay any price for the Oracle's cookie recipe.

JORGE J. E. GRACIA holds the Samuel P. Capen Chair and is SUNY Distinguished Professor of Philosophy at the State University of New York at Buffalo. His most recent books include: *How Can We Know What God Means?* (2001); *Hispanic/Latino Identity* (2000); *Metaphysics and Its Task* (1999); *Texts* (1996); and *A Theory of Textuality* (1995). It's the questions that drive him. It's the questions that brought him here.

CHARLES L. GRISWOLD, JR. is Professor of Philosophy at Boston University. He is author of *Self-Knowledge in Plato's Phaedrus* (Yale, 1986; reprinted by Penn State Press, 1996), *Adam Smith and the Virtues of Enlightenment* (Cambridge, 1999), and editor of *Platonic Writings/Platonic Readings* (Routledge, 1988; reprinted by Penn State Press, 2001). He knows an Agent when he sees one.

THOMAS S. HIBBS is Associate Professor of Philosophy at Boston College. His most recent book is *Virtue's Splendor: Wisdom, Prudence and the Good Life* (Fordham University Press, 2001). He has also published *Shows About Nothing: Nihilism in Popular Culture from The Exorcist to Seinfeld* and an essay on *Buffy the Vampire Slayer*, "Evil Meets its Match," in the Autumn 2000 issue of *Notre Dame Magazine*. Hibbs is in desperate need of debugging.

JASON HOLT teaches philosophy at the University of Manitoba. He has published scholarly and popular articles on a variety of philosophical topics. His books include a forthcoming monograph on blindsight and the nature of consciousness, the novel *Fragment of a Blues* (2001), and several volumes of poetry. He's less of a ψ-ϕ fan than he'd care to admit.

WILLIAM IRWIN is Assistant Professor of Philosophy at King's College, Pennsylvania. He is the author of *Intentionalist Interpretation: A Philosophical Explanation and Defense* (1999), and the co-author of *Critical Thinking: An Introduction* (2001). He is the editor of *Seinfeld and Philosophy* (2000) and *The Death and Resurrection of the Author?* (2002) and co-editor of *The Simpsons and Philosophy* (2001). Bill's other life is lived in computers, where he goes by the hacker alias 'KooKeeMonzzzTer' and is guilty of virtually every computer crime we have a law for.

DEBORAH KNIGHT is Associate Professor of Philosophy and Queen's National Scholar at Queen's University, Kingston, Canada. She has recent publications running the gamut from *The Simpsons* to Borges, Eco, and Calvino. In her spare time, there's a trick with a helicopter she's learning to do.

CAROLYN KORSMEYER is Professor of Philosophy at the State University of New York at Buffalo. She writes in the areas of aesthetics and philosophy of art, feminist philosophy, and emotion theory; at the moment she is especially interested in disgust. Her most recent book is *Making Sense of Taste: Food and Philosophy* (Cornell University Press, 1999). She figures that Neo and Trinity are too hungry to worry about ruining their black leather outfits with kung-fulishness.

JAMES LAWLER is Associate Professor of Philosophy at the State University of New York at Buffalo. He is the author of *The Existentialist Marxism of Jean-Paul Sartre*, and *IQ, Heritability, and Racism*, and is the editor of *Dialectics of the U.S. Constitution: Selected Writings of Mitchell Franklin*. Jim writes articles on Kant, Hegel, and Marx. In his previous life he also taught the truth.

GEORGE MCKNIGHT is Associate Professor of Film Studies in the School for Studies in Art and Culture at Carleton University, Ottawa. He recently edited *Agent of Challenge and Defiance: The Films of Ken Loach* and with Deborah Knight co-authored "Suspense and its Master," in *Hitchcock: Centenary Essays*. Oprah, Rosie, and Martha are all interested in publishing excerpts from his new cookbook, *From Tasty Wheat to Tasty Oats: Scottish Fusion Cuisine after The Matrix*.

JENNIFER L. MCMAHON is Assistant Professor of Philosophy at Centre College. She has published articles on Sartre, Eastern Philosophy, and aesthetics. Though a committed vegetarian, Jennifer is quite sure she could enjoy eating a virtual steak.

DAVID MITSUO NIXON is a graduate instructor at the University of Washington, Seattle, where he is working to complete his dissertation on the epistemology of perception. In the winter of 2000, David designed and taught a class called "The Philosophy of *The Matrix*," in which students examined a number of philosophical issues that the movie raises. Due to a little inverted spectrum problem, David accidentally chose the blue pill, and consequently is still here.

DAVID RIEDER teaches in the English department at the University of Texas at Arlington and is writing his dissertation, *Weightless Writing: Rhetoric and Writing in an Age of Blur*. He is co-editor of *Enculturation: A Journal of Rhetoric, Writing, and Culture*, as well as a column writer for the online journal, *The Writing Instructor*. David knows there is no spoon.

JONATHAN J. SANFORD is Assistant Professor of Philosophy at Franciscan University of Steubenville. He has published articles in Ancient and Medieval philosophy and is co-editing (with Michael Gorman) *Categories Old and New* (Catholic University of America Press, forthcoming). He has a social security number, he pays his taxes, and he helps his landlady carry out her garbage.

THEODORE SCHICK, JR. is Professor of Philosophy at Muhlenberg College and co-author (with Lewis Vaughn) of *How to Think About Weird Things* (McGraw-Hill), and *Doing Philosophy* (McGraw-Hill). His most recent book is *Readings in the Philosophy of Science: From Positivism to Postmodernism* (McGraw-Hill). Ted can bend spoons with his bare hands.

BARRY SMITH is Professor of Philosophy at the State University of New York at Buffalo and is Editor of *The Monist*. His most recent publications include: "True Grid," "The Metaphysics of Real Estate," "The Chinese Rune Argument," "The Cognitive Geometry of War," "The Last Days of the Human Race," and "The Worst Cognitive Performance in History." In 2001 Professor Smith was given a two-million dollar Wolfgang Paul Award from the Alexander von Humboldt Foundation, Germany, the largest single prize ever awarded to a philosopher. Asked about an earlier conversation in a restaurant, Barry responded: "I don't remember nothing. Nothing. You understand?"

DAVID WEBERMAN is Assistant Professor of Philosophy at Georgia State University in Atlanta, Georgia. He has degrees from the University of Munich, Germany and Columbia University. His publications focus on twentieth-century European philosophy and the philosophy of history. He was last seen at a telephone booth at the corner of Wabash and Lake looking for the exit.

SARAH E. WORTH is Assistant Professor of Philosophy at Furman University in Greenville, SC. Her primary work is in the field of aesthetics and has been published in the *Journal of Aesthetics and Art Criticism,* the *British Journal of Aesthetics*, and the *Journal of Aesthetic Education*. Sarah was happy to comply when the Wachowski brothers asked to use her as the model for the character of Trinity.

SLAVOJ ŽIŽEK is Professor of Philosophy at the University of Ljubljana and a former candidate for the Presidency of the Republic of Slovenia. Recent publications include *On Belief* (2001), *The Fright of Real Tears* (2001), *Did Somebody Say Totalitarianism?* (2001), *Enjoy Your Symptom! Jacques Lacan in Hollywood and Out* (2000), *The Fragile Absolute, Or Why the Christian Legacy is Worth Fighting For* (2000). The name is pronounced Leh-nerd Skin-nerd. Most guys think he's a guy.

The Oracle's Index

"Doubting Thomas," 111
Douglass, Fredrick, 11
Dozer, 14, 45, 64
dualism, 76, 85
Duchamp, Marcel, 254, 255
dukkha, 104, 107

Eastern religions on time, 115
Eddington, Sir Arthur, 96
Edmundson, Mark, 165; *Nightmare on Main Street*, 161
egotism, 142, 145, 152
Eightfold Path, 108, 109
eliminative materialism, 76, 80–82; objections to, 81–82
empiricism, 237
employee surveillance, 216
Enlightenment, 141, 155, 241; critique of, 156–58; and freedom, 157–58, 159–160; and nihilism, 156, 158
Epicurus, 96
Epictetus, 11
eudaimonia, 135
Euthyphro, 6
evil scientist scenarios, 21
existentialism, 166–68; on anxiety, 175; on authenticity/inauthenticity, 166–68, 173
eXistenZ, 178, 179; the body in, 205, 206, casting of, 212–13, eroticism in, 212; as fleshy, 211, 212; penetration in, 211–12; surprise ending of, 213, 214; as undermining stereotypes, 211; virtual reality in, 205–06, 213
experience machine, 89–90
expert knowledge, conflicting, 248
extreme pluralism, 117

fallibilism, 23
false belief, amount of, 37
Farewell, My Lovely, 244
fatalism, 91
fate, 91
feminist philosophers, on Western philosophy, 206–07

fiction; emotional response to, 180, 181–83, 184–85; explanation for, 184, 186; paradox of, 180–81; and reality, blurring of, 185–86
fictional genre film, 197
Fight Club, 10, 178
film technology, blurring fiction and reality, 182, 187
Flourens, Pierre, 265
The Fly, 210
Forms (Platonic), 13–14, 238
Foster, Gloria, 210
Fourier, Charles, 156
Four Noble Truths, 107–08
Frankenstein, 163, 195
Frankfurt School, 241
Frankl, Viktor, 11
freedom, 87–88
free will, 96–97
Freud, Sigmund, 254, 262
Frost, Robert, 15
Frye, Northrop, 197; *The Anatomy of Criticism*, 190
fundamental teachings pluralism, 118

Gable, Clark, 207
Galileo Galilei, 247
Gardner, Martin, 24
Garner, James, 243
Gautama, Siddhartha, 101
Geller, Allegra, 211–12, 213, 214
genre categories, 190, 197
genre characters, 198
genre films, 188, 189–90; characteristics of, 197; demarcation of, 191; philosophical themes in, 199
genre heroes, 198
globalization, 225
Gnosticism, 114
Grant, Cary, 244

Habermas, Jürgen, 246
happiness, 126–27; and activity, 135–36; and anxiety, 135; basis for, 145; and contentment, difference between, 131–32, 133, 134; and desire, 134–35; long-term,